T0339614

The Economics of Screening and Risk Sharing in Higher Education

The Economics of Screening and Risk Sharing in Higher Education

Human Capital Formation, Income Inequality, and Welfare

Bernhard Eckwert
Bielefeld University, Bielefeld, Germany

Itzhak Zilcha
Tel Aviv University and the College of Management Academic Studies, Tel Aviv, Israel

ELSEVIER

AMSTERDAM • BOSTON • HEIDELBERG • LONDON
NEW YORK • OXFORD • PARIS • SAN DIEGO
SAN FRANCISCO • SINGAPORE • SYDNEY • TOKYO
Academic Press is an imprint of Elsevier

Academic Press is an imprint of Elsevier
125 London Wall, London, EC2Y 5AS, UK
525 B Street, Suite 1800, San Diego, CA 92101-4495, USA
225 Wyman Street, Waltham, MA 02451, USA
The Boulevard, Langford Lane, Kidlington, Oxford OX5 1GB, UK

Copyright © 2015 Elsevier Inc. All rights reserved.

No part of this publication may be reproduced or transmitted in any form or by any means, electronic or mechanical, including photocopying, recording, or any information storage and retrieval system, without permission in writing from the publisher. Details on how to seek permission, further information about the Publisher's permissions policies and our arrangements with organizations such as the Copyright Clearance Center and the Copyright Licensing Agency, can be found at our website: www.elsevier.com/permissions.

This book and the individual contributions contained in it are protected under copyright by the Publisher (other than as may be noted herein).

Notices
Knowledge and best practice in this field are constantly changing. As new research and experience broaden our understanding, changes in research methods, professional practices, or medical treatment may become necessary.

Practitioners and researchers must always rely on their own experience and knowledge in evaluating and using any information, methods, compounds, or experiments described herein. In using such information or methods they should be mindful of their own safety and the safety of others, including parties for whom they have a professional responsibility.

To the fullest extent of the law, neither the Publisher nor the authors, contributors, or editors, assume any liability for any injury and/or damage to persons or property as a matter of products liability, negligence or otherwise, or from any use or operation of any methods, products, instructions, or ideas contained in the material herein.

Library of Congress Cataloging-in-Publication Data
A catalog record for this book is available from the Library of Congress

British Library Cataloguing in Publication Data
A catalogue record for this book is available from the British Library

ISBN: 978-0-12-803190-2

For information on all Academic Press publications
visit our website at http://store.elsevier.com/

Working together
to grow libraries in
developing countries

www.elsevier.com • www.bookaid.org

Publisher: Nikki Levy
Acquisition Editor: J. Scott Bentley
Editorial Project Manager: Susan Ikeda
Production Project Manager: Nicky Carter
Designer: Mark Rogers

Typeset by SPi Global, India
Printed and bound in the USA

Contents

Preface vii

1. Uncertainty and Screening: Preliminary Notions 1
   - 1.1 Information System 2
   - 1.2 Real State and Signal Spaces 4
   - 1.3 Informativeness Orderings 4
     - 1.3.1 The Blackwell Criterion 4
     - 1.3.2 The Kim Criterion 9
     - 1.3.3 Uniform Signal Distribution 9
   - Appendix to Chapter 1 10

2. Screening Information in Equilibrium 13
   - 2.1 Value of Information in Exchange Economies 13
   - 2.2 Value of Information in Production Economies 18
     - 2.2.1 Complete Risk Sharing Arrangements 19
     - 2.2.2 Incomplete Risk Sharing Arrangements 26
   - Appendix to Chapter 2 34

3. Evidence on Higher Education and Economic Performance 39
   - 3.1 Higher Education and Economic Development 39
   - 3.2 Higher Education and Income Inequality 40
   - 3.3 Income Inequality and Growth 43
   - 3.4 Credit Constraints in Higher Education 45

4. Screening and Economic Growth 47
   - 4.1 Better Screening in a Dynamic Framework 47
   - 4.2 Description of the Framework 49
   - 4.3 Screening in the Absence of Risk Sharing 53
   - 4.4 Screening in the Presence of Risk Sharing 56
   - 4.5 Concluding Remarks 60
   - Appendix to Chapter 4 61

5. Higher Education Financing 67
   - 5.1 Basic Framework with Multiple Funding Schemes 69
     - 5.1.1 Regime I: Unrestricted Access to Credit Markets 72

5.1.2 Regime II: Unrestricted Insurance of Loans 74
5.1.3 Regime III: Restricted Insurance of Loans 76
5.1.4 Remarks on the Implementation of the Regimes 77
5.2 Human Capital Accumulation 78
5.3 Welfare Comparison 81
5.4 The Effect of Better Screening 84
5.4.1 Screening and Human Capital Formation 87
5.4.2 Screening and Welfare 88
Appendix to Chapter 5 93

6. The Role of Government in Financing Higher Education 101

6.1 Subsidizing Tuition Versus Subsidizing Student Loans 102
6.1.1 The Model 104
6.1.2 Exogenous Subsidization Policies 110
6.1.3 Endogenous Subsidization Policies 117
6.1.4 Tax-Deductible Investment 117
6.1.5 Policy Implications 118
6.2 Should Diverse Funding Schemes Coexist in Higher Education? 119
6.2.1 The Model 121
6.2.2 Funding Structure and Social Welfare 128
6.2.3 Access Restriction to Higher Education 129
6.2.4 A Generalization 131
6.2.5 Policy Implications and Conclusion 132
Appendix to Chapter 6 133

7. Screening and Income Inequality 141

7.1 Inequality of Income Opportunities 142
7.1.1 Theoretical Framework 143
7.1.2 Screening and Inequality Without Risk Sharing 148
7.1.3 Screening and Inequality with Risk Sharing 152
7.2 Inequality of Income Distribution 154
7.2.1 The Framework and Assumptions 155
7.2.2 Formation of Human Capital and Income Inequality 158
7.2.3 The Case of CEIS Preferences 162
7.2.4 Discussion and Policy Implications 164
Appendix to Chapter 7 164

Bibliography 171
Index 177

Preface

Higher education plays an important role in promoting economic development and generating personal incomes. While these links have been established in theoretical models (e.g., Glomm and Ravikumar, 1992; Barro, 1998; Restuccia and Urrutia, 2004; Blankenau, 2005; De La Croix and Michel, 2007) they also have solid empirical support (Bassanini and Scarpetta, 2002; Checchi, 2006).

Consistent with these scientific results, past decades have witnessed an enormous expansion of the higher education systems in all developed countries and in most developing countries (Barr and Crawford, 1998; Checchi, 2006). At the same time, advances in information technologies and in statistical and social sciences have significantly improved the reliability of techniques that can be used for screening large populations. These advances are important for higher education worldwide, because they affect many of the mechanisms that are commonly used for rationing the available supply of higher educational services. In most countries, institutions of higher education are overcrowded, admission is therefore restricted and normally based on some mechanism through which students are screened (or tested) for their abilities. In Germany, for instance, new laws recently allowed publicly funded universities to select students on the basis of their scores in specifically designed admission tests. Presumably, this reform will greatly improve the availability and reliability of screening information about students' abilities.

These observations beg important questions. What are the likely economic consequences, if selection procedures in higher education depend to an increasing degree on better screening techniques? Will such development improve the allocation of scarce resources in the higher education sector, thus leading to higher growth and economic welfare? If so, will the positive growth effects necessarily come at the cost of higher income inequality? And which government policies are suited for controlling or counteracting possible detrimental side effects of these developments? Focusing on different scenarios, we illustrate in this book how the answers to these questions vary with the funding structures for investments in higher education as well as with the students' attitudes toward risk and with the availability of arrangements for sharing individual talent risks.

For the most part of our study we think of investments in higher education as being *private* investments, so that the returns to improved skills accrue to the students themselves. Thus we view higher education mainly as an investment opportunity for the individuals. Typically, the returns on such investments vary with the unknown abilities of the individuals. For some agents, investing in higher education may not be a profitable strategy. In modern societies, therefore, students are screened (or tested) for their abilities. The screening process generates noisy information about the students' abilities that can be used in the decision-making process. Rational individuals will base their investment decisions on *estimates* about their abilities. The precision of these estimates, which depends on the reliability of the screening mechanism, thus affects the allocation of educational investments and, consequently, the growth path of the economy as well.

Insofar as economic growth is driven by aggregate human capital accumulation, better screening may have ambiguous implications for the efficiency of the growth process. One channel through which screening affects economic growth originates from the individuals' decisions whether or not to invest in higher education. For agents with low abilities, the net returns on educational investments are negative. Yet, despite their low abilities, some of these agents will receive favorable signals (test results) that induce them to invest. Better screening reduces these misdirected investments as signals become less noisy, thereby reflecting the individual abilities more accurately.

Another channel originates from the individuals' decisions how to relate investment volumes to the favorability of signals. Normally, the marginal return on educational investment is higher for individuals with higher abilities or talents. Thus, a given stock of *aggregate* human capital can be generated with less aggregate investment, if agents with more favorable signals invest more than agents with less favorable signals. Yet, as it turns out, in a rational agent's decision problem investment in education is not always positively related to the favorability of a received signal. Depending on individual attitudes toward risk and on the availability of risk-sharing arrangements, agents with more favorable signals may choose to invest less in higher education. In that case, the equilibrium alignment of individual investment volumes and signals is detrimental to economic growth. More reliable screening further worsens the alignment of signals and investments, thus reducing economic growth through less efficient aggregate human capital formation.

Similar ambiguities arise when one tries to link the reliability of screening in higher education to the inequality of the income distribution. Individuals with more favorable signals have higher income prospects. Therefore, if more favorable signals induce higher investments in education, the distribution of incomes will become more unequal under more reliable screening. As argued above, however, there also exist plausible constellations where higher individual investments correspond to less favorable signals which imply lower income prospects. These are constellations in which more reliable screening in higher education may, in fact, reduce the inequality of the equilibrium income distribution.

The varied and diverse economic implications of more reliable screening in higher education raise a question about the role of government policy in this process. The government may influence the incentives for educational investments through tax-financed subsidies, through loan guarantees, or through a system of publicly provided student loans. While such policies may mitigate some negative side effects resulting from more reliable screening techniques, they also have the potential of generating new distortions in the higher education sector. For instance, tax-financed subsidies and loan guarantees may trigger investments in education that have negative net returns. And a system of publicly provided student loans may generate negative externalities if it coexists with competitive credit markets.

While subsequent chapters look at these questions from different perspectives, our analysis essentially uses a common theoretical framework throughout the book. This framework is laid out in detail in Chapter 4 and will be referred to in later chapters.

Chapter 1 presents basic concepts related to uncertainty and screening information. We define some notions of "informativeness" and discuss general conditions under which more reliable screening information is desirable. Chapter 2 studies the value of information in general equilibrium models. We show that more reliable information may be harmful, and we illustrate why the role of information tends to be less favorable in exchange economies than in production economies. Chapter 3 lays out some stylized facts regarding higher education and economic performance, and it relates the empirical evidence to the main research questions of the book.

In Chapter 4, we construct a dynamic model of production, screening, educational investment, and human capital accumulation. Physical capital is internationally mobile while human capital (labor) is immobile. All young individuals are tested (screened) for their unknown abilities. Educational investments are chosen after the individuals have learned their test results and have updated their beliefs accordingly. This economic set up serves as a benchmark model for the remainder of the book. As it turns out, more reliable screening does not necessarily lead to higher growth or higher welfare. Instead, the growth and welfare effects are determined by the interplay between the agents' risk aversion and the available risk-sharing tools.

Markets for higher education financing tend to be imperfect, mainly because young individuals cannot provide sufficient collateral that would allow them to borrow against their future incomes. In addition, and further complicating loan arrangements, the beginning of repayment often lags behind the origination of a student loan by a long period of time. Chapter 5 explores the consequences of alternative forms of education financing that remove financial barriers for individuals, thereby allowing them to participate in the higher education system. Of special interest are loan programs with income contingent repayments that may accomplish some diversification of individual income risks. Friedman (1955, 1962) argues that such diversification is of prime importance, because it ensures that individuals can finance their educational investments on favorable terms and prevents an economy-wide underinvestment in education.

In the first part of Chapter 5, we compare three alternative funding schemes for higher education. These schemes differ with regard to the extent to which individual income risks are pooled and diversified. We find that the *intermediate* funding scheme with some, but restricted, risk sharing is first choice for financing higher education. In particular, this scheme is most efficient in terms of transforming educational investment into human capital formation. The second part of Chapter 5 further analyzes this preferred intermediate funding scheme and explores how its performance is affected by more reliable screening.

Income-contingent education finance strengthens the functioning of the higher education sector, but does not fully restore efficiency. Considering this background, Chapter 6 studies some government options to further improve the performance of the higher education system. These options include tax-financed tuition subsidies and student loans subsidies as well as access restrictions to higher education. We find that the two subsidy types may have opposing effects on the formation of human capital and on the social desirability of the income distribution. Access restrictions are particularly relevant if the students are allowed to choose between standard loans from the credit market and income-contingent loans provided by the government. Such funding diversity may create severe misallocation of educational investments which raises the financing costs of all individuals participating in the income-contingent loans program. In such a situation, a policy that restricts access to higher education to students with sufficiently favorable test results (signals) may restore full efficiency of the educational investment process.

Chapter 7 links the reliability of screening in higher education to the distribution of incomes and of income opportunities across the population. Actual incomes are determined *ex post*, that is, *after* signals have been observed and beliefs have been updated. Income opportunities, by contrast, refer to expected individual incomes *ex ante*, that is, *before* signals are observed. Income opportunities are more equal, if disparities in endowments (which may be related to social origins) are less consequential in determining future income prospects. We find that better screening affects the inequality of incomes and the inequality of income opportunities in different ways. Indeed, under plausible restrictions on the individuals' attitudes toward risk, less income inequality involves more inequality of income opportunities.

Chapter 1

Uncertainty and Screening: Preliminary Notions

Chapter Outline

1.1 Information System **2**
Favorableness Ordering of Signals: Good News and Bad News 3
1.2 Real State and Signal Spaces **4**
1.3 Informativeness Orderings **4**
1.3.1 The Blackwell Criterion 4
Information and Welfare 6
Real State and Signal Spaces 8
1.3.2 The Kim Criterion 9
1.3.3 Uniform Signal Distribution 9
Appendix to Chapter 1 **10**

The concepts of uncertainty and screening information are intimately related, because screening information affects the uncertainty under which individuals make decisions. As a preparation for subsequent chapters, at this point we present a benchmark model under uncertainty and propose formalizations of the concept of information.

The uncertain environment of our economy is characterized by a probability distribution over the states of the world Ω. For now let Ω be a finite set and denote by $\pi(\omega)$ the probability of the generic element $\omega \in \Omega$. We think of $\pi(\omega)$ as the probability for state ω before any information has become known. $\pi(\omega)$ is therefore called the *prior* probability of ω. Next, suppose that in advance to his action a decision maker observes a random signal y that is correlated with the unknown state of the world. If the decision maker knows the joint distribution of the signals and the states, he can update his prior probability beliefs about the states of the world using Bayes' rule and the signal observation. We denote the set of signals by Y. For now, Y is assumed to be a finite set.

Our economy extends over three points in time, denoted "ex ante," "ex interim," and "ex post." Ex ante, nature chooses randomly the state $\omega \in \Omega$ which, at this time, is unobservable. Ex interim, the decision maker takes an action after observing the realization of a random signal that is correlated to the random state variable. Ex post, the state variable realizes which means that the state (chosen by nature at the ex ante date) becomes observable (Figure 1.1).

The Economics of Screening and Risk Sharing in Higher Education
© 2015 Elsevier Inc. All rights reserved.

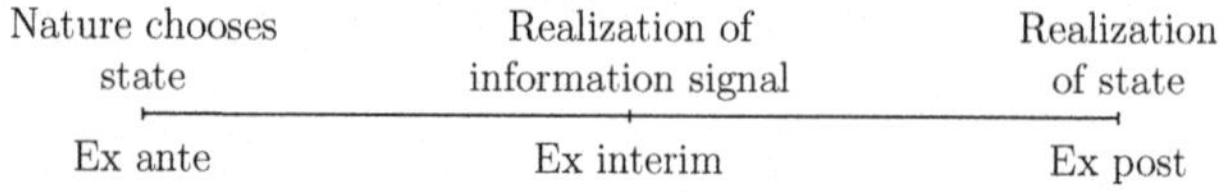

FIGURE 1.1 Temporal sequence of events.

1.1 INFORMATION SYSTEM

We assume that our economy is endowed with an information system. An information system specifies a stochastic transformation ν from Ω to Y. $\nu(y|\omega)$ represents the conditional probability of signal y given that state ω prevails.

Definition 1.1. *An information system with signal space Y is a tuple (Y, ν), where ν is a stochastic transformation from the state space Ω to Y that specifies for each state a conditional probability function over the set of signals,*

$$\nu : Y \times \Omega \to [0, 1]\,; \quad (y, \omega) \to \nu(y|\omega) \tag{1.1}$$

with

$$\sum_{y \in Y} \nu(y|\omega) = 1 \quad \forall \omega \in \Omega. \tag{1.2}$$

When the state space and the signal space are both finite we will identify the information system (Y, ν) with the stochastic matrix

$$\nu = [\nu(y|\omega)]_{\omega \in \Omega, y \in Y}, \tag{1.3}$$

where the rows of ν correspond to the states and the columns of ν correspond to the signals. The entries in each row sum up to unity, representing a probability distribution over the signal space conditional on the associated state.

We assume that the decision maker is endowed with the prior belief π and the information system (Y, ν). Using Bayes' rule, this allows him to update his prior belief about the states of the world after observing the signal realization. The unconditional probability that the information system generates signal y is

$$\nu(y) = \sum_{\omega \in \Omega} \nu(y|\omega)\pi(\omega), \quad y \in Y. \tag{1.4}$$

Without loss of generality we can assume that $\nu(y) > 0$ for all $y \in Y$, as any signal with zero probability can be deleted from the information system. With some abuse of notation, the updated (posterior) probability of state ω after signal y has been observed is

$$\nu(\omega|y) = \frac{\nu(y|\omega)\pi(\omega)}{\nu(y)}, \quad \omega \in \Omega, y \in Y. \tag{1.5}$$

The action of the decision maker at the interim date will be based on the posterior probability distribution $\nu(\cdot|y)$ induced by the signal y over the states in Ω.

Favorableness Ordering of Signals: Good News and Bad News

In our informational setting, signals matter for the decision maker, because they affect the posterior state distribution. A meaningful ordering concept for signals must therefore be based on an ordering of the induced state posteriors. Milgrom (1981) introduces a notion of signal favorableness that is related to the first-order stochastic dominance order of state posteriors. To illustrate this concept, let Ω and Y be ordered sets and assume for the sake of convenience that $\Omega \subset \mathbb{R}$, $Y \subset \mathbb{R}$.

Let $\bar{\pi}$ and $\hat{\pi}$ be two probability distributions over Ω. $\bar{\pi}$ *dominates* $\hat{\pi}$ in the sense of first-order stochastic dominance (FOSD), if for any strictly increasing function $U : \Omega \to \mathbb{R}$,

$$\sum_{\omega \in \Omega} U(\omega)\bar{\pi}(\omega) > \sum_{\omega \in \Omega} U(\omega)\hat{\pi}(\omega). \tag{1.6}$$

Thus, $\bar{\pi}$ dominates $\hat{\pi}$ in the sense of FOSD, if any expected utility maximizer with strictly increasing elementary utility function prefers the lottery $\bar{\pi}$ over the lottery $\hat{\pi}$. It is well known that this condition is equivalent to

$$\sum_{\omega \leq \omega'} \left[\bar{\pi}(\omega) - \hat{\pi}(\omega)\right] \leq 0 \tag{1.7}$$

for all $\omega' \in \Omega$, with strict inequality for some $\omega' \in \Omega$.

Recall that each signal induces a posterior state distribution. A signal is said to be more favorable, if it leads to a better (in the sense of FOSD) posterior distribution.

Definition 1.2. *Let $\bar{y}, \hat{y}$ be two signals in Y. $\bar{y}$ is more favorable than $\hat{y}$, if for every nondegenerate prior state distribution π the posterior $\nu(\cdot|\bar{y})$ dominates the posterior $\nu(\cdot|\hat{y})$ in the sense of FOSD.*

This notation of favorableness can be expressed in terms of a property of the conditional signal probabilities.

Theorem 1.1. *Signal $\bar{y}$ is more favorable than signal $\hat{y}$, if and only if*

$$\nu(\bar{y}|\bar{\omega})\nu(\hat{y}|\hat{\omega}) - \nu(\bar{y}|\hat{\omega})\nu(\hat{y}|\bar{\omega}) > 0 \tag{1.8}$$

for all $\bar{\omega} > \hat{\omega}$.

For a proof of this theorem we refer the reader to Milgrom (1981).

Finally, an information system is said to have the monotone likelihood ratio property (MLRP), if Eq. 1.8 holds for all $\bar{y} > \hat{y}$ and $\bar{\omega} > \hat{\omega}$. Under MLRP, the likelihood ratio $\nu(y|\bar{\omega})/\nu(y|\hat{\omega})$ is strictly monotone increasing in y for $\bar{\omega} > \hat{\omega}$. Using Definition 1.2, Theorem 1.1 can be written as:

Corollary 1.1. *The information system (Y, ν) has the MLRP, if and only if $\bar{y}$ is more favorable than $\hat{y}$ whenever $\bar{y} > \hat{y}, \bar{y}, \hat{y} \in Y$.*

Under an information system which satisfies MLRP, higher signals are more favorable. This implies, in particular, that the favorableness ordering on the signal space is complete. The property that higher signals are more favorable is called *signal monotonicity*. In view of Corollary 1.1, MLRP implies signal monotonicity under *any* prior. For fixed prior, therefore, the concept of signal monotonicity is weaker than MLRP.

1.2 REAL STATE AND SIGNAL SPACES

We briefly discuss the formalization of an information system when the state space Ω and the signal space Y are subsets of the real line. In this setting, an information system specifies for each state a conditional Lebesgue density function over the set of signals.

Definition 1.3. *Let $\Omega \subset \mathbb{R}$. An information system with signal space $Y \subset \mathbb{R}$ is a tuple (Y, ν), where ν is a stochastic transformation from Ω to Y that can be represented by a conditional Lebesgue density function over the set of signals,*

$$\nu : Y \times \Omega \to \mathbb{R}_+; \quad (y, \omega) \to \nu(y|\omega) \tag{1.9}$$

with

$$\int_Y \nu(y|\omega)\,\mathrm{d}y = 1 \quad \forall \omega \in \Omega. \tag{1.10}$$

When the signal space is fixed, at times we will identify the information system (Y, ν) with the stochastic transformation ν.

Let $\pi : \Omega \to \mathbb{R}_+$ be a Lebesgue density for the prior state distribution. A density for the unconditional signal probability distribution is given by

$$\nu(y) = \int_\Omega \nu(y|\omega)\pi(\omega)\,\mathrm{d}\omega, \quad y \in Y. \tag{1.11}$$

Assuming $\nu(y) > 0$ for all $y \in Y$, the updated (posterior) probability density of state ω after observation of signal y is

$$\nu(\omega|y) = \frac{\nu(y|\omega)\pi(\omega)}{\nu(y)}, \quad \omega \in \Omega, y \in Y. \tag{1.12}$$

1.3 INFORMATIVENESS ORDERINGS

For later reference, this section presents two informativeness criteria for the comparison of information systems. Both criteria give rise to an incomplete informativeness order; hence, in general, there will be pairs of information systems that cannot be ranked. Intuitively, a system is more informative, if the statistical relationship between signals and states is stronger. Below we present formalizations of this intuitive idea.

1.3.1 The Blackwell Criterion

Blackwell (1951, 1953) defines a ranking criterion for information systems that differ by a noisy transmission of signals. Starting out from an information system (Y, ν^1), suppose that the signals are subjected to a randomization process before they can be observed by the decision maker. More precisely, in the course of the transmission to the decision maker each signal

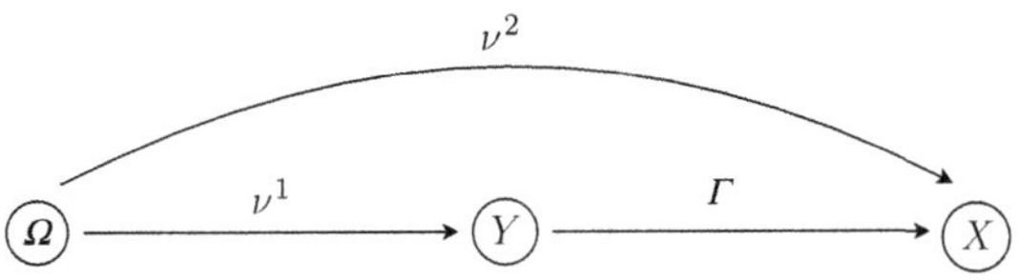

FIGURE 1.2 Signal randomization.

$y \in Y$ is stochastically transformed into a new signal $x \in X$ with probability $\gamma(x, y)$. The Markov-matrix $\Gamma = [\gamma(x, y)]_{y \in Y, x \in X}$ describes the signal randomization process, called Γ-randomization. We denote by (X, ν^2) the information system obtained from the former system by subjecting its signals to the Γ-randomization. It is intuitively clear that the Γ-randomization reduces the statistical correlatedness between the signals and the states thereby watering down the informational content of the signals. Blackwell therefore regards the system (Y, ν^1) as more informative than (X, ν^2), if the latter can be obtained from the former via a Γ-randomization of the signals (Figure 1.2).

Definition 1.4. *The information system (Y, ν^1) is more informative than (X, ν^2), denoted $(Y, \nu^1) \succsim_{\text{inf}} (X, \nu^2)$, if there exists a stochastic transformation Γ from Y to X represented by a function*

$$\gamma : X \times Y \to [0, 1] \quad (x, y) \to \gamma(x, y) \tag{1.13}$$

with

$$\sum_{x \in X} \gamma(x, y) = 1, \quad \forall y \in Y \tag{1.14}$$

such that

$$\nu^2(x|\omega) = \sum_{y \in Y} \gamma(x, y)\nu^1(y|\omega) \tag{1.15}$$

holds for all $\omega \in \Omega$ and $x \in X$.

Note that the stochastic transformation Γ is itself an information system with state space Y and signal space X, where $\gamma(x, y)$ represents the conditional probability that the decision maker observes the transformed signal x when originally the signal y was sent. Since the stochastic signal transformation process Γ does not depend on the state ω, the signals of the system (Y, ν^1) are statistically sufficient for the signals of (X, ν^2). This implies that a signal observation from (X, ν^2) cannot convey more information about the state variable than a signal observation from (Y, ν^1).

As long as both signal sets are finite, the stochastic signal transformation can be identified with the matrix

$$\Gamma = [\gamma(x, y)]_{y \in Y, x \in X} \tag{1.16}$$

and Eq. 1.15 can be written as

$$\nu^2 = \nu^1 \Gamma. \tag{1.17}$$

An information system (Y, ν) is said to be *uninformative* and, hence, represents null information, if $\nu(y|\omega) = \nu(y)\ \forall \omega, y$. Under an uninformative system, each state induces the same probability distribution over the signals. (Y, ν) is said to be *fully informative* and, hence, represents perfect information, if, for any $\omega \in \Omega$, there exists $y_\omega \in Y$ such that

$$\nu(y|\omega) = \begin{cases} 1; & y = y_\omega \\ 0; & y \neq y_\omega \end{cases}.$$

Under a fully informative system the signal reveals the exact state of nature.

Information and Welfare

A decision maker is not interested in the informativeness of a system per se. Instead he cares about the welfare he can achieve under a given information system. This raises the question whether, and in what sense, individuals can be expected to benefit from a more informative system.

Consider an expected utility maximizer with von-Neumann Morgenstern utility function $u(a, \omega)$. The agent chooses an action $a \in A$ at the ex interim date after he has observed a signal y from the information system (Y, ν). In combination with the state ω, the action a determines his elementary utility at the ex post date. The agent maximizes ex interim expected utility[1]:

$$\max_{a \in A} E[u(a, \tilde{\omega})|y] = \max_{a \in A} \sum_{\omega \in \Omega} u(a, \omega)\nu(\omega|y). \tag{1.18}$$

Let $a^*(\nu(\cdot|y))$ be a solution for this problem. Note that this solution depends on the signal only through the posterior state distribution. We define the value function for Problem 1.18,

$$\hat{V}(y) := V(\nu(\cdot|y)) = \sum_{\omega \in \Omega} u(a^*(\nu(\cdot|y)), \omega)\nu(\omega|y) \tag{1.19}$$

as the maximum ex interim expected utility level. The real-valued function V is defined on the set $\mathbb{P}$ of all probability distributions over Ω,

$$\mathbb{P} := \left\{ p : \Omega \to [0, 1] \,\middle|\, \sum_{\omega \in \Omega} p(\omega) = 1 \right\}. \tag{1.20}$$

Thus,

$$V : \mathbb{P} \to \mathbb{R}, p \to \sum_{\omega \in \Omega} u(a^*(p), \omega)p(\omega). \tag{1.21}$$

1. Throughout this book, random variables have a tilde (˜) while their realizations do not.

This value function has an important property that will later be related to the welfare implications of the information system.

Lemma 1.1. *The value function, $V : \mathbb{P} \to \mathbb{R}$, is convex.*

We define the welfare of the decision maker as his ex ante expected utility,

$$\begin{aligned} W(Y, \nu) :&= E[\hat{V}(\tilde{y})] \\ &= E\left[\sum_{\omega\in\Omega} u(a^*(\nu(\cdot|\tilde{y})), \omega)\nu(\omega|\tilde{y})\right] \\ &= \sum_{y\in Y} \nu(y) \sum_{\omega\in\Omega} u(a^*(\nu(\cdot|y)), \omega)\nu(\omega|y). \end{aligned} \tag{1.22}$$

Being an ex ante concept, the decision maker's welfare depends on the entire information system rather than on the signal realizations. The agent weakly prefers information system (Y, ν^1) over (X, ν^2), if $W(Y, \nu^1) \geq W(X, \nu^2)$ holds.

Blackwell (1951, 1953) has shown that the welfare criterion in Eq. 1.22 and the informativeness criterion in Definition 1.4 give rise to the same ordering on the set of information systems: an information system is more informative, if and only if it leads to higher welfare for any expected utility maximizer.

Theorem 1.2 (Blackwell). *Let (Y, ν^1) and (X, ν^2) be two information systems with state space Ω. $(Y, \nu^1) \succsim_{\text{inf}} (X, \nu^2)$ if and only if $W(Y, \nu^1) \geq W(X, \nu^2)$ holds for every expected utility maximizer.*

Most economic applications of this theorem make use only of the necessity part, that is, they draw welfare conclusions from the information order. The necessity part of the proof can be found in the appendix to this chapter. For the sufficiency part, we refer the reader to Crémer (1982).

According to Theorem 1.2, a system is more informative if all decision makers prefer it, that is, if the allocation improves in the Pareto sense from an ex ante perspective. However, Blackwell's theorem applies only if the individual action set, A, is independent of the signal observation. In many economic situations, this condition is not satisfied, because publicly revealed information tends to change prices and other economic variables that affect individual action sets. In such a case, information may have positive value even if Blackwell's criterion is not applicable. In some cases, due to favorable price changes, the action set of the decision maker may expand under the more informative system.

Surprisingly though, larger action sets under the more informative system are not sufficient for higher welfare. Indeed, Sulganik and Zilcha (1997) consider a generalized framework that allows for signal-dependent action sets. They show that better information may reduce welfare, even if for each signal realization the action set expands under the more informative system (see also Hermelingmeier (2010) for an elaborate discussion of the welfare-informativeness link with variable action sets).

Sulganik and Zilcha's result underscores the necessity of a more tractable characterization of Blackwell's criterion—a characterization that does not require action sets to remain fixed after the observation of a signal. To address this issue we begin with a definition.

Definition 1.5. *A function $F : \mathbb{P} \to \mathbb{R}$ is called convex (concave), if for all $p_1, p_2 \in \mathbb{P}$, and all $\alpha \in [0, 1]$*

$$F(\alpha p_1 + (1-\alpha)p_2) \overset{(\geq)}{\leq} \alpha F(p_1) + (1-\alpha)F(p_2) \tag{1.23}$$

is satisfied.

By Lemma 1.1, the value function of an individual with decision Problem 1.18 satisfies Eq. 1.23.

Theorem 1.3 (Kihlstrom). *Let (Y, ν^1) and (X, ν^2) be two information systems with state space Ω.*

(i) $(Y, \nu^1) \succ_{\text{inf}} (X, \nu^2)$ *if and only if* $E[H(\nu^1(\cdot|\tilde{y}))] \geq E[H(\nu^2(\cdot|\tilde{x}))]$ *for every convex function H, $H : \mathbb{P} \to \mathbb{R}$.*

(ii) $(Y, \nu^1) \succ_{\text{inf}} (X, \nu^2)$ *if and only if* $E[H(\nu^1(\cdot|\tilde{y}))] \leq E[H(\nu^2(\cdot|\tilde{x}))]$ *for every concave function $H : \mathbb{P} \to \mathbb{R}$.*

A proof of this theorem can be found in Kihlstrom (1984). The theorem says that a more informative system raises the expectation of any convex function of posterior beliefs, and lowers the expectation of any concave function of posterior beliefs. Note that Kihlstrom's theorem is applicable to decision problems with arbitrary action sets. In particular, the action sets may depend on the signal observations.

To illustrate the usefulness of Kihlstrom's theorem, consider a decision maker endowed with an information system. Since his welfare equals the expectation of the value function, convexity (concavity) of the value function in posterior beliefs implies higher (lower) welfare under a more informative system. In combination with Lemma 1.1, Blackwell's theorem follows immediately. Moreover, if an optimal decision is convex (concave) in posterior beliefs, the average (i.e., ex ante expected) value of the decision variable will be higher (lower) under a more informative system.

Real State and Signal Spaces

We now adapt Blackwell's concept of informativeness to the framework developed in Section 1.2, where the state space and the signal space are subsets of $\mathbb{R}$.

Definition 1.6. *The information system (Y, ν^1) is more informative than (X, ν^2), denoted $(Y, \nu^1) \succ_{\text{inf}} (X, \nu^2)$, if there exists an integrable function, $\gamma : (X \times Y) \to \mathbb{R}_+, (x, y) \to \gamma(x, y)$, with*

$$\int_X \gamma(x, y)\,\mathrm{d}x = 1 \quad \forall y \in Y, \tag{1.24}$$

such that

$$\nu^2(x|\omega) = \int_Y \nu^1(y|\omega)\gamma(x, y)\,\mathrm{d}y \tag{1.25}$$

holds for all $\omega \in \Omega$ and $x \in X$.

With this modified definition of informativeness, Kihlstrom's theorem 1.3 holds in the following form.

Theorem 1.4 (Kihlstrom). *Information systems (Y, ν^1) is more informative than information system (X, ν^2), if and only if for every real-valued convex (concave) function H on the set of density functions over Ω,*

$$\int_Y H(\nu^1(\cdot|y))\nu^1(y)\,dy \geq \int_X H(\nu^2(\cdot|x))\nu^2(x)\,dx \tag{1.26}$$

is satisfied.

The proof of this theorem follows the same lines as the proof of Theorem 1.3 and it is omitted.

1.3.2 The Kim Criterion

Kim (1995) points out that for many economic applications Blackwell's concept of informativeness is overly restrictive. He proposes a weaker ranking criterion for information systems that is based on the sensitivity of the conditional signal distributions. Let (Y, ν) be an information system in the sense of Definition 1.3 and assume that ν is differentiable. Kim expresses the state-sensitivity of the conditional signal distribution by the ratio

$$\frac{\nu_\omega}{\nu}(y|\omega), \tag{1.27}$$

and defines for each state ω a likelihood ratio distribution function as

$$L_\nu^\omega(z) := \text{prob}\left[\frac{\nu_\omega}{\nu}(\tilde{y}|\omega) \leq z\right]. \tag{1.28}$$

$L_\nu^\omega(z)$ is the probability that state ω generates a signal with sensitivity less than z. Kim (1995) calls an information signal *more reliable* if the likelihood ratio distribution is more dispersed in the sense of a mean preserving spread (MPS).

Definition 1.7. *The information system (Y, ν^1) is more reliable than (X, ν^2), denoted $(Y, \nu^1) \succ_{\text{rel}} (X, \nu^2)$, if $L_{\nu^1}^\omega$ is an MPS of $L_{\nu^2}^\omega$ for all $\omega \in \Omega$.*

Kim's reliability criterion is less restrictive than Blackwell's informativeness criterion. A proof of the following theorem can be found in Kim (1995).

Theorem 1.5. *Let (Y, ν^1) and (X, ν^2) be two information systems satisfying the assumptions in this section. Then*

$$(Y, \nu^1) \succ_{\text{inf}} (X, \nu^2) \Longrightarrow (Y, \nu^1) \succ_{\text{rel}} (X, \nu^2).$$

1.3.3 Uniform Signal Distribution

Regardless of the chosen information concept and without loss of generality, an analysis of information systems can always proceed on the assumption that signals are uniformly distributed on $[0, 1]$. Indeed, any information system $\nu(y|\omega)$ with strictly positive marginal signal density can be transformed into an informationally equivalent system with uniformly distributed signals on $[0, 1]$.

To see this, consider the transformation $\tilde{\pi} = F(\tilde{y})$, where F is the cumulative distribution function of the marginal signal density. Clearly, $\tilde{\pi}$ is uniformly distributed on $[0, 1]$ and signal monotonicity (if satisfied by ν) is preserved, since the transformation is monotonic. Moreover, the transformed signal $\tilde{\pi} = F(\tilde{y})$ fully reveals the realization of the original signal $\tilde{y}$ in terms of quantiles and, therefore, conveys exactly the same information.

APPENDIX TO CHAPTER 1

Proof of Lemma 1.1. Let $p^1, p^2 \in \mathbb{P}$ and $\alpha \in [0, 1]$. The claim in Lemma 1.1 follows from

$$\begin{aligned} V(\alpha p^1 + (1-\alpha)p^2) &= \max_{a\in A} \sum_{\omega\in\Omega} u(a,\omega)[\alpha p^1(\omega) + (1-\alpha)p^2(\omega)] \\ &\leq \alpha \max_{a\in A} \sum_{\omega\in\Omega} u(a,\omega)p^1(\omega) + (1-\alpha) \max_{a\in A} \sum_{\omega\in\Omega} u(a,\omega)p^2(\omega) \\ &= \alpha V(p^1) + (1-\alpha)V(p^2). \end{aligned}$$

□

Proof of Theorem 1.4 (Necessity). Bayes' formula implies

$$\nu^1(y)\nu^1(\omega|y) = \pi(\omega)\nu^1(y|\omega) \quad \forall \omega \in \Omega,\ y \in Y \tag{A.1.1}$$

$$\nu^2(x)\nu^2(\omega|x) = \pi(\omega)\nu^2(x|\omega) \quad \forall \omega \in \Omega,\ x \in X, \tag{A.1.2}$$

where variables with upper index 1 refer to information system (Y, ν^1) and variables with upper index 2 refer to information system (X, ν^2). By assumption, $(Y, \nu^1) \succcurlyeq_{\text{inf}} (X, \nu^2)$ and, hence, there exists a Markov-matrix $\Gamma = [\gamma(x, y)]_{y\in Y, x\in X}$ with

$$\nu^2(x|\omega) = \sum_{y\in Y} \nu^1(y|\omega)\gamma(x, y). \tag{A.1.3}$$

Combining Eqs. A.1.1 and A.1.3 yields

$$\begin{aligned} \pi(\omega)\nu^2(x|\omega) &= \pi(\omega) \sum_{y\in Y} \nu^1(y|\omega)\gamma(x,y) \\ &\overset{(A.1.1)}{=} \sum_{y\in Y} \gamma(x,y)\nu^1(y)\nu^1(\omega|y). \end{aligned} \tag{A.1.4}$$

With the help of the last equality we rewrite welfare under information system (X, ν^2) as

$$\begin{aligned} W(X,\nu^2) &\overset{(1.22)}{=} \sum_{x\in X} \nu^2(x) \sum_{\omega\in\Omega} u(a^{2*}(\nu^2(\cdot|x)),\omega)\nu^2(\omega|x) \\ &\overset{(A.1.2)}{=} \sum_{x\in X} \sum_{\omega\in\Omega} \pi(\omega)\nu^2(x|\omega)u(a^{2*}(\nu^2(\cdot|x)),\omega) \end{aligned}$$

$$\stackrel{(A.1.4)}{=} \sum_{x \in X} \sum_{\omega \in \Omega} \sum_{y \in Y} \gamma(x,y)\nu^1(y)\nu^1(\omega|y)u(a^{2*}(\nu^2(\cdot|x)),\omega)$$

$$= \sum_{y \in Y} \nu^1(y) \sum_{x \in X} \gamma(x,y) \sum_{\omega \in \Omega} \nu^1(\omega|y)u(a^{2*}(\nu^2(\cdot|x)),\omega). \quad \text{(A.1.5)}$$

Since $a^{1*}(\nu^1(\cdot|y))$ solves the decision problem under (Y, ν^1) for signal y,

$$\sum_{\omega \in \Omega} \nu^1(\omega|y)u(a^{2*}(\nu^2(\cdot|x)),\omega) \leq \sum_{\omega \in \Omega} \nu^1(\omega|y)u(a^{1*}(\nu^1(\cdot|y)),\omega). \quad \text{(A.1.6)}$$

But Eqs. A.1.5 and A.1.6 imply

$$W(X, \nu^2) \leq \sum_{y \in Y} \nu^1(y) \underbrace{\sum_{x \in X} \gamma(x,y)}_{=1} \sum_{\omega \in \Omega} \nu^1(\omega|y)u(a^{1*}(\nu^1(\cdot|y)),\omega)$$

$$= W(Y, \nu^1),$$

which completes the proof of necessity. □

Chapter 2

Screening Information in Equilibrium

Chapter Outline

2.1 Value of Information in Exchange Economies **13**
Null Information 14
Full Information 15
A Generalization of the Hirshleifer Example 15
2.2 Value of Information in Production Economies **18**
2.2.1 Complete Risk Sharing Arrangements 19
2.2.1.1 Description of the Model 19
2.2.1.2 Economic Welfare 21
2.2.1.3 The Value of Information in the Absence of Risk Sharing 22
2.2.1.4 The Value of Information with Complete Risk Sharing 23
2.2.2 Incomplete Risk Sharing Arrangements 26
Information and Economic Welfare 29
2.2.2.1 The Value of Information on the Nontradable Risk 30
2.2.2.2 The Value of Information on the Tradable Risk 31
Appendix to Chapter 2 **34**

This chapter studies how economic welfare is related to screening information in various competitive equilibrium settings. We find that such information can be harmful and tends to have lower value in economies with less efficient production technologies and/or more effective risk sharing arrangements.

2.1 VALUE OF INFORMATION IN EXCHANGE ECONOMIES

This section presents and discusses three examples in which information has negative value meaning that all agents suffer welfare losses from being better informed. The examples illustrate special cases of a more general result on the negative value of information known as Schlee's theorem.

Example 2.1 (No Value to Information; Hirshleifer, 1971). Consider an exchange economy with a single consumption good and many identical consumers. The individuals consume in two periods: $t = 0$ and $t = 1$. While

© 2015 Elsevier Inc. All rights reserved.

period 0 endowment ω_0 is known with certainty, endowment in period 1 is random (as of date 0). In period 1, two states of nature, a and b, exist that occur with probabilities π_a and π_b. Endowment is ω_{1a}, if state a occurs, and ω_{1b}, if state b occurs. Consumers are expected utility maximizers. The economy is competitive and, at date 0, there exists a market for consumption at date 0 as well as contingent claims markets for consumption at date 1. The initial endowment vector $(\omega_0, \omega_{1a}, \omega_{1b})$ can be modified via trade only. The price of the consumption good at date 0 is normalized to 1. The prices of contingent claims for consumption in state a and state b are p_{1a} and p_{1b}, respectively. An individual consumption plan (c_0, c_{1a}, c_{1b}) is feasible if, given the prices p_{1a} and p_{1b}, its cost does not exceed the individual's income, I, which is the value of his initial endowment.
The von-Neumann Morgenstern (vNM) utility function $v(c)$ is assumed to be increasing and strictly concave. Expected utility is given by:

$$U(c_0, c_{1a}, c_{1b}) = v(c_0) + \pi_a v(c_{1a}) + \pi_b v(c_{1b}). \tag{2.1}$$

Since all consumers in this exchange economy are identical, no trade takes place in equilibrium. Hence, $(c_0, c_{1a}, c_{1b}) = (\omega_0, \omega_{1a}, \omega_{1b})$. This implies that the prices for contingent claims are equal to the intertemporal marginal rates of substitution at the initial endowment:

$$p_{1a} = \frac{\pi_a v'(\omega_{1a})}{v'(\omega_0)} \quad p_{1b} = \frac{\pi_b v'(\omega_{1b})}{v'(\omega_0)}. \tag{2.2}$$

In equilibrium, each consumer maximizes expected utility in Eq. 2.1 subject to the budget constraint,

$$c_0 + p_{1a}c_{1a} + p_{1b}c_{1b} = \omega_0 + p_{1a}\omega_{1a} + p_{1b}\omega_{1b} =: I,$$

where prices are given by Eq. 2.2. In this economy, information has no value, because it does not affect the equilibrium behavior of individuals. Indeed, under any information system, individuals always consume their initial endowments. Ex ante expected utility is therefore independent of the underlying information system. In place of a detailed proof, we illustrate this result by comparing the cases of null information and full information. We also choose a specific form of the utility function and specific values for endowments and probabilities:

$$v(c) = \ln c, \quad \pi_a = 0.6, \quad \pi_b = 0.4.$$
$$\omega_0 = 100, \quad \omega_{1a} = 200, \quad \omega_{1b} = 80$$

Null Information

Under an uninformative system, signals convey no information about the state of nature. Hence, the posterior state probabilities coincide with the prior state probabilities, $\pi_a = 0.6$ and $\pi_b = 0.4$. The contingent claim prices are calculated as

$$p_{1a} = 0.3, \quad p_{1b} = 0.5, \quad I = 200.$$

Since no trade takes place in equilibrium, the expected utility of each consumer is

$$U = \ln 100 + 0.6 \ln 200 + 0.4 \ln 80 = 9.5370.$$

Full Information

Under a fully informative system, agents know at $t = 0$ with certainty whether the future state will be a or b. Again, no trade takes place. Yet, the information does affect the state probabilities and the prices. If, based on the information, state a occurs with certainty ($\pi_a = 1$), then $p_{1a} = 0.5$ and $p_{1b} = 0$. By contrast, conditional on the information that state b occurs with certainty, $p_{1b} = 1.25$ and $p_{1a} = 0$. Utility in state a is

$$U_a = \ln 100 + \ln 200 = 9.9035,$$

and utility in state b is

$$U_b = \ln 100 + \ln 80 = 8.9873.$$

Ex ante expected utility, $\pi_a U_a + \pi_b U_b$, is, once again, 9.5370. Thus, information has no value in this example.

A Generalization of the Hirshleifer Example

The above example may produce the impression that the derived result of information being worthless requires special restrictions on preferences, parameters, or information systems. This is, in fact, not the case. Rather, information is worthless whenever there is no trade in equilibrium. To see this, consider an exchange economy with arbitrary state set $\mathcal{A}$ and signal set Y. Assume further that in equilibrium no trade takes place and denote by $c(a, y)$ an individual's consumption in state a when the signal y was observed. Then,

$$\begin{aligned}
E\left\{E\left[v\left(c\left(\tilde{a}, y\right)\right) |y\right]\right\} &= \int_Y \left[\int_{\mathcal{A}} v(c(a, y))\nu(a|y)\, da\right] \nu(y)\, dy = \\
&= \int_Y \int_{\mathcal{A}} v(\omega(a))\nu(a|y)\, da \nu(y)\, dy = \\
&= \int_{\mathcal{A}} v(\omega(a)) \left[\int_Y \nu(a|y)\nu(y)\, dy\right] da = \\
&= \int_{\mathcal{A}} v(\omega(a))\pi(a)\, da = E\left[v\left(\omega\left(\tilde{a}\right)\right)\right].
\end{aligned}$$

Thus, if there is no trade in equilibrium, then, under any information system, an individual's welfare is equal to his unconditionally expected utility of the initial endowment. In particular, information has no value.

Example 2.2 (Risk-Neutral Pricing). Consider an economy with states a_σ and prices for state-contingent consumption $p_\sigma, \sigma = 1, \ldots, S$. The price system is normalized and satisfies $\sum_{\sigma=1}^{S} p_\sigma = 1$. Let $q = (q_1, \ldots, q_S)$, where q_σ is the (posterior) probability for state a_σ. There exist two agents, $i = 1, 2$ with endowments ω_σ^i and budget constraints

$$\sum_{\sigma=1}^{S} p_\sigma (c_\sigma^i - \omega_\sigma^i) = 0, \quad i = 1, 2, \tag{2.3}$$

where c_σ^i denotes consumption of agent i in state a_σ. Both agents take prices as given. Agent 1 is risk neutral. His decision problem is:

$$\max_{c_1^1, \ldots, c_S^1} \sum_{\sigma=1}^{S} c_\sigma^1 q_\sigma, \quad \text{s.t. Eq. 2.3 is satisfied for } i = 1. \tag{2.4}$$

The first-order conditions for Problem 2.4 imply

$$p_\sigma = q_\sigma, \quad \sigma = 1, \ldots, S. \tag{2.5}$$

The second agent is risk averse with strictly concave vNM-utility function, $u : \mathbb{R}_+ \to \mathbb{R}$. This agent solves

$$\max_{c_1^2, \ldots, c_S^2} \sum_{\sigma=1}^{S} u(c_\sigma^2) q_\sigma, \quad \text{s.t. Eq. 2.3 is satisfied for } i = 2. \tag{2.6}$$

The first-order conditions for Problem 2.6 imply

$$\frac{u'(c_\sigma^2)}{u'(c_S^2)} \frac{q_\sigma}{q_S} = \frac{p_\sigma}{p_S}, \ \sigma = 1, \ldots, S. \tag{2.7}$$

Equation 2.7 in combination with Eq. 2.5 yield

$$c_\sigma^2 = c_2 : \ = \sum_{\sigma'=1}^{S} \omega_{\sigma'}^2 q_{\sigma'}. \tag{2.8}$$

Thus, the agents' value functions in the competitive equilibrium with posterior belief $q = (q_1, \ldots, q_S)$ are

$$V_1(q) = \sum_{\sigma=1}^{S} q_\sigma \omega_\sigma^1 \tag{2.9}$$

$$V_2(q) = u\left(\sum_{\sigma=1}^{S} q_\sigma \omega_\sigma^2\right). \tag{2.10}$$

Since $V_1(\cdot)$ is linear and $V_2(\cdot)$ is strictly concave in q, Kihlstrom's Theorem 1.3 implies that agent 1 is indifferent about information while agent 2 strictly dislikes better information.

In this example, economic welfare declines in a Pareto sense if the economy becomes better informed. Intuitively, this adverse information effect can be understood in terms of the operation of the equilibrium risk sharing mechanism. Since in equilibrium $p_\sigma = q_\sigma$ holds for all σ, the budget constraints in Eq. 2.3 imply for both agents that average consumption is equal to average endowment. Thus, each agent's *average* consumption is independent of the information system. This implies, in particular, that the risk-neutral agent 1 is indifferent about information. Welfare of the risk-averse agent 2 is higher if, from an ex ante perspective, his consumption is less risky, that is, less responsive to the information. Economic welfare is therefore highest under null information and declines when the information system becomes more informative.

The negative value of information in this example can also be interpreted in terms of the interaction between information and the equilibrium risk allocation. Conditional on the information, the risk allocation is efficient: the entire aggregate consumption risk is born by the risk-neutral agent 1. In particular, if the information system is uninformative, then the equilibrium allocation is *unconditionally* efficient and economic welfare is maximized. By contrast, if the information system is informative about the state of the world then, from an ex ante perspective, agent 2's consumption becomes random as it depends on the revealed information. The unconditional risk allocation is therefore no longer efficient because consumption risks are not shifted entirely toward the risk-neutral individual. As a consequence, economic welfare declines.

Example 2.3 (Risk Aversion). We modify the exchange economy in Example 2.2 as follows: now both agents have identical risk-averse preferences with expected utility given by

$$\sum_{\sigma=1}^{S} q_\sigma \ln c^i_\sigma. \tag{2.11}$$

Anything else is kept unchanged, and we stick to the same notation as in the previous example. Agent i's first-order conditions consist of the budget constraint and

$$\frac{p_\sigma}{p_S} = \frac{q_\sigma}{q_S}\frac{c^i_S}{c^i_\sigma}, \qquad \sigma = 1, \ldots, S-1. \tag{2.12}$$

For this economy, equilibrium prices can be calculated as

$$p_\sigma = \frac{q_\sigma}{\omega_\sigma} \tag{2.13}$$

where ω_σ is the total endowment in state a_σ. Combining Eq. 2.13 with the individual budget constraints we find that

$$c^i_\sigma(q) = \omega_\sigma \sum_{\sigma'=1}^{S} q_{\sigma'} \frac{\omega^i_{\sigma'}}{\omega_{\sigma'}}, \qquad i = 1, 2. \tag{2.14}$$

From Eqs. 2.11 and 2.14, agent i's value function when the belief is q can be derived as

$$V^i(q) = \sum_{\sigma=1}^{S} q_\sigma \ln \omega_\sigma + \ln \left(\sum_{\sigma=1}^{S} q_\sigma \frac{\omega_\sigma^i}{\omega_\sigma} \right), \quad i = 1, 2. \tag{2.15}$$

The value functions are strictly concave as long as individual endowments are not proportional to aggregate endowment. Hence under this nonproportionality assumption both agents suffer welfare losses under a better information system.

These three examples in which information was shown to have negative value constitute special cases of a more general result derived in a seminal paper by Schlee (2001). Schlee showed that information is detrimental in the Pareto sense for a large class of exchange economies. These economies satisfy some restrictions on individual preferences; and they have market structures which lead to interim efficient allocations, that is, allocations are efficient conditional on the released information. The latter condition is satisfied, in particular, whenever the market structure is complete at the interim date.

Theorem 2.1 (Schlee's Theorem). *In competitive exchange economies with efficient interim allocations, better information reduces ex ante expected utility for all individuals under any of the following conditions:*

(i) *The economy has no aggregate risk.*
(ii) *Some agents are risk neutral (and they are wealthy enough).*
(iii) *The economy admits a representative agent with concave vNM-preferences.*

Part (iii) of the above theorem postulates that the economy admits a representative agent. This assumption means that the economy's aggregate demand is equal to the demand of a hypothetical individual (with suitably chosen preferences) who owns all resources of the economy.

The assumption that the interim allocation is efficient is critical for the validity of the theorem. If the market structure is incomplete and, hence, the equilibrium allocation is (generically) inefficient at the interim date, then information may play a much more favorable role in an exchange economy (for further details, see Gottardi and Rahi, 2014).

2.2 VALUE OF INFORMATION IN PRODUCTION ECONOMIES

According to Schlee's Theorem 2.1, better information has negative value in a large class of exchange economies with efficient risk sharing arrangements. In this section, we extend the theoretical framework by allowing for production as well as for risks that are not necessarily shared efficiently at the interim date. Both modifications have the potential of making information more valuable. In production economies, better information may improve the allocation of resources leading to higher output, consumption, and welfare. Similarly, if, at the interim date, risks are not efficiently shared, then better information may raise economic welfare by improving the overall risk allocation.

2.2.1 Complete Risk Sharing Arrangements

This section analyzes how the introduction of complete risk sharing arrangements affects the value of information in a production economy. Risk sharing arrangements are said to be complete, if the equilibrium risk allocation is efficient conditional on the information released at the interim date.

We consider the model of a two-period economy in which agents make intertemporal decisions. Firms use factor inputs to produce a consumption good after the state of nature has been revealed. Thus, production takes place under certainty. Consumers own endowments of capital and labor. They commit to savings and consumption decisions before the state of nature becomes known, but after they have observed an information signal.

Broadly speaking, we find that the value of information tends to be low when risk sharing arrangements are complete. Indeed, under efficient risk sharing at the interim date, better information is even Pareto-inferior if the economy is highly risk averse. When risk sharing markets are absent, by contrast, better information is highly valuable as it improves the equilibrium allocation in a Pareto sense.

2.2.1.1 Description of the Model

The model describes a two-period economy with homogeneous risk-averse consumers, homogeneous risk-neutral producers, and a single commodity. The commodity can either be consumed or used as an input in production. We will refer to this commodity as capital even though it can also be used for consumption. Consumers live for two periods, consume in both periods, and supply (inelastically) one unit of labor at each date t, $t = 0, 1$. In period 0, the aggregate capital stock is fixed, while the capital stock at date 1 will be affected by the aggregate savings of the households in period 0. The interest rate paid on savings from period 0 until period 1 will depend on the marginal product of capital at date 1 and, hence, is random at the time when savings decisions are made. In period 0, individuals supply labor, earn wages, w, and choose savings. Yet, their total income at this date, I_0, may include other sources of income as well.

At date 0, there is uncertainty regarding the output next period, which will be resolved at the beginning of date 1. The production process is subject to random shocks. Hence, period 1 wages w and the interest rate r (on savings during period 0) are random variables, when individuals choose consumption and savings at date 0.

Each household maximizes expected utility, defined over lifetime consumption. We assume that the vNM utility index is time-separable and has the following form:

$$U(c_0, c_1) = u(c_0) + \beta u(c_1), \quad \beta > 0,$$

where $u(\cdot)$ is a strictly concave and strictly increasing utility function. If s denotes individual savings, the typical consumer chooses c_0, c_1, and s such that:

$$\begin{aligned} &\max E[u(c_0) + \beta u(c_1)] \quad \text{s.t.} \\ &c_0 = I_0 - s \\ &c_1 = (1+r)s + w, \end{aligned} \tag{2.16}$$

where E stands for the expectation operator conditional on the information known at date 0.

The aggregate production function is stochastic. We denote by $\tilde{\theta}$ the random shock to the production technology and let $\tilde{\theta}$ assume values in $\Theta := [\underline{\theta}, \overline{\theta}]$, where $0 < \underline{\theta} < \overline{\theta} < \infty$. $\tilde{\theta}$ is the state variable that realizes at the beginning of period 1. The aggregate output is given by $\tilde{\theta}F(K,L)$,where K is the capital input and L is the labor input. $F(K,L)$ is a neoclassical production function with constant returns to scale and satisfies: $F_K(0,L) = \infty, F_L(K,0) = \infty, F_K > 0, F_L > 0, F_{KK} < 0$, and $F_{LL} < 0$.

The uncertainty about period 1 arises from the randomness of the state variable $\tilde{\theta}$. In period 0, all agents observe the realization of a signal $\tilde{y}$ which takes values in $Y \subset \mathbb{R}$ and is correlated to the unknown state variable. Thus, the relevant expectation for $\tilde{\theta}$ at date 0 is the updated posterior belief after the signal has been observed.

Let $\pi : \Theta \to \mathbb{R}_+$ be the (Lebesgue-) density function for the prior distribution over Θ, and let (Y, ν) be the economy's information system. The marginal signal density is given by

$$\nu(y) = \int_\Theta \nu(y|\theta)\pi(\theta)\, d\theta \quad \text{for all } y.$$

The density function for the updated posterior state distribution is

$$\nu(\theta|y) = \nu(y|\theta)\pi(\theta)/\nu(y).$$

Figure 2.1 illustrates the timing of events in the economy.

The per capita production function is given by $\tilde{\theta}f(k)$, where $k = K/L$, and f satisfies $f' > 0, f'' < 0$, and $f'(0) = \infty$. We also assume that capital depreciates

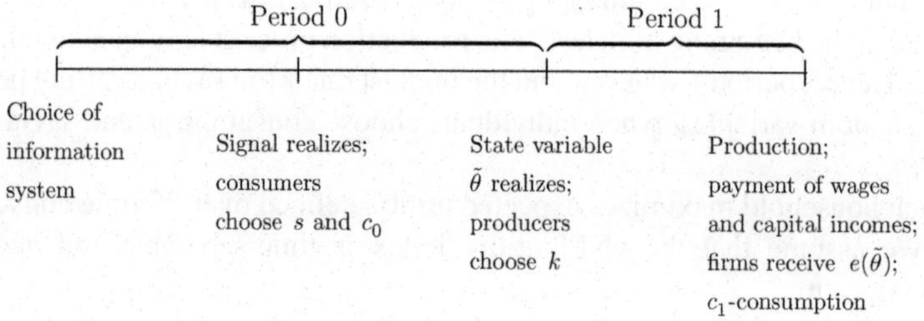

FIGURE 2.1 Temporal sequence of events.

completely. Each firm (owner) possesses some endowment $e(\tilde{\theta})$ at date 1. In period 1, firms rent capital and hire labor in competitive markets after $\tilde{\theta}$ has realized. This implies that the interest factor $1+r$ is given by the marginal product of capital and the wage rate w is equal to the marginal product of labor. In a competitive equilibrium, optimal individual behavior is consistent with market clearing for all signal realizations:

Definition 2.1. *Given the first period per capita capital stock k_0 and any realization of the signal $y \in Y$, $[c_0^*, c_1^*(\theta), s^*, \ r^*(\theta), w^*(\theta)]$ is a competitive equilibrium, if $c_0^*, s^* \in \mathbb{R}_+$; $c_1^*(\theta), r^*(\theta), w^*(\theta)$ are functions defined on Θ into $\mathbb{R}_+$ and*

(i) *Given the random interest rate $r^*(\tilde{\theta})$ and wages $w^*(\tilde{\theta})$ for period 1, consumers' optimum in Problem 2.16 is attained at $[c_0^*, c_1^*(\tilde{\theta}), s^*]$, where period 0 income is $I_0 = f(k_0)$.*
(ii) *The aggregate capital stock at date 1 equals aggregate savings at date 0, hence $k^* = s^*$, where k^* is the per capita capital at date 1.*
(iii) *Factors markets are competitive:*

$$1 + r^*(\theta) = \theta f'(k^*) \qquad \text{for all } \theta \in \Theta \tag{2.17}$$

$$w^*(\theta) = \theta[f(k^*) - k^* f'(k^*)] \qquad \text{for all } \theta \in \Theta \tag{2.18}$$

The above definition specifies the equilibrium vector $[c_0^*, c_1^*(\theta), s^*, r^*(\theta), w^*(\theta)]$ for each signal realization y. Hence, a competitive equilibrium consists of a profile of such vectors indexed by the elements of Y.

In view of Eqs. 2.17 and 2.18, for each state of nature the rate of return to capital equals the marginal product of capital, and the wage rate equals the marginal product of labor. These conditions are implied by our assumption that firms observe the state of nature prior to their decision about borrowing capital and hiring labor.

2.2.1.2 Economic Welfare

The households make their consumption and savings decision in period 0 after observing the information signal. Since the uncertainty to which the consumers are exposed depends on the informativeness of the signal, economic welfare is affected by the underlying information system.

Under information system (Y, ν), optimal savings, s, are determined uniquely (due to the strict concavity of u) by the first-order condition to Problem 2.16:

$$u'(I_0 - s) = \beta E_\theta \left[(1 + r(\theta)) u' \left([1 + r(\theta)]s + w(\theta) \right) \middle| y \right], \quad (y \in Y). \tag{2.19}$$

Let $s(y)$ be the solution to Eq. 2.19, and let $c_0(y)$ and $c_1(y, r(\theta), w(\theta))$ be the corresponding optimal consumption at dates 0 and 1. For any realization of the signal y, the value function $V(y)$ equals the level of a typical agent's expected utility,

$$V(y) := u[c_0(y)] + \beta E_\theta\left[u(c_1(y, r(\theta), w(\theta)))|y\right].$$

In equilibrium, economic welfare, $W(Y, \nu)$, depends on the information system and is defined as the ex ante expected utility of the households at the beginning of period 0,[1]

$$W(Y,\nu) = E_y[V(y)] = E_y\left[u(I_0 - s(y)) + \beta E_\theta[u([1 + r(\theta)]s(y) + w(\theta))|y]\right]. \tag{2.20}$$

Information has value, if agents are better off under a more informative system: $W(Y, \nu^1) \geq W(X, \nu^2)$ whenever $(Y, \nu^1) \succ_{\text{inf}} (X, \nu^2)$, that is, whenever (Y, ν^1) is more informative than (X, ν^2) in the sense of Definition 1.6.

2.2.1.3 The Value of Information in the Absence of Risk Sharing

In our model, the individual opportunity sets are signal-dependent because the signals affect wages and interest rates. As was mentioned earlier, even in partial equilibrium better information may be disadvantageous, if individual opportunity sets depend on signals and information systems. In view of this fact, it appears unlikely that Blackwell's Theorem holds in a full equilibrium context. However, surprisingly it does hold in our model: the Blackwell result is robust as long as the agents have no access to risk sharing markets.

Theorem 2.2. *Let* (Y, ν^1) *and* (X, ν^2) *be two information systems with* $(Y, \nu^1) \succ_{\text{inf}} (X, \nu^2)$. *Economic welfare is (weakly) higher under* (Y, ν^1) *than under* (X, ν^2), *that is,* $W(Y, \nu^1) \geq W(X, \nu^2)$.

According to Theorem 2.2 information always has nonnegative value in our economy. For the class of utility functions with constant relative risk aversion γ, it can be shown that better information has strictly positive value as long as $\gamma \neq 1$ (for a proof see Eckwert and Zilcha, 1998). When $\gamma = 1$ (logarithmic utility), the optimal saving is determined by the equation:

$$(I_0 - s)^{-1} = \beta f'(s) f(s)^{-1}.$$

Thus, in the logarithmic utility case, it is optimal for consumers not to react to information signals. Consequently, more precise information does not have value because the information is effectively ignored by the agents.

In particular, welfare losses of the type found in the partial equilibrium framework of Sulganik and Zilcha (1997) do not occur in the equilibria of our model. Sulganik and Zilcha identify the dependency of individual opportunity sets upon the information system and signals as the main channel through which, in certain situations, better information may trigger disadvantageous allocational changes. Although in our model, the information system and the signals both

1. Note that the ex ante expected utility of the producers, $E_y\{E_\theta[e(\theta)|y]\} = E[e(\theta)]$, is independent of the information system. The producers can therefore be neglected in our welfare analysis.

affect the opportunity sets via endogenously determined factor prices, adverse welfare effects as the result of more precise information can be ruled out. This finding suggests that the sufficient conditions for welfare improving information discussed by Theorem 4.1 of Sulganik and Zilcha (1997) may be sustainable in our general equilibrium framework.

2.2.1.4 The Value of Information with Complete Risk Sharing

Next we introduce a futures market where contracts for contingent delivery of the commodity can be traded. The futures market is open at date 0 after the signal y has been observed and before θ is revealed. A futures contract pays off θ units of the commodity at the end of period 1, if θ is the true state. Since there exist risk-neutral agents in the economy, namely, the owners of the firms, the futures market clears at a price $p(y)$ (which falls due at the end of period 1) equal to the conditional mean of a contract's payoff,[2]

$$p(y) = \overline{\theta}_y := E_\theta[\theta|y]. \tag{2.21}$$

Let h be the sale (or purchase, if negative) of an agent on the futures market. Under information system (Y, ν), given some signal y, the constraints of Problem 2.16 become:

$$\begin{aligned} c_0 &= I_0 - s \\ c_1(\theta) &= (1 + r(\theta))s + w(\theta) + h(p(y) - \theta) \end{aligned}$$

For the purpose of this section we choose the utility function to be of the constant relative risk aversion type, $u(c) = c^{1-\gamma}/(1-\gamma), \gamma > 0$. Due to the strict concavity of the expected utility in s and h, necessary and sufficient conditions for an optimum are:

$$u'(I_0 - s) = \beta E_\theta \left\{(1 + r)u'[(1 + r)s + w + h(p(y) - \theta)]|y\right\} \tag{2.22}$$

$$E_\theta \left\{u'[(1 + r)s + w + h(p(y) - \theta)](p(y) - \theta)|y\right\} = 0. \tag{2.23}$$

In view of Eqs. 2.17 and 2.18, future consumption can be written as $c_1 = \theta f(s) + h(p(y) - \theta)$. Since $E_\theta[p(y) - \theta|y] = 0$ by virtue of Eq. 2.21, Eq. 2.23 implies $\mathrm{Cov}\,(\theta, u'(c_1(\theta))) = 0$. Combining the last two equations yields $h = f(s)$, hence

$$c_1 = p(y)f(s). \tag{2.24}$$

Using Eq. 2.24 in Eq. 2.22 and referring to our specification of the utility function, $u(c) = c^{1-\gamma}/(1-\gamma)$, we arrive at

$$(I_0 - s)^{-\gamma} = \beta \left(\overline{\theta}_y\right)^{1-\gamma} f'(s)f(s)^{-\gamma}. \tag{2.25}$$

2. Assuming that producers are risk neutral is just for convenience. This assumption spares us the technical difficulty of calculating the equilibrium risk premium on the futures market. It also allows us to focus our welfare analysis exclusively on consumers.

Let $s(\overline{\theta}_y)$ be the solution to Eq. 2.25. It is easily verified that $s'(\overline{\theta}_y) \overset{(\leq)}{\geq} 0$ if $\gamma \overset{(\geq)}{\leq} 0$.

The value function can now be written as

$$V\left(\overline{\theta}_y\right) = \frac{1}{1-\gamma}\left[I_0 - s\left(\overline{\theta}_y\right)\right]^{1-\gamma} + \frac{\beta}{1-\gamma}\left[\overline{\theta}_y f\left(s\left(\overline{\theta}_y\right)\right)\right]^{1-\gamma}, \tag{2.26}$$

and the welfare level attained in equilibrium is

$$W(Y, \nu^1) = E_y\left[V\left(\overline{\theta}_y\right)\right] = \frac{1}{1-\gamma} E_y\left\{\left(I_0 - s\left(\overline{\theta}_y\right)\right)^{1-\gamma} + \beta\left[\overline{\theta}_y f\left(s\left(\overline{\theta}_y\right)\right)\right]^{1-\gamma}\right\}.$$

With these preparations we are ready to prove the following result:

Theorem 2.3 (Possibility of Harmful Information). *Let (Y, ν^1) and (X, ν^2) be two information systems with $(Y, \nu^1) \succ_{inf} (X, \nu^2)$. Assume further that the individual utility functions exhibit constant relative risk aversion $\gamma > 0$, and that a futures market of the type described above exists. Economic welfare is higher under (X, ν^2) than under (Y, ν^1), if γ exceeds $1 - \epsilon$ for some $\epsilon > 0$.*

In the presence of a risk sharing market, more precise information has two opposing effects on the welfare of the agents in this economy. First, by anticipating the uncertain future economic situation in a more reliable way, the consumers are able to improve the quality of their current period saving decision and thereby attain a higher level of expected utility. This positive welfare effect becomes small, if relative risk aversion, γ, is close to unity. In fact, in the limit, $\gamma = 1$, the saving decision is independent of the information system; that is, deriving better information from the signal is of no help for decision making in the current period.

Second, the more precise the information revealed by the signal, the stronger is the Hirshleifer effect (Hirshleifer, 1971) which constraints the risk sharing opportunities provided by the futures market. To see how this effect works, consider the extreme case where the signal is fully informative and hence reveals the state θ. Since the futures market opens *after* the signal has been observed, there is no scope left for risk sharing at the time when the hedging decisions can be made, because the risk has already materialized via the realization of the signal. Similarly, if the signal is less than fully informative, the futures market allows agents to share only those risks which have not yet been resolved through the signal. In a nutshell, the less informative the signal, the more risks become insurable and the higher is, ceteris paribus, (ex ante) expected utility.

The Hirshleifer effect becomes small if relative risk aversion, γ, is close to zero. To verify this denote by $s_\gamma(\bar{\theta}_y)$ optimal savings parameterized by relative risk aversion, γ; that is, $s_\gamma(\bar{\theta}_y)$ is the solution to

$$\left[\frac{I_0 - s\left(\bar{\theta}_y\right)}{f\left(s\left(\bar{\theta}_y\right)\right)}\right]^{-\gamma} = \beta\left(\bar{\theta}_y\right)^{(1-\gamma)} f'\left(s\left(\bar{\theta}_y\right)\right).$$

For $\gamma \downarrow 0$ the above equation implies

$$f'\left(s_\gamma\left(\bar{\theta}_y\right)\right) \underset{\gamma \downarrow 0}{\longrightarrow} \frac{1}{\beta \bar{\theta}_y} \tag{2.27}$$

and, hence

$$f''\left(s_\gamma\left(\bar{\theta}_y\right)\right) s'_\gamma\left(\bar{\theta}_y\right) \underset{\gamma \downarrow 0}{\longrightarrow} -\frac{1}{\beta\left(\bar{\theta}_y\right)^2}. \tag{2.28}$$

Combining Eqs. 2.27 and 2.28 we arrive at

$$f'\left(s_\gamma\left(\bar{\theta}_y\right)\right) + \bar{\theta}_y f''\left(s_\gamma\left(\bar{\theta}_y\right)\right) s'_\gamma\left(\bar{\theta}_y\right) \underset{\gamma \downarrow 0}{\longrightarrow} 0. \tag{2.29}$$

Now, from the expression for V'' in Eq. A.2.5 we find that

$$\lim_{\gamma \downarrow 0} \frac{V''\left(\bar{\theta}_y\right)}{\beta} = \lim_{\gamma \downarrow 0} \left\{ \left(\bar{\theta}_y\right)^{-\gamma} f^{-\gamma} s'_\gamma\left(\bar{\theta}_y\right) \left[2f'\left(s_\gamma\left(\bar{\theta}_y\right)\right) + \bar{\theta}_y f''\left(s_\gamma\left(\bar{\theta}_y\right)\right) s'_\gamma\left(\bar{\theta}_y\right) \right] \right\}.$$

Using Eqs. 2.27 and 2.28 in the last equation yields

$$\lim_{\gamma \downarrow 0} \frac{V''\left(\bar{\theta}_y\right)}{\beta} = \lim_{\gamma \downarrow 0} \frac{s'_\gamma\left(\bar{\theta}_y\right)}{\beta \bar{\theta}_y}.$$

Since $s'_\gamma(\bar{\theta}_y)$ is positive for $\gamma < 1$, we conclude that the value function $V''(\cdot)$ is strictly convex for small (but positive) γ. Hence, by the Kihlstrom's Theorem 1.4 better information has positive value. Accordingly, for γ close to zero, the existence of a risk sharing market does not invalidate Theorem 2.2 because, due to low risk aversion, the Hirshleifer effect becomes negligible.

We may summarize the discussion of Theorem 2.3 as follows: when moving to a more informative system, the first (welfare enhancing) effect is weak as long as γ is close to or above unity. This is because the higher reliability of the signal does not significantly improve the agents' savings decision. As a consequence, the Hirshleifer effect is dominant and overall welfare declines. On the other hand, with γ close to zero, the Hirshleifer effect tends to disappear, because missing risk sharing opportunities do not hurt agents who are (almost) risk neutral. In this case, the first (positive) welfare effect is dominant and, hence, more accurate information is beneficial.

Discussion

For decades economists have conjectured that the value of information may not necessarily be positive in equilibrium. In general equilibrium, individual opportunity sets are determined endogenously and thus they vary with the information system through which agents interpret signals. Blackwell's Theorem, in contrast, which claims that the value of information is positive, is based on the assumption of fixed opportunity sets and thus lacks applicability to equilibrium analysis in economics. This section has presented an approach which allows, within the context of a standard two-period production economy, a generalization of Blackwell's result to an equilibrium framework.

The incorporation of production into the model is important for two reasons: First, modeling the interaction between consumers and producers explicitly allows the information signal to affect individual opportunity sets via factor prices. This implies that Blackwell's basic assumption of fixed opportunity sets is violated. Hence, to make this point, there is no need to introduce further heterogeneity among agents. Second, the special structure of our model (homogeneous consumers, constant returns to scale, risk-neutral producers) implies that the interactions in equilibrium among opportunity sets, prices, and information are somewhat restricted. The result in Theorem 2.2 may therefore not be entirely robust. Even so, since in a production economy better information may lead to improved allocation of inputs, information can be expected to have positive value in a wider range of circumstances than is suggested by models of pure exchange.

It was further demonstrated that the introduction of risk sharing markets may result in a failure of Blackwell's Theorem. In our model, the Hirshleifer effect dominates the Blackwell effect, if the measure of relative risk aversion is greater than or equal to 1; in that case, better information is harmful to all agents. This finding generalizes Hirshleifer's result on the possible negative value of information: better information constraints the operation of risk sharing arrangements, and the resulting welfare losses are higher if consumers are more risk averse.

Theorem 2.3 in this section bears some resemblance with an old result in economics according to which the introduction of an additional risk sharing market into an incomplete market system can make all agents worse off (e.g., Hart, 1975). In fact, at some level better information plays a similar role in the agents' decision problems as an additional risk sharing market: in both cases, agents are able to make decisions under less uncertainty. However, unlike the incomplete markets literature, our analysis uses a welfare criterion which is based on an ex ante expected utility evaluation. Therefore, the respective results are not easily comparable.

2.2.2 Incomplete Risk Sharing Arrangements

In a next step, we generalize our theoretical framework to include two different sources, or factors, of production risk. The first risk factor will be assumed to be tradable while the second risk factor is nontradable. In equilibrium, the tradable risk is allocated efficiently while the allocation of the nontradable risk is inefficient. We study the welfare implications of better information about the tradable risk and the nontradable risk, respectively. As it turns out, the interaction between the Blackwell effect and the Hirshleifer effect and, hence, the value of information are closely related to the efficiency properties of the equilibrium risk allocation.

In particular, we shall find that better information about the nontradable, inefficiently allocated risk has always positive value; in this case, the Hirshleifer effect is absent and, hence, the Blackwell effect is dominant. By contrast, better information about the tradable, efficiently allocated risk has negative value (for all agents), if the relative measure of risk aversion is not too low; in that case, the Hirshleifer-effect is negative and dominates the Blackwell effect.

We consider, again, an economy which extends over two periods. The economy has two types of homogeneous agents and a single commodity (capital) that can be either consumed or used as an input in a production process. We will refer to the first type of agents as consumers and to the second type of agents as firm owners. Consumers live for two periods, consume in both periods and supply (inelastically) one unit of labor at each date $t, t = 0, 1$. Firm owners also live for two periods but consume only in the last period. Each firm owner possesses a firm which produces under constant returns to scale. The production process, which takes place in period 1, is affected by random shocks. Aggregate output is given by $\tilde{\theta} F(K, L)$, where K is the aggregate capital input and L is the aggregate labor input. The random shock $\tilde{\theta}$ to the production technology realizes in period 1. The production function $F(K, L)$ has the same properties as in Section 2.2.1.

We assume that the production shock is composed of two additive components, $\tilde{\theta} = \tilde{\lambda} + \tilde{\phi}$. The random variables $\tilde{\lambda}$ and $\tilde{\phi}$ are stochastically independent. And they take values in $\Lambda := [\lambda_1, \lambda_2]$ and $\Phi := [\phi_1, \phi_2]$, where $0 < \lambda_1 < \lambda_2 < \infty$, $0 < \phi_1 < \phi_2 < \infty$. All agents have access to a futures market in which the λ-risk can be traded. The ϕ-risk, by contrast, is nontradable. More precisely, on the futures market, which is open at date 0, contracts for contingent delivery of the commodity are traded. *A* futures contract pays off λ units of the commodity at the end of period 1, if the realization λ occurs.

Let $k = K/L$ and denote by $\tilde{\theta} f(k)$ per capita production function. Our previous specifications imply: $f' > 0$, $f'' < 0$, and $f'(0) = \infty$. At the outset of period 1, after the production shock $\tilde{\theta}$ has realized, profit maximizing firms rent capital and hire labor in competitive markets. Again, the interest factor $1 + r$ is given by the marginal product of capital, and the wage rate w is equal to the marginal product of labor.

The uncertainty in period 1 is represented by the lack of knowledge of the state variable $(\lambda, \phi) \in \Lambda \times \Phi$. In period 0, all agents observe a signal $\tilde{y}$ which takes values in Y and is correlated to the unknown state variable. We specify this signal in greater detail below. The relevant expectation for $(\tilde{\lambda}, \tilde{\phi})$ is the updated posterior belief after the signal has been observed.

The firm owners are risk neutral. Each firm owner possesses some (per capita) endowment e at date 1 which is large enough to ensure nonnegative total income, that is,[3]

$$e \geq f(I_0)(\lambda_2 - \lambda_1) \quad \text{for all} \quad (\lambda, \phi) \in \Lambda \times \Phi. \tag{2.30}$$

3. For simplicity we assume that e is a constant. All of our results remain valid if e is contingent on the state (λ, ϕ).

I_0 denotes the total income of each consumer in period 0, which is derived from labor and capital incomes. Risk neutrality on the part of the firm owners in combination with Eq. 2.30 implies that the futures market is unbiased, that is, this market clears at a price $p(y)$ (which is due at the end of period 1) equal to the conditional mean of the contract's payoff,

$$p(y) = E\left[\tilde{\lambda}|y\right]. \tag{2.31}$$

Since on average profits from speculation on the futures market are zero, average consumption of the firm owners at date 1 equals e.

At the beginning of period 0, the level of the aggregate capital stock is *fixed* (which implies fixed factor prices at date 0 in equilibrium). The capital stock at the outset of date 1 will be determined by the aggregate savings of the consumers in period 0. Each consumer maximizes expected utility, defined over lifetime consumption. We assume that the vNM utility index is time-separable and has the following form:

$$U(c_0, c_1) = v(c_0) + u(c_1)$$

where $v(\cdot)$ and $u(\cdot)$ are strictly concave and strictly increasing utility functions. If s denotes individual savings and h denotes the sale (or purchase, if negative) on the futures market, the typical consumer chooses s, h such that:

$$\max E[v(c_0) + u(c_1)|y] \quad \text{s.t.} \tag{2.32}$$
$$c_0 = I_0 - s$$
$$c_1 = (1 + r)s + w + h(p(y) - \lambda),$$

where E stands for the expectation operator conditional on the information, y, revealed at date 0.

The timing of events in the economy is the same as in Section 2.2.1. In a competitive equilibrium, prices are determined such that the futures market and the factor markets clear.

Definition 2.2. *Given the first period per capita capital stock k_0 and any realization of the signal $y \in Y$, $[p^*, c_0^*, c_1^*(\lambda, \phi), s^*, r^*(\lambda, \phi), w^*(\lambda, \phi)]$ is a* competitive equilibrium, *if $p^* = p(y)$ satisfies Eq. 2.31, $c_0^*, s^* \in \mathbb{R}_+$; $h^* \in \mathbb{R}$; $c_1^*(\lambda, \phi), r^*(\lambda, \phi), w^*(\lambda, \phi)$ are functions defined on $\Lambda \times \Phi$ into $\mathbb{R}_+$ and*

(i) *Given the random interest rate $r^*(\lambda, \phi)$, and wages $w^*(\lambda, \phi)$ for period 1, consumers' optimum in Problem 2.32 is attained at $[c_0^*, c_1^*(\lambda, \phi), s^*, h^*]$, where $I_0 = f(k_0)$.*

(ii) *The aggregate capital stock at date 1 equals aggregate savings at date 0, hence $k^* = s^*$, where k^* is the per capita capital at date 1.*

(iii) *Factors markets are competitive:*

$$1 + r^*(\lambda, \phi) = (\lambda + \phi)f'(k^*) \quad \textit{for all} \quad (\lambda, \phi) \in \Lambda \times \Phi \tag{2.33}$$

$$w^*(\lambda, \phi) = (\lambda + \phi)[f(k^*) - k^* f'(k^*)] \quad \textit{for all} \quad (\lambda, \phi) \in \Lambda \times \Phi \tag{2.34}$$

Let $\pi : \Lambda \times \Phi \to \mathbb{R}_+$ be the (Lebesgue-) density function for the prior distributions over $\Lambda \times \Phi$. Since the random variables $\tilde{\lambda}$ and $\tilde{\phi}$ are stochastically independent, we can write $\pi(\lambda, \phi) = \pi(\lambda)\pi(\phi)$ in obvious notation. Before trading on the goods market and futures market begins at date 0, all agents observe the signal $\tilde{y} = (\alpha \tilde{y}_\lambda, \beta \tilde{y}_\phi) \in Y \subset \mathbb{R}^2$. The constants α and β take values in $\{0, 1\}$. If, for example, $\alpha = 0$ and $\beta = 1$, then only the second component of the signal contains information on the unknown state variable $(\tilde{\lambda}, \tilde{\phi})$. This specification captures the case where agents can observe only the signal (component) y_ϕ but not y_λ. $\alpha = 1, \beta = 1$ implies that both signals can be observed. We assume that $\tilde{y}_\lambda$ and $\tilde{\phi}$ are stochastically independent, that is, $\tilde{y}_\lambda$ contains information related only to the risk factor $\tilde{\lambda}$. Similarly, $\tilde{y}_\phi$ and $\tilde{\lambda}$ are stochastically independent such that $\tilde{y}_\phi$ contains information related only to the risk factor $\tilde{\phi}$.

Information and Economic Welfare

The firm owners make their production decision in the absence of uncertainty after the state of nature (λ, ϕ) has become known. Since the technology exhibits constant returns to scale, no profits accrue from the production process itself. Also, speculation on the futures market results in zero average profits since in equilibrium this market is unbiased. Being risk neutral, the expected utility of the firm owners therefore does not depend on information and, hence, the firm owners can be neglected in our welfare analysis. By contrast, expected utility of the consumers is affected by the underlying information system.

Consider the information system (Y, ν). Due to the strict concavity of the utility function, optimal savings, s, and futures market hedging, h, are determined uniquely by the first-order conditions to Problem 2.32:

$$v'(I_0 - s) = E\left[\left(\tilde{\lambda} + \tilde{\phi}\right) f'(s) u'\left(\left(\tilde{\lambda} + \tilde{\phi}\right) f(s) + h\left(p(y) - \tilde{\lambda}\right)\right) \Big| y\right], \quad (y \in Y) \quad (2.35)$$

$$E\left[\left(p(y) - \tilde{\lambda}\right) u'\left(\left(\tilde{\lambda} + \tilde{\phi}\right) f(s) + h\left(p(y) - \tilde{\lambda}\right)\right) \Big| y\right] = 0, \quad (y \in Y). \quad (2.36)$$

In Eqs. 2.35 and 2.36, we have used the market clearing factor prices from Eqs. 2.33 and 2.34; namely, $c_1 = (\lambda + \phi)f(s) + h[p(y) - \lambda]$. Since the futures market is unbiased, Eq. 2.36 implies $\mathrm{Cov}(\tilde{\lambda}, u'(c_1)) = 0$ and hence, due to the strict monotonicity of u', we must have $h = f(s)$. Using this equality in Eq. 2.35 we arrive at[4]

$$v'(I_0 - s) = E\left[\left(p(y) + \tilde{\phi}\right) f'(s) u'\left(\left(p(y) + \tilde{\phi}\right) f(s)\right) \Big| y\right], \quad (y \in Y). \quad (2.37)$$

4. Note that equilibrium savings are strictly positive because f satisfies the Inada conditions.

If we denote by $s(y)$ the unique solution to Eq. 2.37, the value function of each consumer is

$$V(y) := v(I_0 - s(y)) + E\left[u\left(\left(p(y) + \tilde{\phi}\right) f(s(y))\right) \Big| y\right]. \tag{2.38}$$

Finally, using Eq. 2.38, economic welfare can be written as

$$W(Y, \nu) := E_y[V(y)] = E_y\left[v(I_0 - s(y)) + E\left[u\left(\left(p(y) + \tilde{\phi}\right) f(s)\right) \Big| y\right]\right]. \tag{2.39}$$

Again, the value of information is positive if all consumers are better off under a more informative information system, that is, $W(Y, \nu^1) \geq W(X, \nu^2)$ whenever $(Y, \nu^1) \succsim_{\text{inf}} (X, \nu^2)$.

We now analyze the value of information in two different settings. The first setting is described by the parameter constellation $\alpha = 0, \beta = 1$ which implies that the signal (component) y_λ is unobservable while y_ϕ is publicly observed. Recall that y_ϕ contains information related only to the nontradable risk factor $\tilde{\phi}$. The second setting corresponds to the parameter constellation $\alpha = 1, \beta = 0$. Under this specification agents cannot observe the signal y_ϕ. Instead, they observe y_λ which contains information related only to the tradable risk factor $\tilde{\lambda}$.

2.2.2.1 *The Value of Information on the Nontradable Risk*

We analyze the value of information under the parameter constellation $\alpha = 0, \beta = 1$, that is, when the agents observe only the signal component y_ϕ. For later reference, we note that in equilibrium the tradable λ-risk is efficiently allocated while the nontradable ϕ-risk is inefficiently allocated. To see this, observe that the future consumption of the consumers $c_1 = (p(y) + \phi)f(s)$ does not depend on λ. Hence, the tradable risk is allocated efficiently because it is fully shifted to the risk-neutral firm owners. On the other hand, the allocation of the nontradable ϕ-risk is fully inefficient, because period 1 consumption of the firm owners, $e + f(s)(\lambda - p(y))$, does not depend on ϕ. Hence, the risk-averse consumers bear the entire nontradable risk in the economy.

In this situation, information always has positive value:

Theorem 2.4. *Let (Y, ν^1) and (X, ν^2) be two information systems and consider the parameter constellation $\alpha = 0, \beta = 1$; that is, the agents observe only the signal y_ϕ which contains information on the nontradable risk factor $\tilde{\phi}$. If $(Y, \nu^1) \succsim_{\text{inf}} (X, \nu^2)$, economic welfare is higher under (Y, ν^1) than under (X, ν^2), that is, $W(Y, \nu^1) \geq W(X, \nu^2)$.*

We remark that the weak inequality in Theorem 2.4 holds as a strict inequality whenever the consumers' utility in the second period is nonlogarithmic. With logarithmic utility, optimal savings are independent of the signal and, hence, information has no value.

Theorem 2.4 differs markedly from Schlee's Theorem 2.1 which holds for the case of pure exchange under efficient risk sharing. Although our equilibrium model allows for risk sharing and both the information system and the signals affect the agents' opportunity sets via endogenously determined factor prices, information on the nontradable risk always has value. In interpreting this finding, we will argue below that the robustness of Blackwell's Theorem in general equilibrium is intimately connected to the efficiency of the risk allocation: information tends to have less value, if risks that are affected by the information are shared more efficiently.

We have noted earlier that in economies where risk sharing mechanisms are active more precise information tends to have two possibly opposing effects: First, by anticipating the uncertain future economic environment in a more reliable way, the agents are able to improve the quality of their decisions. This is the *Blackwell effect* where more information has a positive impact on economic welfare. Second, the more precise is the information revealed by the signal, the more limited are the risk sharing opportunities in this economy. This mechanism, which may have negative welfare implications, is the *Hirshleifer effect*.

The interaction of the Blackwell effect and the Hirshleifer effect determines the value of information in our equilibrium model. Under the specification $\alpha = 0, \beta = 1$ in Theorem 2.4, the signal y contains only information on the ϕ-risk. Accordingly, while it is true that the Hirshleifer effect limits the risk sharing opportunities in the economy, this does not result in welfare losses, because the allocation of the ϕ-risk is perfectly inefficient and, hence, cannot deteriorate any further. As the Blackwell effect is always benign, better information increases economic welfare under the assumption of Theorem 2.4.

2.2.2.2 The Value of Information on the Tradable Risk

Now we consider the other setting $\alpha = 1, \beta = 0$, under which the agents observe only the signal component y_λ. Define $\gamma(c_1) = -\frac{c_1 u''(c_1)}{u'(c_1)}$ as the measure of relative risk aversion of the consumers' second period utility function. The following theorem relates the value of information on the tradable risk to the measure of relative risk aversion.[5]

Theorem 2.5. *Let* (Y, ν^1) *and* (X, ν^2) *be two information systems with* $(Y, \nu^1) \succ_{\text{Inf}} (X, \nu^2)$ *and consider the parameters* $\alpha = 1, \beta = 0$*; that is, the agents observe only the signal* y_λ *which contains information on the insurable risk factor* $\tilde{\lambda}$*. Economic welfare is higher under* (X, ν^2) *than under* (Y, ν^1)*, that*

5. The condition in Theorem 2.5 is merely sufficient and might be stronger than necessary, if the production function, utility in period 0, and the priors are given. It is therefore natural to ask whether the condition is necessary, if the stated result is to hold for *arbitrary* parameterizations of the model. While we do not have a complete answer to this question, it is possible to show that the following is true: whenever $\gamma(c_1)$ is less than 1/2 but larger than 1/4, then it is possible to construct an economy such that the assertion in Theorem 2.5 does not hold for a suitably chosen pair of information systems. The details are tedious and therefore omitted.

is, $W(X, \nu^2) \geq W(Y, \nu^1)$, if relative risk aversion of the consumers, $\gamma(c_1)$, is greater than or equal to 1/2 for all $c_1 \geq 0$.

Comparing Theorems 2.4 and 2.5, the impact of more precise information on economic welfare appears to be less favorable (or even harmful) the better agents can hedge the risks to which the information is related. This observation is surprising at first sight, because well-developed insurance markets can normally be expected to benefit agents by enabling them to capitalize on their information more effectively. Yet, in view of the above theorems, just the opposite is true: information tends to be less valuable, if the market system offers better hedging opportunities against the risk on which information is revealed. Looked at more closely, however, our results for this equilibrium economy can be reconciled with more traditional views on the value of information, attained usually in partial equilibrium settings.

According to Theorem 2.5, better information can (but need not) be harmful, if the risks which are affected by the information are efficiently allocated. The Hirshleifer effect now plays an important role. Intuitively, the signal is more informative the more closely the stochastic fluctuations of the signal are linked to the fluctuations of the state variable. In particular, a signal that does not fluctuate at all contains no information. In view of Eq. 2.37, a volatile (i.e., informative) signal induces instabilities in the savings behavior and thus tends to reduce ex ante expected utility. Crucially, the market allocates risks efficiently only conditional on the signal. The risks emanating from a volatile signal, however, cannot be insured and result in welfare losses. This is the mechanism through which the Hirshleifer effect translates more informative signals into lower ex ante expected utility.

The Hirshleifer effect may also be interpreted in terms of the ex ante efficiency of the λ-risk allocation. In our model, the futures market allows agents to share that part of the λ-risk which has not yet been resolved through the signal. Thus, from an ex ante point of view, in equilibrium only part of the tradable λ-risk is allocated efficiently: the more informative the signal, the less tradable risks are efficiently allocated and the lower is economic welfare.

In Theorem 2.5, the Hirshleifer effect is complemented by the Blackwell effect. Figure 2.2 gives the intuition of the interaction between these two effects. In order to simplify the illustration the figure is drawn for the case of *constant* relative risk aversion γ.

Since ex post (i.e., conditional on the signal) the λ-risk is allocated efficiently, the Hirshleifer effect causes a deterioration of the ex ante λ-risk allocation and, therefore, reduces economic welfare. The strength of the Hirshleifer effect depends on the risk aversion of the consumers. If the consumers are only slightly risk averse, then the welfare loss caused by inefficiently allocated risks is small; hence, the Hirshleifer effect will be dominated by the Blackwell effect and overall welfare increases with better information. Yet, in case the workers are strongly risk averse, their welfare will be severely affected by inefficiently allocated risks. In Figure 2.2, the critical value of relative risk aversion, beyond

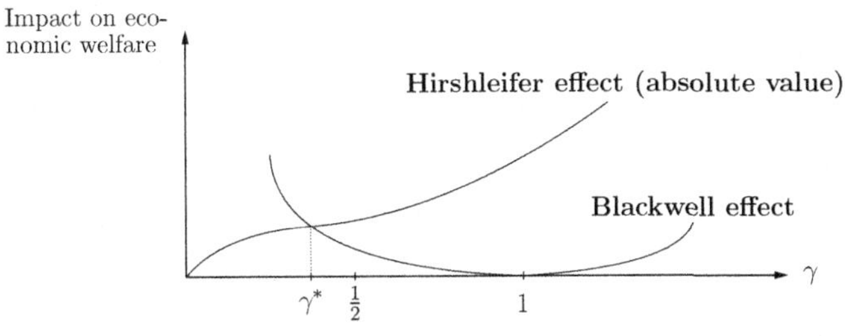

FIGURE 2.2 Welfare components of information.

which the Hirshleifer effect outweighs the Blackwell effect, is γ^*. In view of Theorem 2.5, we have $\gamma^* \leq \frac{1}{2}$.[6]

We have learned from Schlee's Theorem 2.1 that in pure exchange economies better information necessarily makes all agents worse off, if in equilibrium risks are shared efficiently and if some agents are risk neutral. Theorem 2.5 demonstrates that this result cannot be generalized to models with production. In an exchange economy, the cake to be distributed across agents does not grow if, due to better information, the agents are able to improve the quality of their decisions. Therefore, as long as better information does not enhance the efficiency of the equilibrium allocation, the Blackwell effect is nil. This is true, in particular, if the allocation is efficient in the Pareto sense. In models with production, by contrast, the size of the cake may grow when the economy becomes better informed. This explains why the welfare consequences of improved information tend to be less detrimental in a production economy than in the context of pure exchange.

The informational specifications $\alpha = 0, \beta = 1$ in Theorem 2.4 and $\alpha = 1$, $\beta = 0$ in Theorem 2.5 are extreme in the sense that the signal $y = (\alpha y_\lambda, \beta y_\phi)$ is either uninformative with respect to the tradable λ-risk or uninformative with respect to the nontradable ϕ-risk. Under the specification $\alpha = 1, \beta = 1$, the agents observe both components of the signal and hence receive information on both risk factors. In this case, the equilibrium allocation of the risks which are affected by the information signal is neither efficient nor perfectly inefficient. Clearly, in our model, the specification $\alpha = 1, \beta = 1$ implies that the effects described in Theorems 2.4 and 2.5 show up in combination: better information can but need not lead to higher economic welfare. Signal components which

6. The Hirshleifer effect and the Blackwell effect are not independent of one another. Since our model is based on the maximization of the expected value of an intertemporally additive utility function, high relative risk aversion goes hand in hand with low intertemporal substitution in consumption (see Hall, 1988; Kocherlakota, 1990). The measure of intertemporal substitution, in turn, affects the Blackwell effect. With $\gamma = 1$ (logarithmic utility), it is optimal for the workers not to react to information signals. Yet, if the information is ignored by the agents, then the Blackwell effect is absent and, hence, only the harmful Hirshleifer effect is active.

reduce the exposure of the agents toward *inefficiently* allocated risks tend to increase the value of the information; and signal components which reduce *efficiently* allocated risks have an ambiguous impact. Such components tend to increase the value of the information, if risk aversion (of the consumers) is low; and they tend to decrease the value of the information, if risk aversion is high.

It is worth pointing out that these findings are not necessarily limited to economies where explicit risk sharing markets exist. Even in the absence of any hedging instrument, some risk sharing may occur through the operation of goods and labor markets; for example, part of the production risk may be shifted to the consumption sector via stochastically fluctuating factor prices. In principle, our analysis is applicable whenever some risk sharing takes place in equilibrium. The mechanism at work in our model, which may lead to lower welfare in better informed economies, has been studied in a different context by Hart (1975), Milne and Shefrin (1987), Newbery and Stiglitz (1984), and others. These authors show that the introduction of new securities (or opening new markets) in an incomplete markets economy may make everybody worse off.

The analysis in this chapter is subject to a number of limitations. First, we have assumed that all consumers and all firm owners are identical. By continuity, under suitable smoothness conditions the conclusions of Theorems 2.2–2.5 will remain valid as long as the diversity among consumers and firm owners are sufficiently small. The theorems may also hold in a weaker form for economies with much diversity among agents. Berk and Uhlig (1993) develop a model with endogenous timing of information. They show that almost surely some agents exist who prefer more information, if there is enough heterogeneity in the population of agents; these are those agents whose net trades under the initial information system are sufficiently small. The basic idea underlying the argument in the paper by Berk and Uhlig can also be applied to the informational structure we have analyzed in Section 2.2.2. This suggests, in particular, that our result in Theorem 2.4 is robust with respect to the introduction of heterogeneity among agents in the weak sense that at least some agents (out of a population with enough diversity) will benefit from better information. Similar considerations apply to Theorem 2.5.

Second, the tradable and the nontradable risks in Section 2.2.2 interact additively. This specification can be generalized without affecting the results as long as the risks are stochastically independent. Third, consumer preferences are additively separable. This is not an innocuous assumption as it shapes the interaction between the Hirshleifer effect and the Blackwell effect.

APPENDIX TO CHAPTER 2

Proof of Theorem 2.2. From the equilibrium conditions in Eqs. 2.17 and 2.18, we observe that the optimal savings in equilibrium $s^*(y)$ satisfy

$$u'(I_0 - s^*(y)) = \beta E\left[\tilde{\theta} f'(s^*(y))u'\left(\tilde{\theta} f(s^*(y))\right)\Big|\, y\right], \qquad (A.2.1)$$

if the economy operates under the information system (Y, ν^1). Each agent attains a level of expected utility equal to

$$V(y) = u(I_0 - s^*(y)) + \beta E\left[u\left(\tilde{\theta} f(s^*(y))\right)\Big| y\right]. \tag{A.2.2}$$

Let us consider the following auxiliary decision problem for a hypothetical decision maker:

$$V_h(y) = \max_{0 \le s \le I_0} \left\{u(I_0 - s) + \beta E\left[u\left(\tilde{\theta} f(s)\right)\Big| y\right]\right\} \tag{A.2.3}$$

The unique solution $\bar{s}(y)$ to Eq. A.2.3 satisfies the necessary and sufficient first-order condition

$$u'\left(I_0 - \bar{s}(y)\right) = \beta E\left[\tilde{\theta} f'\left(\bar{s}(y)\right) u'\left(\tilde{\theta} f\left(\bar{s}(y)\right)\right)\Big| y\right]. \tag{A.2.4}$$

Comparing Eqs. A.2.1 and A.2.4 we find that $s^*(y) = \bar{s}(y)$ which implies $V(y) = V_h(y), y \in Y$. Thus in equilibrium a typical consumer attains the same welfare level as the hypothetical decision maker, that is, $W(Y, \nu^1) = W_h(Y, \nu^1)$ in obvious notation.

We also note that Problem A.2.3 of the hypothetical decision maker satisfies the conditions of Blackwell's Theorem 1.2, since the feasible set of action $s \in [0, I_0]$ does not depend on the information system or the revealed signal. Thus the hypothetical decision maker is weakly better off under the information system (Y, ν^1) than under (X, ν^2), that is, $E_y[V_h(y)] \ge E_x[V_h(x)]$. Since $V(y) = V_h(y)$ holds for all y, we conclude that

$$W(Y, \nu^1) = E_y\left[V(y)\right] = E_y\left[V_h(y)\right] \ge E_x\left[V_h(x)\right] = E_x\left[V(x)\right] = W(X, \nu^2),$$

which proves the theorem. □

Proof of Theorem 2.3. In view of Theorem 1.4, it is sufficient to show that under the assumptions of the theorem the value function is concave in the updated posterior belief $\nu(\cdot|y)$ about the technological shock θ. Since $\overline{\theta}_y$ is linear in $\nu(\cdot|y)$, the value function will be concave in $\nu(\cdot|y)$, if it is concave in $\overline{\theta}_y$. Differentiation of Eq. 2.26 yields

$$\begin{aligned}\frac{V''\left(\overline{\theta}_y\right)}{\beta} &= -\frac{\gamma}{\beta}\left(s'\left(\overline{\theta}_y\right)\right)^2\left[I_0 - s\left(\overline{\theta}_y\right)\right]^{-(1+\gamma)} \\ &\quad + \left(\overline{\theta}_y\right)^{1-\gamma} f''\left(s\left(\overline{\theta}_y\right)\right)\left(f\left(s\left(\overline{\theta}_y\right)\right)\right)^{-\gamma}\left(s'\left(\overline{\theta}_y\right)\right)^2 \\ &\quad + \left[2A - \gamma(1+A)^2\right]\left(\overline{\theta}_y\right)^{-(1+\gamma)}\left(f\left(s\left(\overline{\theta}_y\right)\right)\right)^{1-\gamma},\end{aligned} \tag{A.2.5}$$

where $A := \overline{\theta}_y s'(\overline{\theta}_y) f'(s(\overline{\theta}_y))/f(s(\overline{\theta}_y))$. The first and second expressions on the right-hand side of Eq. A.2.5 are both negative. The third term is also negative for any $\gamma > 1$ (in which case $s'(\overline{\theta}_y) < 0$ holds) and for $\gamma < 1$ as long as $(1-\gamma)$ is sufficiently small.

Thus, under the conditions spelled out in the theorem, the value function is concave in the updated posterior beliefs which completes the proof. □

Proof of Theorem 2.4. Since the signal y is uninformative with respect to the tradable risk factor λ, the price of a futures contract is constant, $\bar{p} = E[\lambda]$. Let $s(y)$ be the equilibrium optimal savings function of the workers, if the economy operates under the information system (Y, ν^1). $s(y)$ satisfies the optimality condition in Eq. 2.37. Each consumer attains a level of expected utility equal to

$$V(y) = v(I_0 - s(y)) + E_\phi \left[u\left((\bar{p} + \phi)f(s(y))\right) \mid y\right].$$

Let us consider the following auxiliary decision problem for a hypothetical decision maker:

$$V_h(y) = \max_{0 \le s \le I_0} \left\{v(I_0 - s) + E_\phi \left[u\left((\bar{p} + \phi)f(s)\right) \mid y\right]\right\}. \tag{A.2.6}$$

Equation A.2.6 has a unique solution, $\bar{s}(y)$, which satisfies the necessary and sufficient first-order condition

$$v'\left(I_0 - \bar{s}(y)\right) = E\left[(\bar{p} + \phi)f'\left(\bar{s}(y)\right)u'\left((\bar{p} + \phi)f\left(\bar{s}(y)\right)\right) \mid y\right]. \tag{A.2.7}$$

Comparing Eqs. 2.37 and A.2.7 we find that $s(y) = \bar{s}(y)$ which implies $V(y) = V_h(y), y \in Y$. Thus, in equilibrium, a typical worker attains the same welfare level as the hypothetical decision maker, that is, $W(Y, \nu^1) = W_h(Y, \nu^1)$ in obvious notation.

Observe that the utility functions v and u in Eq. A.2.6 do not depend on the revealed signal. The problem of the hypothetical decision maker therefore satisfies the conditions of Blackwell's Theorem 1.2. Thus the hypothetical decision maker is weakly better off under the information system (Y, ν^1) than under (X, ν^2), that is, $E_y[V_h(y)] \ge E_x[V_h(x)]$. Since $V(y) = V_h(y)$ holds for all y, and $V(x) = V_h(x)$ holds for all x, we conclude $W(Y, \nu^1) \ge W(X, \nu^2)$, which proves the theorem. □

Proof of Theorem 2.5. The informational specification in Theorem 2.5 describes an economic environment where the information system acts on a single risk factor $\tilde{\lambda}$. In view of Theorem 1.4, we have to show that under the conditions of the theorem the value function in Eq. 2.38 is concave in the updated posterior belief $\nu(\lambda|y)$.

The first-order condition for optimal savings is

$$v'(I_0 - s) = E\left[\left[p(y) + \tilde{\phi}\right]f'(s)u'\left(\left[p(y) + \tilde{\phi}\right]f(s)\right)\right] \quad (y \in Y). \tag{A.2.8}$$

Let $s(p(y))$ be the solution. The value function in Eq. 2.38 can now be written as

$$V\left(p(y)\right) = v\left(I_0 - s(p(y))\right) + E\left[u\left(\left[p(y) + \tilde{\phi}\right]f(s(p(y)))\right)\right]. \tag{A.2.9}$$

Since $p(y) := E[\tilde{\lambda}|y]$ is linear in the posterior belief $\nu(\lambda|y)$, the value function will be concave in $\nu(\lambda|y)$, if it is concave in $p(y)$. Differentiating Eq. A.2.9 with respect to $p(y)$ and using the envelope theorem, we get

$$V'(\cdot) = E\left[f\,(s(\cdot))\,u'\left(\left[p(y)+\tilde{\phi}\right]f\,(s(\cdot))\right)\right]$$

and, hence, (omitting arguments of functions)

$$V'' = E[f's'u'] + E\left[fu''\left(f + \left(p+\tilde{\phi}\right)f's'\right)\right]. \tag{A.2.10}$$

Now, multiply Eq. A.2.8 by s' and differentiate with respect to p to obtain

$$\begin{aligned} 0 = s'^2 v'' &+ E\left[\left(f's' + \left(p+\tilde{\phi}\right)f''s'^2\right)u'\right] \\ &+ E\left[\left(f + \left(p+\tilde{\phi}\right)f's'\right)\left(p+\tilde{\phi}\right)u''f's'\right]. \end{aligned} \tag{A.2.11}$$

Adding Eq. A.2.11 to the right-hand side of Eq. A.2.10 and rearranging yields

$$\begin{aligned} V'' = s'^2 v'' &+ E\left[\left(p+\tilde{\phi}\right)s'^2 f'' u'\right] \\ &+ E\left[\left(f + \left(p+\tilde{\phi}\right)f's'\right)^2 u'' + 2f's'u'\right]. \end{aligned} \tag{A.2.12}$$

The first and second term on the right-hand side of Eq. A.2.12 are both negative. The third term can be rewritten as

$$E\left[\frac{u'f(1+A)^2}{p+\tilde{\phi}}\left(\frac{2A}{(1+A)^2} - \gamma(c_1)\right)\right], \tag{A.2.13}$$

where $A := (p+\tilde{\phi})s'f'/f$, and $\gamma(c_1) := -c_1 u''(c_1)/u'(c_1)$. The above expression is nonpositive, as long as $\gamma(c_1) \geq 2A/(1+A)^2$, $\forall c_1$. The last inequality is satisfied if $\gamma(c_1) \geq 1/2, \forall c_1$, since $2A/(1+A)^2$ is bounded from above by $1/2$.

We have shown that under the conditions of Theorem 2.5, the value function is strictly concave in the updated posterior beliefs. The proof is complete. □

Chapter 3

Evidence on Higher Education and Economic Performance

Chapter Outline

3.1 Higher Education and Economic Development 39
3.2 Higher Education and Income Inequality 40
3.3 Income Inequality and Growth 43
3.4 Credit Constraints in Higher Education 45

There exists extensive empirical evidence on the role of higher education in modern societies. To a considerable extent, however, this evidence is inconclusive, or even contradictory, raising questions about the mechanisms through which higher education is related to other macroeconomic variables. Here, we review some disputed empirical evidence and suggest explanations that will be laid out in greater detail in subsequent chapters.

3.1 HIGHER EDUCATION AND ECONOMIC DEVELOPMENT

Investment in higher education fuels human capital formation which, in turn, constitutes an input factor for the aggregate production process. In many cases, this technological link led economists to conclude that higher education is positively related to economic growth. Under a long-term perspective, the conclusion has, in fact, solid empirical support. Using pooled-country time series data from the OECD Analytical database, Bassanini and Scarpetta (2002) estimate that one additional year of education raises the long-term steady-state level of output per capita by about 6%. Yet, the short-term dynamics are inconclusive. In the short-run, the authors find a negative (although not significant) link between education and output. Other studies have also failed to identify a significant contribution of investment in education to economic growth (Caselli et al., 1996; Topel, 1999; Forbes, 2000).

De Meulemeester and Rochat (1995) use cointegration and Granger-causality tests to evaluate the existence of causality from higher education to economic growth. They find the presence of such causal short-term relationship in Japan, the UK, France, and Sweden. Yet, no causal link could be found for Italy and Australia.

© 2015 Elsevier Inc. All rights reserved.

These inconclusive and sometimes contradictory empirical results raise questions about the nature of the complex link between education and growth. To be consistent with the empirical evidence, a theoretical model of educational investment and human capital formation must be able to identify channels that allow for the possibility of both positive and negative relationships between education and growth.

To resolve this issue, it is important to keep in mind that the aggregate return of an additional dollar investment in higher education depends on the specific individual who receives the education. The better talented this individual is, the more will the invested dollar contribute to aggregate human capital. In other words, the aggregate level of human capital in the economy depends not only on aggregate investment in education but also on the distribution of educational investments across the population. Indeed, policies that stimulate aggregate investment in education may lead to *less* aggregate human capital and *lower* output if the allocation of educational investment deteriorates in the process.

Suppose, for instance, that screening techniques for individual talent become more reliable over time. Such technological development may enhance or reduce the efficiency of the educational investment allocation depending on whether, on average, more reliable screening induces better talented individuals to invest more or less in education. This mechanism can be linked to some puzzles in the empirical literature. Chapter 4 therefore explores in greater detail the delicate screening-induced interaction between investment in higher education and economic growth.

3.2 HIGHER EDUCATION AND INCOME INEQUALITY

Changes in income inequality are poorly explained by standard human capital models which rely on variables like experience and higher education. Lemieux (2006) finds that such variables explain only about one-third of the total income variance. Rubinstein and Tsiddon (2004) arrive at a similar conclusion arguing that such weakness may be caused by technological changes and the irreversible nature of investments in education.

Over the last four decades, income inequality has grown due to higher within-group inequality and due to higher between-group inequality. Within-group inequality captures the income dispersion among individuals with the same average levels of education and experience but with different unobserved skills or abilities. Reducing this dispersion can be viewed as giving more "equal opportunities" to individuals in their early stages of life. By contrast, between-group inequality captures the dispersion of income prospects across individuals with different education levels. Lemieux (2006) finds that changes in the distribution of income opportunities and changes in the distribution of income prospects have both contributed significantly to the history of income inequality.

Figures 3.1 and 3.2 show the between-group variances of US log wages for men and women over the time interval 1975-2005. In the 1970s, the

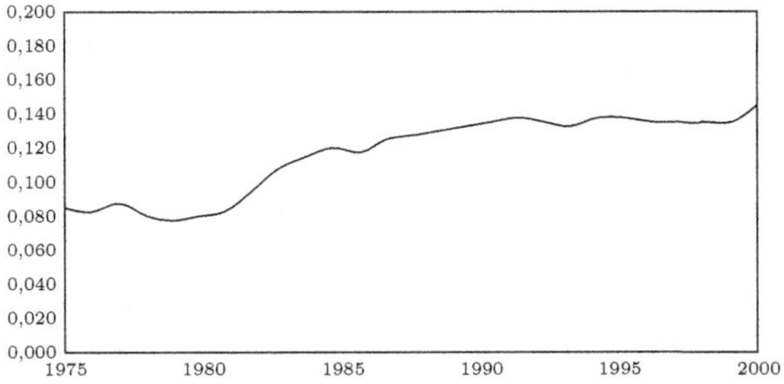

FIGURE 3.1 Between-group variance of log wages, men. *Source: Lemieux (2006).*

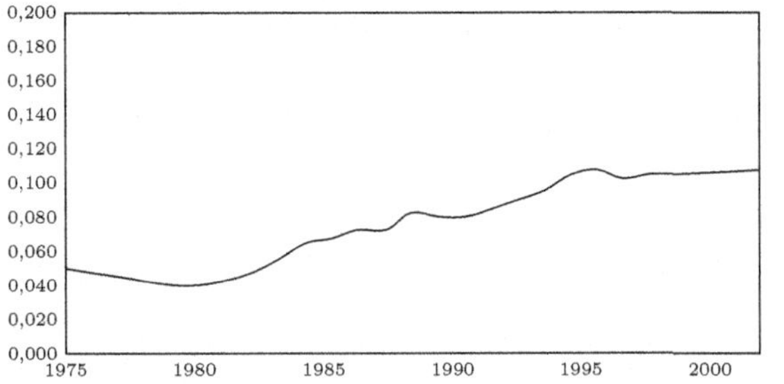

FIGURE 3.2 Between-group variance of log wages, women. *Source: Lemieux (2006).*

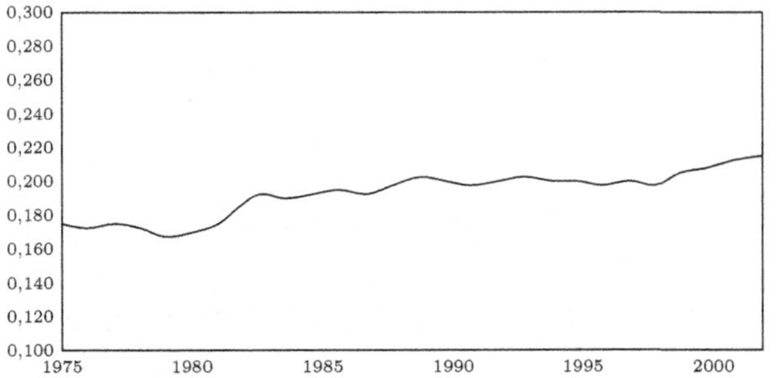

FIGURE 3.3 Within-group variance of log wages, men. *Source: Lemieux (2006).*

between-group variances declined for women and were more or less constant for men. From the 1980s onwards the variance kept increasing for men and women alike.

Figures 3.3 and 3.4 visualize the within-group variances of US log wages for men and women. In the 1970s, the within-group variances were more or less constant, and grew thereafter for men and women alike.

This empirical evidence shows that the inequality of income prospects and the inequality of income opportunities have not always grown in step with each

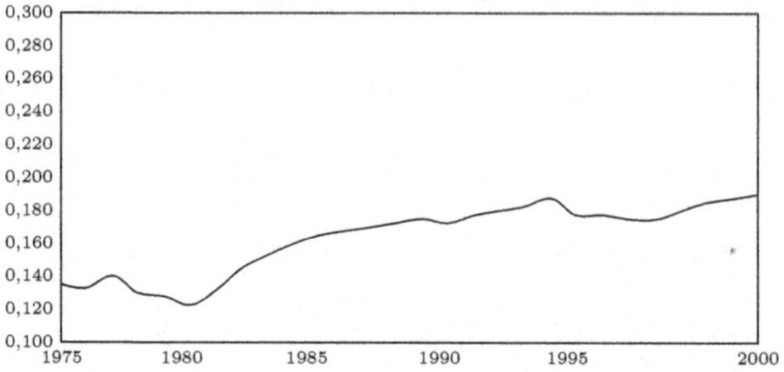

FIGURE 3.4 Within-group variance of log wages, women. *Source: Lemieux (2006).*

other. At times, moreover, the pattern of inequality has developed differently for men and women. In the 1970s, for instance, the inequality of income prospects declined for women and remained roughly constant for men. Many of these empirically documented opposing effects on inequality are not adequately included in standard human capital models.

Given these empirical ambiguities, Chapter 7 analyzes in which circumstances screening and risk sharing in higher education may drive a wedge between changes in the inequality of income prospects and of income opportunities. Individuals with more favorable signals have higher income prospects but not necessarily better income opportunities. Moreover, a more favorable signal may induce higher or lower investment in higher education, depending on the available risk sharing arrangements and on individual attitudes toward risk. The link between investment behavior and screening, in turn, affects the inequality of income prospects but not the inequality of income opportunities. Under plausible restrictions, the interaction of these mechanisms explains why sometimes higher inequality of income prospects goes hand in hand with less inequality of income opportunities.

For Latin American countries, Cruces et al. (2011) found that countries with high inequality in the distribution of education tend to exhibit high income inequality. Yet, this association is rather loose. At least temporarily, equalizing effects on educational investments appear to have generated unequalizing changes in the distribution of incomes. In the 1990s, inequality in the distribution of education has increased in all Latin American countries, while during the first decade of the 2000s, it shrunk in several countries. These developments did not have a visible equalizing impact on the income distributions in the 1990s, but had a strong equalizing effect on the distribution of incomes in the 2000s.

This observation raises a question about the nature of the relationship between the distribution of education and the distribution of incomes. Chapters 5 and 6 elaborate on this link. Will government policies that provide incentives or reduce barriers for educational investments lead to less income inequality? Can this goal be achieved, if the policy is combined with suitable funding schemes for higher education?

3.3 INCOME INEQUALITY AND GROWTH

The relationship between inequality and growth has become a centerpiece of economic research. While there was a time when economists seemed to broadly agree that there exists a trade-off between reducing inequality and stimulating growth (Kuznets, 1955), this view has been challenged more recently by various empirical studies. In particular, postwar data show that some East Asian economies with low levels of inequality grew at a higher rate than some Latin American countries with higher levels of inequality.

Forbes (2000) uses data generated from a sample of 45 countries to estimate the effect of inequality on growth. The data span the period from 1965 to 1995. Mean income is measured as the logarithm of real GNP per capita while income inequality is measured by the Gini coefficient. The data relevant for our purposes are reported in Table 3.1. The graph of these data, which is plotted in Figure 3.5, suggests that there exists no statistically significant effect of inequality on income levels.

TABLE 3.1 Income-Inequality Data

Year	Mean Income (ln of Real GNP/Capita)	Inequality (Gini Coefficient)
1965	7.62	37.8
1970	7.68	40.3
1975	8.19	39.9
1980	8.38	38.1
1985	8.0	37.4
1990	8.28	38.0

Source: Forbes (2000).

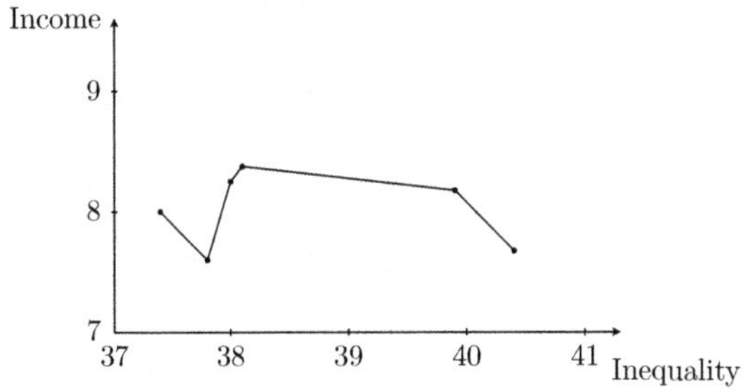

FIGURE 3.5 Income and inequality.

TABLE 3.2 Growth-Inequality Data

Period	Mean Income	Inequality
1965-1969	0.06	37.8
1970-1974	0.51	40.3
1975-1979	0.19	39.9
1980-1984	−0.38	38.1
1985-1989	0.28	37.4
1990-1994	0.02	38.0

Source: Forbes (2000).

Table 3.2 reports the relevant data for a comparison of mean income growth and inequality. The first variable is calculated as the change of mean income during the respective period while the second variable represents the inequality measure at the beginning of the period. A positive (negative) statistical relationship between the two variables thus suggests that higher inequality stimulates (weakens) subsequent economic growth.

In Figure 3.6, we plot the growth data from Table 3.2 against the inequality data. While, again, the relationship appears to be rather loose, the statistical coefficient of inequality on growth is clearly positive. Indeed, using a variety of different estimation techniques, Forbes (2000) finds that this coefficient is never negative.

Some other studies, however, have reached opposite conclusions. These studies use different data sets and, in many cases, different estimation techniques. Perotti (1996) finds a negative effect of inequality on growth. Persson and Tabellini (1994) also find that the coefficient is of negative sign, both in historical panel data and in postwar cross section data, and that the negative sign is almost always statistically significant.

The inconclusiveness of these empirical studies suggests that inequality and growth are aligned through various interacting mechanisms. Chapters 4, 5, and 7

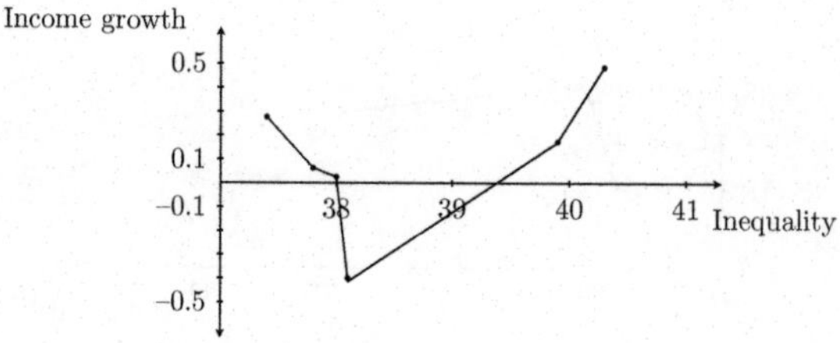

FIGURE 3.6 Inequality and income growth.

discuss some mechanisms in higher education that can explain positive as well as negative links between inequality and growth. The mechanisms will be based on the varied role of improved screening techniques for the distribution of investments and returns in higher education. The role of screening is shaped by the existence and nature of risk sharing arrangements, by the specifics of the funding schemes for educational investments, by attitudes toward risk as well as by government transfer and tax policies.

3.4 CREDIT CONSTRAINTS IN HIGHER EDUCATION

The process of aggregate human capital formation will be plaqued by inefficiencies unless individual investments in higher education are chosen by equating marginal costs and marginal aggregate returns. The marginal returns vary across the population as they depend on individual abilities or potentials. It is therefore important that talented children from poor families are able to raise funds to finance their enrollment in college. Yet, competitive asset markets are unlikely to achieve that goal. Financial markets for education financing tend to be imperfect. Indeed, often such markets do not even exist because human capital cannot be traded, nor can it easily serve as collateral for human capital investments. As a consequence, credit constraints facing poor families may distort the equilibrium allocation of educational investments thus creating inefficiencies in the human capital formation process.

A large body of empirical research shows persistently strong correlation between the income distribution in a society and per capita incomes. Galor and Zeira (1993) argue that this correlation may be caused by credit constraints in higher education. Picking up on this conjecture, Carneiro and Heckman (2002) have analyzed the evidence on credit constraints in post-secondary schooling. Figure 3.7 provides a first indication by showing the relationship between family incomes and college participation rates. The figure refers to 18- to 24-year-old American males classified by their parental incomes. The figure shows that college participation varies substantially across family income classes. Persons from families with higher incomes are more likely to enroll in college. Carneiro and Heckman (2002) point out that similar patterns are found in many other countries.

While these patterns may be interpreted in several ways, the most plausible explanation for the relationship in Figure 3.7 are credit constraints facing poorer families. For one thing, credit constraints impose limitations on the resources those families can use to finance college education. For another, restricted access to credit markets implies higher funding costs. Both factors limit the enrollment in college for the children of the poor.

Cameron and Heckman (1999) use a more direct approach to testing the importance of credit constraints on college attendance. They estimate the effect of a \$1000 increase in gross tuition on college entry probabilities of American high school completers classified by parental incomes. The results are reported

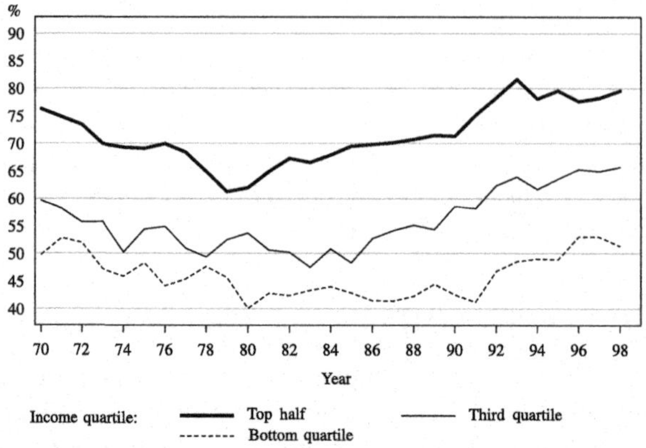

FIGURE 3.7 College attendance rates by parental family income quartiles. *Source: Carneiro and Heckman (2002).*

TABLE 3.3 Effect of Gross Tuition Increase on College Entry Probabilities

Family Income Quartiles	Whites	Blacks	Hispanics
Top quartile	−0.04	−0.01	−0.04
Second quartile	−0.06	−0.03	−0.05
Third quartile	−0.07	−0.07	−0.08
Bottom quartile	−0.06	−0.05	−0.08

Source: Cameron and Heckman (1999).

in Table 3.3. Higher gross tuition reduces the college entry probability of Whites, Blacks, and Hispanics in all income quartiles. However, the negative impact is substantially larger for families in the two lower income quartiles than for families in the two upper income quartiles. This evidence suggests, once again, that credit constraints facing low income families affect college enrollment rates.

In Chapters 5 and 6, we pick up on these empirical findings by focusing on the financial barriers that prevent talented individuals from participating in the higher education system. Credit constraints can be mitigated by government guarantees or by loan programs with income contingent repayments. Income contingent loan programs may offer different degrees of diversification for individual income risks. Overcoming credit constraints and risk diversification problems holds out the prospect of efficiency gains for the human capital formation process. We will also explore how these gains are affected by more reliable screening and by some government policy options such as tax-financed tuition subsidies or student loans subsidies.

Chapter 4

Screening and Economic Growth

Chapter Outline

4.1 Better Screening in a Dynamic Framework 47
4.2 Description of the Framework 49
4.3 Screening in the Absence of Risk Sharing 53
4.4 Screening in the Presence of Risk Sharing 56
4.5 Concluding Remarks 60
Appendix to Chapter 4 61

4.1 BETTER SCREENING IN A DYNAMIC FRAMEWORK

The theory of economic growth has focused on endogenous growth models since the mid-1980s of the twentieth century. The main engine for economic growth is the formation of human capital. Following the seminal contributions of Becker (e.g., Becker, 1964), economic models have included explicitly investment in education, its effects on productivity and its consequences to growth. Endogenous growth models in which human capital operates as the engine for growth have been widely used in the literature to analyze implications of economic policy. This literature includes the seminal papers by Lucas (1988), Azariadis and Drazen (1990), Eckstein and Zilcha (1994), Galor and Tsiddon (1997), and Orazem and Tesfatsion (1997).

Information about unknown individual ability affects the decision-making process in which agents choose their investment in education following the compulsory schooling. Since this decision is made at an early stage when individual ability is still uncertain, the informativeness of signals about ability plays an important role. We assume that the provision of compulsory education has a uniform impact on all young individuals and that it is fully financed by the public sector. For now, we also abstract from government subsidies at the tertiary education stage and focus instead on the role of private investment in higher education for economic development over time. This type of investment depends on family background as well as on the availability and the design of student

© 2015 Elsevier Inc. All rights reserved.

loan arrangements. In particular, the financial terms of loan repayments and the involved risk diversification are important determinants of private investment in higher education.

The process of human capital formation is known to be extremely complex and needs to be simplified in theoretical analysis. Education systems typically include a public schooling system, where part of the elementary education is compulsory, and other parts are noncompulsory. Private education institutions also play a significant role, in particular in tertiary education. Moreover, the human capital formation process is also affected by "home education" and the social environment. Some discussion related to these issues can be found in Jovanovic and Nyarko (1995), Laitner (1997), and Orazem and Tesfatsion (1997).

We consider a framework in which young agents with finished compulsory education obtain a public signal correlated with their true innate ability (which is yet unknown). Each agent's decision about private investment in higher education will be based on the signal obtained as well as on the cost of the investment. The information system determines the precision of these signals. Thus, updated beliefs about uncertain ability and future incomes will be affected by the information system. Unlike in static models of information (e.g., Hirshleifer, 1971; Green, 1981; Schlee, 2001), the information system in a dynamic model affects all future generations via its impact on the investment in human capital.

It is widely recognized that investment in education involves considerable risk. In addition, the possibilities for diversification are quite limited, because human capital cannot be traded on markets and cannot be separated from individuals (see Levhari and Weiss, 1974). In some cases, insurance contracts which are contingent on the level of individual incomes may be tradable, thereby allowing the agents to share part of their idiosyncratic risks. Our study therefore compares the welfare effects of information under two different scenarios. The first scenario is characterized by the absence of any risk sharing arrangements; and under the second scenario agents are able to obtain partial insurance for the risky returns of their investments in human capital.

Our analysis uses the framework of an overlapping generations (OLG) economy with production (see, Diamond, 1965) and no population growth. Individuals in the same generation differ in their innate abilities. We assume that the human capital of an individual depends upon innate ability as well as the "environment," represented by the average human capital level of the older generation (the generation of the teachers and parents). When ability is still unknown each individual decides how much "effort" to invest in his/her education and training. The return to this investment, in terms of wages during the working period, is random since it depends on the realization of ability. Before investment decisions are made, each agent observes a signal which reveals in a Bayesian manner some information about his personal ability. In this way, individuals are screened for their abilities. The invest decisions and, hence, the accumulation of human capital, depend on the reliability of the screening process. The reliability of the screening process corresponds to the informativeness of the signals.

We shall find that better screening affects economic welfare in two ways. First, as signals become more informative agents are exposed to less uncertainty when they make their decisions. This reduction in uncertainty has an impact on welfare which is called the *direct* effect. Second, better screening creates an externality through its impact on the accumulation of human capital: future generations benefit from a higher accumulation rate, because they inherit part of their human capital from the previous generation. This mechanism is called the *indirect* welfare effect.

If no risk sharing is available, then the direct effect on welfare is always positive. By contrast, the indirect effect, that is, the welfare effect via growth, is positive in economies with moderately risk-averse agents, and negative in economies with highly risk-averse agents. If a risk sharing market exists, its operation can potentially interfere with the informational structure of the economy. More precisely, if part of the human capital risk can be insured, both the direct and the indirect welfare effects are negative in economies with highly risk-averse agents, and positive in economies with moderately risk-averse agents. Thus, if the consumers are highly risk-averse, better screening during the youth period can be harmful and may reduce growth and welfare of all generations.

The value of information, too, depends heavily on the existing risk sharing arrangements. In particular, it matters whether the screening information relates to risks that can be insured or to risks that are uninsurable.

4.2 DESCRIPTION OF THE FRAMEWORK

Our theoretical set up consists of an OLG economy with a single commodity. Individuals live for three periods: in the first period, called the "youth period," they acquire higher education while they are still supported by their parents. In the second period, called "middle-aged" period, agents work, receive income and also consume part of their resources. In the third period, called the "retirement" period, agents consume the returns on their savings. Generation t, denoted G_t, $t = 0, 1, 2, \ldots$, consists of all individuals born at date $t - 1$.

One of the main features of our economy is the heterogeneity of individuals with regard to their human capital generated by different levels of innate ability. Nature assigns abilities to agents deterministically but, when young, no agent knows nature's choice. We assume that the distribution of abilities across agents is the same in each generation. Let $\nu(A)$ denote the (time-invariant) density of agents with ability A and, for convenience, normalize the measure of agents in each generation to 1:

$$\int_{\mathbb{R}_+} \nu(A)\,\mathrm{d}A = 1.$$

Agents learn their abilities at the beginning of their middle-age period. Hence, they act under uncertainty in their first period of life. Observe, however, that there is no risk in the aggregate since the distribution ν is fixed. This approach follows the modeling technique in Feldman and Gilles (1985, Proposition 2), which produces individual uncertainty but aggregate certainty.

In order to specify the human capital formation process, we assume that individual human capital is determined by three factors. The first factor is individual innate ability A^i. The second factor is effort, e^i, invested in learning and practicing. The third factor is the average human capital, H_{t-1}, of the "older generation," which includes the individual's parents, teachers, etc. The parameter H_{t-1} is sometimes called "the environment" in which the individual grows up. Thus, we specify for agent i in G_t:

$$\tilde{h}^i = \tilde{A}^i g(H_{t-1}, e^i) \tag{4.1}$$

with

$$g : \mathbb{R}^2_+ \to \mathbb{R}_+, \quad g(H,e) = \hat{g}(H)e^\alpha, \tag{4.2}$$

where $\hat{g} : \mathbb{R}_+ \to \mathbb{R}_+$ is strictly increasing, and $\alpha \in (0,1)$.

Before agent i chooses an effort level in the youth period, nature assigns to him a signal $y^i \in Y \subset \mathbb{R}$. The signals assigned to agents with ability A are distributed according to the density $\nu_A(y)$ which satisfies strict MLRP. The distribution of signals received by agents in the same generation has the density

$$\mu(y) = \int_{\mathbb{R}_+} \nu_A(y)\nu(A)\, dA. \tag{4.3}$$

Denoting by $\nu_y(\cdot)$ the density of the conditional distribution of A given the signal y, average ability of all agents who have received the signal y is

$$\bar{A}(\nu_y) := \int_{\mathbb{R}_+} A\nu_y(A)\, dA. \tag{4.4}$$

We assume that signals are public information while the effort employed by each individual is private information. This assumption will be relaxed later on.

Individuals derive negative utility from "effort" while they are young. We denote consumption in the working period by c_1, and in the retirement period by c_2. For each agent, the lifetime utility function is given by

$$U(e, c_1, c_2) = v(e) + u_1(c_1) + u_2(c_2), \tag{4.5}$$

where the period utility functions belong to the family of CRRA:

$$u_1(c_1) = \frac{c_1^{1-\gamma_u}}{1-\gamma_u}; \quad u_2(c_2) = \beta\frac{c_2^{1-\gamma_u}}{1-\gamma_u}; \quad v(e) = -\frac{e^{\gamma_v+1}}{\gamma_v+1}. \tag{4.6}$$

γ_u and γ_v are strictly positive constants. γ_v parameterizes the curvature of the utility function in the youth period, v; and γ_u parameterizes the curvature of the utility functions in the middle-age period and the retirement period, u_i, $i = 1, 2$.

In models with additively separable intertemporal preferences, the curvatures of the utility functions have elements of both risk aversion and intertemporal substitution: high relative risk aversion goes hand in hand with low intertemporal substitution in consumption (see, Kihlstrom and Mirman, 1981; Hall, 1988; Epstein and Zin, 1989; Kocherlakota, 1990). However, since in our model, the utility of an agent in his youth period is nonrandom, γ_v represents a measure for the reciprocal of the elasticity of intertemporal substitution (rather than a measure of relative risk aversion). By contrast, γ_u needs to be interpreted as a measure of the agent's relative risk aversion in his middle-age period and retirement period. This is because in these periods price induced intertemporal substitution effects play no role as prices are fixed by the international rate of interest.

The following assumptions about the production process in our economy will be maintained throughout the remainder of this book. Production is carried out by competitive firms who use two factors of production: physical capital K and human capital H. The process is described by an aggregate production function $F(K,H)$ which exhibits constant returns to scale.

The aggregate human capital employed in the production process is measured in "efficiency units" of labor: if individual i with human capital h^i supplies l^i units of labor during the working period, his supply of human capital in efficiency units equals $l^i h^i$. Labor supply is inelastic, hence l^i is constant across individuals and will be normalized, $l^i = 1$ for all i.

Assumption 4.1. *$F(K,H)$ is concave, homogeneous of degree 1, and satisfies $F_K > 0$, $F_H > 0$, $F_{KK} < 0$, and $F_{HH} < 0$.*

We assume full international mobility of physical capital. Human capital, by contrast, is assumed to be immobile. Thus, the interest rate $\bar{r}_t$ is exogenously given at each date t. This implies that the marginal productivity of aggregate physical capital K_t must be equal to $1 + \bar{r}_t$, assuming full depreciation of capital in each period. On the other hand, given the aggregate stock of human capital, H_t, the stock K_t adjusts in equilibrium such that

$$1 + \bar{r}_t = F_K(K_t, H_t) \quad t = 1, 2, 3, \ldots \tag{4.7}$$

holds. Assumption 4.1 then implies that $\frac{K_t}{H_t}$ is determined by the international rate of interest $\bar{r}_t$. Hence, the wage rate w_t (price of one unit of human capital), which is equal to the marginal product of aggregate human capital, is also determined once $\bar{r}_t$ is given. Thus, we may write

$$w_t = F_L\left(\frac{K_t}{H_t}, 1\right) =: \zeta\left(\bar{r}_t\right) \quad t = 1, 2, 3, \ldots. \tag{4.8}$$

Agents in G_t choose optimal levels of saving and investment in education at time $t-1$ by maximizing their lifetime expected utility. They take as given the relevant prices of physical capital and labor $(\bar{r}_t, w_t)$, as well as the externality parameter, H_{t-1}, representing the average human capital of middle-aged agents. The investment (effort) decision is made when ability $\tilde{A}$ is still unknown, but after the signal y^i has been observed. The saving decision, s^i, is made in the middle-aged period, after $\tilde{A}$ has realized and human capital, h^i, has become known. s^i will therefore depend on h^i via the wage earnings $w_t h^i$.

For given levels of h^i, w_t, and $\bar{r}_t$, the optimal saving decision of individual $i \in G_t$ is determined by

$$\max_{s^i} u_1(c_1^i) + u_2(c_2^i), \quad \text{s.t. } c_1^i = w_t h^i - s^i, \quad c_2^i = (1 + \bar{r}_t)\, s^i \tag{4.9}$$

and satisfies the necessary and sufficient first-order condition

$$-u_1'(w_t h^i - s^i) + (1 + \bar{r}_t)\, u_2'\left((1 + \bar{r}_t)\, s^i\right) = 0. \tag{4.10}$$

From Eq. 4.10 we derive optimal saving as a function of h^i, that is, $s^i = s_t(h^i)$. The optimal level of effort invested in education, e^i, is determined by

$$\max_{e^i} E\left[v(e^i) + u_1\left(\tilde{c}_1^i\right) + u_2\left(\tilde{c}_2^i\right) \middle| y^i\right], \quad \text{s.t. } \tilde{c}_1^i = w_t \tilde{h}^i - \tilde{s}^i, \quad \tilde{c}_2^i = (1 + \bar{r}_t)\, \tilde{s}^i, \tag{4.11}$$

where $\tilde{h}^i$ is given by Eq. 4.1 and $\tilde{s}^i$ satisfies Eq. 4.10. Due to the Envelope theorem and the strict concavity of the utility functions, Problem 4.11 has a unique solution determined by the first-order condition

$$v'(e^i) + w_t g_2(H_{t-1}, e^i) E\left[\tilde{A} u_1'\left(w_t \tilde{h}^i - \tilde{s}^i\right) \middle| y^i\right] = 0. \tag{4.12}$$

Since u_1' is a decreasing function we also conclude from Eq. 4.10 that $s_t(h^i)$ and $w_t h^i - s_t(h^i)$ are both increasing in h^i. This implies, in particular, that the LHS in Eq. 4.12 is strictly decreasing in e^i. Similarly, from Eq. 4.11 we obtain the optimal level of effort as a function of the conditional distribution ν_{y^i}, that is, $e^i = e_t(\nu_{y^i})$. Note that any two agents in generation t who receive the same individual signal will choose the same effort level.

Using Eqs. 4.3 and 4.4 the aggregate stock of human capital at date t can be expressed as

$$H_t = E_y\left[\bar{h}_t(\nu_y)\right] = \int_Y \bar{h}_t(\nu_y)\mu(y)\, dy, \tag{4.13}$$

where

$$\bar{h}_t(\nu_y) := \bar{A}(\nu_y) g(H_{t-1}, e_t(\nu_y)) \tag{4.14}$$

is the average human capital of agents in G_t who have received the signal y. Next we define the dynamic equilibrium for our economy given the exogenous rates of interest and initial human capital stock, H_0.

Definition 4.1. *Given the international interest rates $(\bar{r}_t)$ and the initial stock of human capital H_0, a competitive equilibrium consists of a sequence $\{(e^i, s^i)_{i \in G_t}\}_{t=1}^{\infty}$, and a sequence of wages $(w_t)_{t=1}^{\infty}$, such that:*

(i) *At each date t, given $\bar{r}_t$, H_{t-1}, and w_t, the optimum for each $i \in G_t$ in Problems 4.11 and 4.9 is given by (e^i, s^i).*
(ii) *The aggregate stocks of human capital, $H_t, t = 1, 2, \ldots$, satisfy Eq. 4.13.*
(iii) *Wage rates $w_t, t = 1, 2, \ldots$, are determined by Eq. 4.8.*

Below, we study the implications of better screening on welfare and economic growth under two different scenarios. The first scenario entails a market structure that precludes the sharing of ability and income risks while, under the second scenario, agents have access to efficient risk sharing arrangements.

4.3 SCREENING IN THE ABSENCE OF RISK SHARING

Since the first generation G_1 lives only for two periods, in which no decision under uncertainty is taken, it will be considered separately from all the subsequent generations. Recall that all agents in the same generation are ex ante identical; namely, before individual signals are received any two agents in $G_t, t \geq 2$, share the same characteristics. Thus, the welfare of G_t can be defined in a natural way as the ex ante expected lifetime utility of each member in G_t.[1] Consistent with this concept, a welfare improvement of an equilibrium allocation requires that ex ante expected utilities (of agents) in all generations increase.

For our further analysis, we recall that any two agents in generation t who receive the same signal face the same posterior distribution of ability. Therefore, agents with the same signal choose the same effort investment in education. Now, consider the optimizations in Problems 4.9 and 4.11 under some given information system ν_A, and denote by $e_t(\nu_{y^i})$ and $s_t(h^i)$ the decision rules for agent i in generation t. The value function, V_t, of generation t associates to any realization of an individual signal, $y^i, i \in G_t$, the level of i's expected utility,

$$V_t(\nu_{y^i}) = v(e_t(\nu_{y^i})) + E_{\tilde{A}^i}\left[u_1\left(w_t\tilde{h}^i - s_t\left(\tilde{h}^i\right)\right) + u_2\left((1+\bar{r}_t)\, s_t\left(\tilde{h}^i\right)\right)\Big|y^i\right], \tag{4.15}$$

where $\tilde{h}^i = \tilde{A}^i g(H_{t-1}, e_t(\nu_{y^i}))$. Economic welfare, W_t, of an individual in generation t is defined as the ex ante expected utility at the outset of his lifetime:

$$\begin{aligned} W_t(\nu_A) &= E_y[V_t(\nu_y)] \\ &= E_y\left\{v(e_t(\nu_y)) + E_{\tilde{A}}\left[u_1\left(w_t\tilde{h}_t - s_t\left(\tilde{h}_t\right)\right) + u_2\left((1+\bar{r}_t)\, s_t\left(\tilde{h}_t\right)\right)\Big|y\right]\right\}, \end{aligned} \tag{4.16}$$

where $\tilde{h}_t = \tilde{A}g(H_{t-1}, e_t(\nu_y))$. W_t does not depend on the particular agent i chosen from G_t. Thus, all individuals in the same generation attain the same level of welfare.

1. Some authors (e.g., Peled, 1984) apply the Pareto criterion to the conditionally expected utilities at the interim stage *after* signals have been observed. Such criterion is more restrictive than ours as it requires the comparison of profiles of expected utilities for each agent.

We say that the *value of screening information is positive* for G_t, if $W_t(\bar{\nu}_A) \geq W_t(\hat{\nu}_A)$, whenever $\bar{\nu}_A \succ_{\inf} \hat{\nu}_A$ (i.e., $\bar{\nu}_A$ is more informative than $\hat{\nu}_A$ in the Blackwell sense of Definition 1.6).

The following proposition formulates a general result which does not require the parameterizations assumed in Eqs. 4.2 and 4.6.

Proposition 4.1. *Let $\bar{\nu}_A$ and $\hat{\nu}_A$ be two information systems satisfying $\bar{\nu}_A \succ_{\inf} \hat{\nu}_A$. Given any initial conditions, all members of G_1 are better-off (or at least nobody is worse-off) under $\bar{\nu}_A$ than under $\hat{\nu}_A$.*

Thus, information has positive value for all agents in G_1, that is, these agents will benefit from better screening. *Future* generations G_t, $t > 1$, differ from G_1 only by their inherited stock of human capital, H_{t-1}. The welfare of future generations therefore depends on two, possibly conflicting, factors. The first factor represents the mechanism characterized in Proposition 4.1. This factor which, in the absence of risk sharing, has a positive impact on the welfare of all generations will be called the *direct* welfare effect. The second factor is the aggregate stock of human capital, H_{t-1}, which affects the human capital and, hence, the welfare of agents in G_t. This factor will be called the *indirect* welfare effect. Future generations benefit from better screening unambiguously, if these two factors work in the same direction, that is, if better screening leads to higher aggregate stocks of human capital at all dates $t > 1$.

Using the functional forms of $u_j, j = 1, 2$, assumed in Eq. 4.6, it follows from Eq. 4.10 that, given $\bar{r}_t$ and w_t, the saving s^i is proportional to the human capital level h^i. In other words, for each t and for each $i \in G_t$ we have:

$$s^i = m_t h^i, \quad 0 < m_t < w_t, \quad t = 1, 2, \ldots. \tag{4.17}$$

Define $\rho = \alpha/[\gamma_v + \alpha(\gamma_u - 1) + 1]$. Obviously, $\rho \geq 1$ implies that γ_u and γ_v are both less than 1, while $\gamma_v > 1$ and $\gamma_u > 1$ both imply that $\rho < 1$. In the remainder of this section, we will distinguish between two constellations which turn out to be critical for our analysis:

(a) $\rho \geq 1$: the economy is moderately risk-averse and exhibits strong intertemporal substitution.

(b) $\gamma_u > 1$: the economy is highly risk-averse.

Since ρ depends on both γ_u and γ_v, under constellation (a) relative risk aversion and intertemporal substitution are jointly restricted. In particular, risk aversion alone is not an effective device to separate the above constellations. Since $\rho \geq 1$ implies $\gamma_u < 1$ and $1/\gamma_v > 1$, we shall refer to constellation (a) as the moderate risk aversion/strong substitution case and to constellation (b) as the high risk aversion case.

In our model, physical capital fully depreciates in the production process while human capital accumulates over time. Economic growth is therefore reflected in the time path of aggregate human capital, H_t. We identify higher growth with higher levels of H_t for all $t \geq 1$. As a first result, we find that in moderately risk-averse economies with strong intertemporal substitution, better screening has positive effects on growth and welfare.

Proposition 4.2 (Moderate Risk Aversion/Strong Substitution). *Assume $\rho \geq 1$, let $\bar{\nu}_A$ and $\hat{\nu}_A$ be two information systems satisfying $\bar{\nu}_A \succ_{\text{inf}} \hat{\nu}_A$, and denote by $H_t(\bar{\nu}_A)$ and $H_t(\hat{\nu}_A)$, $t = 0, 1, \ldots$, the corresponding stocks of human capital in equilibrium.*

(i) *Better screening enhances growth, that is, $H_t(\bar{\nu}_A) > H_t(\hat{\nu}_A)$ for all $t \geq 1$.*
(ii) *In any competitive equilibrium, screening information has positive value in the sense that all generations are (weakly) better-off under $\bar{\nu}_A$ than under $\hat{\nu}_A$.*

The growth effects of better screening are very different, if individual preferences exhibit high risk aversion. Indeed, for highly risk-averse economies, our next proposition implies an inverse link between information and growth.

Proposition 4.3 (High Risk Aversion). *Assume $\gamma_u > 1$. Better screening reduces growth: $H_t(\bar{\nu}_A) < H_t(\hat{\nu}_A)$, for all $t \geq 1$, whenever $\bar{\nu}_A \succ_{\text{inf}} \hat{\nu}_A$.*

Better screening changes the return on investment in education, which in turn affects effort decisions through the mechanism of intertemporal substitution. By changing effort, the information also affects the volatility of random human capital, thereby causing risk effects. This is why the parameter ρ depends on both γ_v and γ_u implying that in Proposition 4.2 intertemporal substitution effects and risk effects show up in combination. If we rule out intertemporal substitution effects by setting $1/\gamma_v = 0$, the risk effects also disappear. As a consequence, aggregate human capital (Eq. A.4.6 in the Appendix) becomes a constant and, hence, screening does not affect growth. Similarly, for $\gamma_u = 1$, human capital $\bar{h}_t(\nu_y)$ (Eq. A.4.4 in the Appendix) is linear in the posterior belief ν_y and, hence, Theorem 1.4 implies that better screening does not affect growth. With $1/\gamma_v > 0$ and $\gamma_u \neq 1$, however, intertemporal substitution and risk aversion jointly determine the growth effects of better screening.

In equilibrium, there are two mechanisms through which the precision of information signals affects economic growth. We illustrate these mechanisms separately for the respective constellations specified in Propositions 4.2 and 4.3. Consider the case $\rho \geq 1$ (moderate risk aversion/strong substitution). First, with better screening, private investment in education will be better in line with the distribution of talent across agents. Indeed, when signals are more reliable, it is less likely that an agent with low ability receives a signal which suggests high talent and induces him to invest heavily in education; or that an agent with high ability receives a signal which suggests low talent, thereby inducing him to invest too little. This allocative effect has a positive impact on growth.

Second, from Eq. A.4.5 in the Appendix we conclude that the conditional expectation $\bar{\tilde{A}}^{1-\gamma_u}(\nu_y) = E[\tilde{A}^{1-\gamma_u}|y]$ aggregates all relevant information conveyed by the signal y. The higher is $\bar{\tilde{A}}^{1-\gamma_u}(\nu_y)$, the more favorable is the signal y. When signals become more informative, agents with good signals invest more in education and agents with bad signals invest less. However, $\rho \geq 1$ implies that $\bar{h}_t$ in Eq. A.4.4 is a convex function of $\tilde{\bar{A}}^{1-\gamma_u}(\nu_y)$. Thus, the additional effort of agents with good signals adds more to the stock of human capital than the reduced effort of agents with bad signals detracts from it. The strength of this positive effect on aggregate human capital is inversely related to risk aversion and positively related to intertemporal substitution, because ρ is decreasing in γ_u and γ_v.

The overall impact of better screening on growth combines these two effects. On the one hand, the allocation of investment in education becomes more efficient; and on the other hand, the distribution of individual effort levels becomes more dispersed. If the economy is moderately risk-averse, these two effects work in the same direction and stimulate economic growth.

We now turn to the case of high risk aversion, where $\gamma_u \geq 1$ (which implies $\rho < 1$), and reexamine the second effect discussed above. Again, the dispersion of individual effort levels increases with better screening. However, now the resulting effect on the stock of human capital is negative, because $\rho < 1$ and Eq. A.4.4 together imply that $\bar{h}_t$ is concave as a function of the aggregated information $\tilde{\bar{A}}^{1-\gamma_u}(\nu_y)$. The first effect, which is due to a more efficient allocation of effort, also works in the opposite direction as before. According to Eq. A.4.5, agents who have received a good signal (and will probably be highly talented) invest less in education than agents with bad signals (and low talent). By responding to low expected talent with higher investment in education, agents attempt to achieve a satisfactory level of human capital in their second period of life. As the signals become more reliable, agents who have received bad signals will step up their effort and invest more in education. By contrast, agents who have received good signals will cut back on their investment in education. While this kind of behavior is efficient from the decision makers' point of view it is clearly detrimental to economic growth. Thus, again, the two effects work in the same direction. In a highly risk-averse economy, however, they depress economic growth.

4.4 SCREENING IN THE PRESENCE OF RISK SHARING

In Chapter 2, we have discussed the link between screening information and risk sharing in a static economic environment. In the dynamic framework of our current analysis, the existence of risk sharing arrangements has further implications for the accumulation of human capital over time which, in turn, affects the link between screening and welfare.

We proceed on the assumption that risk sharing arrangements are incomplete. Hence, only part of the perceived uncertainty about individual ability is insurable. For this purpose, assume that individual ability is composed of two factors, $A = A_1 \cdot A_2$, with $(A_1, A_2) \in \mathcal{A} := \mathbb{R}_+^2$. The distributions of A_1 and of A_2 across agents in H_t are stochastically independent. Before agents choose effort, they can insure the perceived risk which is associated with the A_1-component of their (unknown) ability. Since there is no aggregate risk in the economy, the insurance market for the A_1-component of ability will be unbiased, that is, the agents can share this part of the perceived risk on fair terms. While in Section 4.3 the signals affected only uninsurable risks, we now assume that the signals contain only information about the insurable risk factor A_1. Since risk sharing takes place on fair terms, any risk-averse decision maker will fully insure the A_1-risk.

To model the risk sharing market, we assume that the A_1-component of individual ability is verifiable by the insurers. The future income of each individual, perceived as random at young age, will then have an insurable component as well as an uninsurable component. Let $\bar{A}_1(\nu_y)$ be the expected value of $\tilde{A}_1$, if the signal y has been observed.

$$\bar{A}_1(\nu_y) := \int_{\mathcal{A}} A_1 \nu_y(A)\, \mathrm{d}A \tag{4.18}$$

Since the insurance market is unbiased, all agents find it optimal to completely eliminate the (perceived) A_1-risk from income in their second period of life. Thus, the optimal saving and effort decisions of individual $i \in G_t$ satisfy the following first-order conditions:

$$(1+\bar{r}_t)u_2'\left((1+\bar{r}_t)s^i\right) - u_1'\left(w_t\bar{A}_1(\nu_{y^i})A_2 g(H_{t-1}, e^i) - s^i\right) = 0, \quad A_2 \in \mathbb{R}_+ \tag{4.19}$$

$$v'(e^i) + w_t g_2(H_{t-1}, e^i) E\left[\bar{\tilde{A}}(\nu_{y^i}) u_1'\left(w_t \bar{\tilde{A}}(\nu_{y^i}) g(H_{t-1}, e^i) - s^i\right) \Big| y^i\right] = 0, \quad y^i \in Y, \tag{4.20}$$

where

$$\bar{\tilde{A}}(\nu_{y^i}) := \bar{A}_1(\nu_{y^i}) \cdot \tilde{A}_2. \tag{4.21}$$

Can better screening enhance economic welfare when the A_1-component of the ability risk is insurable? In Chapter 2 of this book, we demonstrated for a class of production economies and risk sharing arrangements that the welfare effects of screening information critically depend on the degree of risk aversion of the consumers. However, it is unclear whether these findings still apply in the present context, because the analysis in Chapter 2 was static and has abstracted from the externality created by private investment into the human capital stock.

Let us first consider the *direct* welfare effect which was shown to be positive in the absence of risk sharing (cf. Proposition 4.1). Denote by $e(\cdot)$ and $s(\cdot)$ the optimal effort and saving decision of an agent in the first generation G_1 (omitting the indices i and t). Recall that the signal affects only the insurable risk $\tilde{A}_1$. Thus, according to Eq. 4.20, $e(\cdot)$ depends on the posterior belief ν_y only via $\bar{A}_1(\nu_y)$. Similarly, in view of Eq. 4.19, $s(\cdot)$ depends on ν_y only via $\underset{\sim}{\tilde{h}} := \underset{\sim}{\tilde{A}}(\nu_y) g(H_0, e(\cdot))$, where $\underset{\sim}{\tilde{A}}(\nu_y)$ has been defined in Eq. 4.21. Thus, we may write the value function as

$$V\left(\bar{A}_1(\nu_y)\right) = v(e(\cdot)) + E\left[u_1\left(w_1\tilde{\bar{h}}(\cdot) - s\left(\tilde{\bar{h}}(\cdot)\right)\right)\right]$$
$$+E\left[u_2\left((1+\bar{r})s\left(\tilde{\bar{h}}(\cdot)\right)\right)\right], \qquad (4.22)$$

where $e(\cdot)$ and $\tilde{\bar{h}}(\cdot)$ are functions of $\bar{A}_1(\nu_y)$.

For agents in the first generation, G_1, only the direct welfare effect matters. In the presence of risk sharing, this effect is negative, if relative risk aversion exceeds $1/2$.

Proposition 4.4. *Let $\bar{\nu}_A$ and $\hat{\nu}_A$ be two information systems satisfying $\bar{\nu}_A \succ_{\text{inf}} \hat{\nu}_A$ and assume that all agents have access to the insurance market. Given any initial conditions, all members of G_1 are worse-off (or at least nobody is better-off) under $\bar{\nu}_A$ than under $\hat{\nu}_A$, if $\gamma_u \geq 1/2$ holds.*

The above result is not limited to the assumed parametric family of utility functions in Eq. 4.6. Indeed, the proposition holds for arbitrary twice differentiable strictly concave period utility functions $u_1(c)$ and $u_2(c)$ that satisfy the following conditions: denote by $R_j(c_j) := -u_j''(c_j)c_j/u_j'(c_j), j = 1, 2$, the relative measures of risk aversion in the agent's working period and retirement period. Then the claim in Proposition 4.4 holds true, if (i) $R_1(c_1) \geq 1/2$, for all $c_1 \geq 0$ and (ii) $R_2(c_2) \geq R_1(c_1)$, for all $c_1, c_2 \geq 0$.

Propositions 4.1 and 4.4 suggest that the *direct* welfare effect, that is, the impact of better screening on the welfare of G_1, is less favorable (or even harmful) when agents are able to hedge against the risk on which information is revealed. This result can be interpreted in terms of two opposing mechanisms that we encountered already in Chapter 2. The first mechanism was pointed out by Blackwell (1953): when agents receive more reliable information they are able to improve the quality of their effort and saving decisions. And better individual decisions result in higher welfare.

The second mechanism captures the Hirshleifer effect (Hirshleifer, 1971, 1975). The Hirshleifer effect rests on a deterioration of the risk allocation due to better information: more reliable information signals typically restrict the risk sharing opportunities in an economy, which leads to lower welfare. In our model, the risk sharing market opens after the signals have been observed. Thus, on this market the agents can only insure that part of the $\tilde{A}_1$-risk, which has not yet been resolved through the signals. Accordingly, with more informative signals the insurable part of the $\tilde{A}_1$-risk will become smaller and economic welfare will decline. The welfare loss caused by the uninsured risks is small, if the economy is only slightly risk-averse, but may assume significant proportions in highly risk-averse economies.

In economies where no risk sharing arrangements are operative, the Hirshleifer effect is nil and, hence, better information increases welfare

(Proposition 4.1). If, by contrast, the $\tilde{A}_1$-risk can be insured, then the *direct* impact of better information on economic welfare depends on a subtle interaction between the positive Blackwell effect and the negative Hirshleifer effect: in weakly risk-averse economies welfare will rise; and in strongly risk-averse economies welfare will decline, when the Hirshleifer effect dominates the Blackwell effect. According to Proposition 4.4, the critical value of relative risk aversion, beyond which the Hirshleifer effect outweighs the Blackwell effect, is less than 1/2.

We now turn to the indirect welfare effect which is due to economic growth.

Proposition 4.5 (Moderate Risk Aversion). *Assume that an insurance market for the $\tilde{A}_1$-risk exists, and let $\gamma_u < 1$. Better screening enhances growth for all $t \geq 1$. When $\gamma_u = 1$, information has no effect on growth.*

Proposition 4.5 contains a similar message as Proposition 4.2(i): loosely speaking, better screening enhances growth in moderately risk averse economies. In the absence of a risk sharing market for the $\tilde{A}_1$-risk, moderate risk aversion was a necessary condition for higher screening-induced growth, too. Therefore, the conditions which guarantee positive growth effects are somewhat less restrictive, if a risk sharing market exists.

Next we consider the case where the economy has strongly risk-averse agents. High risk aversion not only weakens the growth and welfare effects of better screening but may actually reverse them.

Proposition 4.6 (High Risk Aversion). *Assume that an insurance market for the $\tilde{A}_1$-risk exists, and let $\gamma_u > 1$; that is, the economy is strongly risk-averse. Then:*

(i) *Better screening reduces growth for all $t \geq 1$.*
(ii) *Screening has negative value in the sense that all generations are (weakly) worse-off under a more informative system.*

It is interesting to note that the results in Propositions 4.5 and 4.6 depend only on relative risk aversion, γ_u, although there exists interaction between the risk effects and the intertemporal substitution effects that are caused by better screening. Yet, with regard to economic growth these effects always work in the same direction if a risk sharing market is available. This explains why the growth effects of better screening can be characterized solely in terms of relative risk aversion.

Better screening may stimulate growth and, at the same time, reduce welfare of the agents in G_1. Combining Propositions 4.4 and 4.5, this happens if $1/2 \leq \gamma_u \leq 1$. If γ_u exceeds 1, better screening depresses growth according to Proposition 4.6(i). In this case, the direct and the indirect welfare effects are both negative and, hence, all generations are worse-off under a more informative system. Future generations are hit harder than the current generation: they suffer not only from the negative direct welfare effect but also from the indirect welfare effect induced by lower growth.

The value of information is unambiguously positive only if the direct and indirect effect are both positive. Under the market structures analyzed in this section and in the previous one, this requirement will be violated unless relative risk aversion γ_u is sufficiently small.[2] In the more realistic case considered in Proposition 4.6 where the $\tilde{A}_1$-risk is insurable and γ_u exceeds 1, screening has negative value in the sense that the economy is better off under a less informative system. This result may explain why in some countries the use of aptitude tests as a screening device for entrance to higher education has recently been subjected to a critical reevaluation.

4.5 CONCLUDING REMARKS

There exists an extensive literature examining the role of screening information in the presence of risk sharing markets. Most of these studies are conducted within a static theoretical set up. We have argued in this chapter that static models are of limited value for an analysis of the welfare implications of screening in higher education, because these models do not explain economic growth that contributes to the welfare of future generations. This chapter proposed a dynamic framework in which the role of screening for growth and economic welfare can be studied.

Better screening creates a *direct* and an *indirect* welfare effect. The direct welfare effect arises because, under a more informative system, agents are able to anticipate the uncertain future economic environment in a more reliable way. In addition, better screening has implications for economic growth through its impact on investment in human capital (indirect effect) thereby affecting the welfare of future generations. The direct and indirect welfare effects can be in conflict with each other. This happens in strongly risk-averse economies, if no risk sharing takes place (direct effect positive, indirect effect negative). In case risk sharing is possible, it also happens in moderately risk-averse economies, if γ_u exceeds 1/2 but is less than 1 (direct effect negative, indirect effect positive).

In either case, that is, with and without risk sharing, both effects are positive, if γ_u and γ_v are sufficiently small. Thus, in slightly risk-averse economies with strong intertemporal substitution better information enhances welfare. By contrast, if a risk sharing market exists and γ_u exceeds 1, both effects are negative implying that all generations are worse-off under a more informative system. As a rule of thumb, the impact of better screening on welfare is less favorable (or even harmful), when risk sharing arrangements are more effective and/or when risk aversion is high.

2. Note from Eq. A.4.8 that, in the presence of risk sharing, $\gamma_u = 0$ implies the convexity of V. Hence, by Theorem 1.4, the direct welfare effect is positive in that case.

APPENDIX TO CHAPTER 4

In this appendix, we prove Propositions 4.1–4.6.

Proof of Proposition 4.1. Denote by $e(\nu_y)$ and $s(h)$ the optimal decision of an agent in G_1 (omitting the indices i and t), and define $U(\tilde{h}, s(\tilde{h})) := u_1(w\tilde{h} - s(\tilde{h})) + u_2((1+\bar{r})s(\tilde{h}))$. With this notation, we may state the value function as

$$V(\nu_y) = v(e(\nu_y)) + \int_{\mathbb{R}_+} U\left(\tilde{h}, s(\tilde{h})\right) \nu_y(A)\, \mathrm{d}A.$$

We show that the value function is convex in the posterior belief ν_y. Assume $\nu_y = \alpha\bar{\nu}_y + (1-\alpha)\hat{\nu}_y, \alpha \in [0,1]$, and denote by $(e(\bar{\nu}_y), \bar{s}(h))$ and $(e(\hat{\nu}_y), \hat{s}(h))$ the optimal decisions under the posterior beliefs $\bar{\nu}_y$ and $\hat{\nu}_y$. We obtain

$$\begin{aligned}
V(\nu_y) &= v(e(\nu_y)) + \int_{\mathbb{R}_+} U\left(\tilde{h}, s\left(\tilde{h}\right)\right) [\alpha\bar{\nu}_y(A) + (1-\alpha)\hat{\nu}_y(A)]\, \mathrm{d}A \\
&= \alpha \left[v(e(\nu_y)) + \int_{\mathbb{R}_+} U\left(\tilde{h}, s\left(\tilde{h}\right)\right) \bar{\nu}_y(A)\, \mathrm{d}A \right] \\
&\quad + (1-\alpha) \left[v(e(\nu_y)) + \int_{\mathbb{R}_+} U\left(\tilde{h}, s\left(\tilde{h}\right)\right) \hat{\nu}_y(A)\, \mathrm{d}A \right] \\
&\le \alpha \left[v\left(e(\bar{\nu}_y)\right) + \int_{\mathbb{R}_+} U\left(\tilde{h}, \bar{s}\left(\tilde{h}\right)\right) \bar{\nu}_y(A)\, \mathrm{d}A \right] \\
&\quad + (1-\alpha) \left[v\left(e(\hat{\nu}_y)\right) + \int_{\mathbb{R}_+} U\left(\tilde{h}, \hat{s}\left(\tilde{h}\right)\right) \hat{\nu}_y(A)\, \mathrm{d}A \right] \\
&= \alpha V(\bar{\nu}_y) + (1-\alpha) V(\hat{\nu}_y).
\end{aligned}$$

The inequality holds because $(e(\bar{\nu}_y), \bar{s}(h))$ and $(e(\hat{\nu}_y), \hat{s}(h))$ maximize expected utility, if the posterior belief is given by $\bar{\nu}_y$ and $\hat{\nu}_y$, respectively.

We have shown that the value function is convex in the posterior beliefs. Now the claim in Proposition 4.1 follows from Kihlstrom's Theorem 1.4. □

The proof of Proposition 4.2 requires some preparatory work. Define

$$\phi(y, y') := \lambda(y', y)\bar{\mu}(y)/\hat{\mu}(y').$$

Note that for any $y' \in Y$, the function $\phi(\cdot, y')$ constitutes a probability density over Y, that is, $\int_Y \phi(y, y')\, \mathrm{d}y = 1$.[3] For any integrable function $\vartheta : Y \to \mathbb{R}$, let $\Gamma(\vartheta(y); y')$ be its expectation with respect to the probability density $\phi(\cdot, y')$, that is,

$$\Gamma\left(\vartheta(y); y'\right) := \int_Y \vartheta(y)\phi(y, y')\, \mathrm{d}y.$$

3. The interpretation of $\phi : Y \times Y \to \mathbb{R}_+$ is the following: If the signal y has realized under the information system $\bar{\nu}_A$, then $\phi(y, y')$ is the probability (density) that y' would have been observed under the information system $\hat{\nu}_A$.

Direct computation yields

$$\hat{\nu}_{y'}(A) = \Gamma\left(\bar{\nu}_y(A); y'\right) \tag{A.4.1}$$

$$\bar{A}(\hat{\nu}_{y'}) = \Gamma\left(\bar{A}(\bar{\nu}_y); y'\right). \tag{A.4.2}$$

Proof of Proposition 4.2.

(i) Since the initial stock of human capital, H_0, is fixed, it suffices to show that for any given $H_{t-1},\ t \geq 1$, the aggregate stock of human capital at date t,

$$H_t = \int_Y \bar{h}_t(\nu_y)\mu(y)\,dy, \tag{A.4.3}$$

is higher under the more informative system. Using Eq. 4.2 in Eq. 4.14 we get

$$\bar{h}_t(\nu_y) = \bar{A}(\nu_y)\hat{g}(H_{t-1})(e_t(\nu_y))^{\alpha}, \tag{A.4.4}$$

where $e_t(\nu_y)$ is given by[4]

$$e_t(\nu_y) = \delta_t\left(E\left[\tilde{A}^{1-\gamma_u}\middle|y\right]\right)^{\frac{1}{\gamma_v+\alpha\gamma_u+1-\alpha}} \tag{A.4.5}$$

with

$$\delta_t := \left[\frac{\alpha w_t\left(\hat{g}(H_{t-1})\right)^{1-\gamma_u}}{(w_t - m_t)^{\gamma_u}}\right]^{\frac{1}{\gamma_v+\alpha\gamma_u+1-\alpha}}.$$

Combining Eqs. A.4.4 and A.4.5 with Eq. A.4.3, we arrive at

$$H_t(\nu_A) = \delta_t^{\alpha}\hat{g}(H_{t-1})\int_Y \bar{A}(\nu_y)\left[\bar{A}^{1-\gamma_u}(\nu_y)\right]^{\rho}\mu(y)\,dy. \tag{A.4.6}$$

By assumption, $\rho \geq 1$ holds which implies $\gamma_u < 1$. From this, in combination with strict Monotone likelihood ratio property (MLRP), we conclude that $\bar{A}(\bar{\nu}_y)$ and $(\bar{A}^{1-\gamma_u}(\bar{\nu}_y))^{\rho}$ are co-monotone in the signal y. The representation in Eq. A.4.6 then implies the following assessment with regard to the information systems $\bar{\nu}_A$ and $\hat{\nu}_A$:

$$\begin{aligned}
H_t(\bar{\nu}_A)/\delta_t^{\alpha}\hat{g}(H_{t-1}) &= \int_Y \bar{A}(\bar{\nu}_y)\left(\bar{A}^{1-\gamma_u}(\bar{\nu}_y)\right)^{\rho}\bar{\mu}(y)\,dy \\
&= \int_Y \Gamma\left(\bar{A}(\bar{\nu}_y)\left(\bar{A}^{1-\gamma_u}(\bar{\nu}_y)\right)^{\rho}, y'\right)\hat{\mu}(y')\,dy' \\
&> \int_Y \Gamma\left(\bar{A}(\bar{\nu}_y), y'\right)\Gamma\left(\left(\bar{A}^{1-\gamma_u}(\bar{\nu}_y)\right)^{\rho}, y'\right)\hat{\mu}(y')\,dy' \\
&\geq \int_Y \bar{A}(\hat{\nu}_{y'})\left(\bar{A}^{1-\gamma_u}(\hat{\nu}_{y'})\right)^{\rho}\hat{\mu}(y')\,dy' \\
&= H_t(\hat{\nu}_A)/\delta_t^{\alpha}\hat{g}(H_{t-1}).
\end{aligned} \tag{A.4.7}$$

4. Equation A.4.5 can be derived from Eq. 4.12 using Eqs. 4.2, 4.12, and 4.17.

In Eq. A.4.7, the first inequality follows from the co-monotonicity property and the second inequality follows from $\rho \geq 1$.

(ii) The future generations G_t, $t \geq 2$, differ from G_1 only by their inherited stocks of human capital. Since the factor prices $\bar{r}_t$ and w_t do not depend on H_t, all future generations will benefit from higher growth. Propositions 4.1 and 4.16(i) therefore imply the claim. □

Proof of Proposition 4.3. $\gamma_u > 1$ implies $\rho < 1$. In this case, both inequalities in Eq. A.4.7 are reversed and the second inequality becomes strict. Thus the same reasoning as in the proof of Proposition 4.2(i) yields the result claimed in the proposition. □

Proof of Proposition 4.4. We prove the more general claim in the paragraph following the proposition. Under the specification in Eq. 4.6, conditions (i) and (ii) in this paragraph boil down to the restriction in Proposition 4.4.

In view of Kihlstrom's Theorem 1.4, we need to show that under the conditions of the proposition the value function in Eq. 4.22 is concave in the posterior belief ν_y. Since $\bar{A}_1(\nu_y)$ is linear in ν_y, the value function will be concave in ν_y if it is concave in $\bar{A}_1$. Making use of the Envelope theorem, differentiation of Eq. 4.22 with respect to $\bar{A}_1$ yields

$$V'(\bar{A}_1) = E\left[u_1'\left(w_1\tilde{\bar{A}}g\left(H_0, e\left(\bar{A}_1\right)\right) - s(\cdot)\right) w_1\tilde{A}_2 g\left(H_0, e\left(\bar{A}_1\right)\right)\right] \quad \text{(A.4.8)}$$

and (omitting the arguments of all functions)

$$V'' = E\left[w_1\tilde{A}_2 g_2 u_1' e' + w_1\tilde{A}_2 g u_1''\left\{w_1\left(\tilde{A}_2 g + \tilde{\bar{A}} g_2 e'\right) - s'\right\}\right]. \quad \text{(A.4.9)}$$

e' and s' denote, respectively, the derivatives of $e(\cdot)$ and $s(\cdot)$ with respect to $\bar{A}_1$. Next, we differentiate Eq. 4.20 with respect to $\bar{A}_1$ and multiply by e' to obtain

$$\begin{aligned} 0 = v'' e'^2 + E\left[\left(\tilde{A}_2 w_1 g_2 e' + \tilde{\bar{A}} w_1 g_{22} e'^2\right) u_1'\right] \\ + E\left[\left\{w_1\left(\tilde{A}_2 g + \tilde{\bar{A}} g_2 e'\right) - s'\right\} w_1 g_2 \tilde{\bar{A}} e' u_1''\right]. \end{aligned} \quad \text{(A.4.10)}$$

Adding Eqs. A.4.9 and A.4.10, and rearranging, yields

$$\begin{aligned} V'' = e'^2 v'' + w_1 g_{22} e'^2 E\left[\tilde{\bar{A}} u_1'\right] \\ + E\left[\left(w_1\tilde{A}_2 g + w_1\tilde{\bar{A}} g_2 e'\right)^2 u_1'' - s' u_1'' w_1\left(\tilde{A}_2 g + g_2\tilde{\bar{A}} e'\right) + 2\tilde{A}_2 w_1 g_2 e' u_1'\right]. \end{aligned} \quad \text{(A.4.11)}$$

The two terms in the first line on the RHS of Eq. A.4.11 are negative. We show that the sign of the term in the second line of Eq. A.4.11 is negative as well. From Eq. 4.19 we get

$$s' = \hat{m}\left(\tilde{\bar{A}}\right)\left(\tilde{A}_2 g + g_2 e' \tilde{\bar{A}}\right), \tag{A.4.12}$$

where

$$\hat{m}\left(\tilde{\bar{A}}\right) := \frac{u_1'' w_1}{(1+\bar{r}_1)^2 u_2'' + u_1''} \le w_1.$$

Using Eq. A.4.12, we rewrite the term in the second line of Eq. A.4.11 as

$$E\left[\left(w_1 - \hat{m}(\tilde{\bar{A}})\right) w_1 \left(\tilde{A}_2 g + \tilde{\bar{A}} g_2 e'\right)^2 u_1'' + 2\tilde{A}_2 w_1 g_2 e' u_1'\right]. \tag{A.4.13}$$

Noting that $\tilde{c}_1 = w_1 \tilde{\bar{A}} g - s$, the expression in Eq. A.4.13 can be transformed into

$$E\left[\frac{u_1' w_1 g(\tilde{A}_2 + B)^2}{\tilde{\bar{A}}}\left\{\frac{2B\tilde{A}_2}{(\tilde{A}_2 + B)^2} - R_1(\tilde{c}_1) + \frac{u_1''}{u_1'}\left[s - \hat{m}\left(\tilde{\bar{A}}\right)\tilde{\bar{A}} g\right]\right\}\right], \tag{A.4.14}$$

where $B := \tilde{\bar{A}} g_2 e'/g$. Since $2B\tilde{A}_2/(\tilde{A}_2 + B)^2 = 2(B/\tilde{A}_2)/[1 + (B/\tilde{A}_2)]^2$ is bounded from above by 1/2, $[2B\tilde{A}_2/(\tilde{A}_2 + B)^2] - R_1(\tilde{c}_1)$ is negative under the assumptions of the proposition. Thus the proof is complete if we can show that

$$s \ge \hat{m}\left(\tilde{\bar{A}}\right)\tilde{\bar{A}} g \tag{A.4.15}$$

is satisfied.

By assumption, $R_2(\tilde{c}_2) \ge R_1(\tilde{c}_1)$ holds for all $\tilde{c}_1, \tilde{c}_2$. From this we conclude, using Eq. 4.19, that

$$\begin{aligned} R_2(\tilde{c}_2) \ge R_1(\tilde{c}_1) &\Longleftrightarrow \frac{u_1'}{u_2'} u_2''(1+\bar{r}_1) \le u_1''\left[\frac{w_1 \tilde{\bar{A}} g}{s} - 1\right] \\ &\Longleftrightarrow (1+\bar{r}_1)^2 u_2'' \le u_1''\left[\frac{w_1 \tilde{\bar{A}} g}{s} - 1\right]. \end{aligned} \tag{A.4.16}$$

If $\tilde{\bar{A}} g$ is locally increasing (decreasing) in $\bar{A}_1$, then Eq. A.4.16 in combination with Eq. 4.19 implies that $w_1 \tilde{\bar{A}} g/s$ is locally increasing (decreasing) in $\bar{A}_1$. Hence, we obtain

$$\begin{aligned} 0 \le \frac{\mathrm{d}}{\mathrm{d}\bar{A}_1}\left(\tilde{\bar{A}} g\right)\frac{\mathrm{d}}{\mathrm{d}\bar{A}_1}\left(\frac{w_1 \tilde{\bar{A}} g}{s}\right) &= \left(\tilde{A}_2 g + \tilde{\bar{A}} g_2 e'\right)\frac{w_1}{s^2}\left[\left(\tilde{A}_2 g + \tilde{\bar{A}} g_2 e'\right)s - s'\tilde{\bar{A}} g\right] \\ &= w_1\left(\frac{\tilde{A}_2 g + \tilde{\bar{A}} g_2 e'}{s}\right)^2\left[s - \hat{m}\left(\tilde{\bar{A}}\right) g\tilde{\bar{A}}\right], \end{aligned} \tag{A.4.17}$$

where in the last equality we have made use of Eq. A.4.12. Obviously, Eq. A.4.17 implies the inequality in Eq. A.4.15. □

Proof of Proposition 4.5. Proceeding along the same lines as in the proof of Proposition 4.2(i) we obtain

$$\bar{h}_t(\nu_y) = \delta_t^{\alpha} \hat{g}(H_{t-1}) \bar{A}_2 \left(\bar{A}_1(\nu_y)\right)^{1+\rho(1-\gamma_u)} \left(E\left[\tilde{A}_2^{1-\gamma_u}\right]\right)^{\rho}, \qquad \text{(A.4.18)}$$

where $\rho > 0$ has been defined in Section 3.3. $\bar{h}_t$ depends on the posterior belief ν_y only via $\bar{A}_1(\nu_y)$. Since $\bar{A}_1(\cdot)$ is linear in ν_y, $\bar{h}_t$ is convex (linear) in ν_y, if and only if $\hat{h} : \mathbb{R}_+ \to \mathbb{R}_+$,

$$\hat{h}(\bar{A}_1) := \bar{A}_2 \bar{A}_1^{1+\rho(1-\gamma_u)} \left(E\left[\tilde{A}_2^{1-\gamma_u}\right]\right)^{\rho}, \qquad \text{(A.4.19)}$$

is a convex (linear) function. Obviously $\hat{h}$ is convex, if $\gamma_u \leq 1$, and linear, if $\gamma_u = 1$ holds. Theorem 1.4 therefore implies the claims in the proposition. □

Proof of Proposition 4.6. $\gamma_u > 1$ implies that $\hat{h}$ in Eq. A.4.19 is a concave function. Thus, the same reasoning as in the proof of Proposition 4.5 yields the result in Part (i).

(ii) By Proposition 4.4, the direct welfare effect is negative for $\gamma_u > 1$. In addition, we have just seen in Part (i) of this proof that the (growth-induced) indirect welfare effect is also negative. Hence, all generations are worse-off under a more informative system. □

Chapter 5

Higher Education Financing

Chapter Outline

5.1 Basic Framework with Multiple Funding Schemes 69
5.1.1 Regime I: Unrestricted Access to Credit Markets 72
5.1.2 Regime II: Unrestricted Insurance of Loans 74
5.1.3 Regime III: Restricted Insurance of Loans 76
5.1.4 Remarks on the Implementation of the Regimes 77
5.2 Human Capital Accumulation 78
5.3 Welfare Comparison 81
5.4 The Effect of Better Screening 84
5.4.1 Screening and Human Capital Formation 87
5.4.2 Screening and Welfare 88
Appendix to Chapter 5 93

Investments in the education sectors of the OECD countries have increased substantially during the second half of the twentieth century (see Greenaway and Haynes, 2003; Checchi, 2006). Yet, the expansion of higher education has created fiscal pressures and a tendency to shift the financial burden from public funding toward private funding. Indeed, most European countries have begun long ago to substitute various forms of income support transfers with nonsubsidized funding schemes for private investment in higher education.

The shift toward private funding of higher education is sometimes justified with reference to a more egalitarian income distribution. On average, students have a better socioeconomic background and, hence, higher income prospects than other members of society (for empirical evidence in various countries, see Chapman, 1997; Carneiro and Heckman, 2002). Public subsidies of higher education are therefore often perceived as an implicit monetary transfer from the poor toward the more affluent individuals. This problematic aspect of public funding was pointed out by Friedman in his famous book *Capitalism and Freedom* in 1962.

Under the idealistic assumption that frictionless markets for private education financing exist, individual abilities will be used efficiently in the production process. In reality, however, markets for education financing are imperfect and sometimes even nonexistent. For instance, young individuals often cannot provide sufficient collateral that would allow them to borrow against their future incomes. The adverse macroeconomic implications of imperfect access

© 2015 Elsevier Inc. All rights reserved.

to loan markets have been extensively discussed in Galor and Zeira (1993). A structural change away from public funding toward private funding therefore requires the provision of suitable loan programs that remove financial barriers for the younger generation, allowing them to participate in the higher education system. Ideally, such loan programs would also provide some diversification of individual income risks within a given cohort of agents. In this chapter, we shall analyze various ways in which the government can support this process.

Moving from public funding toward private funding of higher education generally induces a trade-off in terms of economic welfare that results from interacting efficiency effects and equity effects. What are the main ingredients of a financing scheme that optimally combines the efficiency and equity effects in light of this trade-off? Friedman (1955, 1962) was the first to raise this issue and to suggest income-contingent financing of students' investments in higher education. Friedman argues that income-contingent loans are particularly well suited for the finance of higher education, because they allow individuals to sell "shares" in their uncertain future income streams. These shares will be bought by investors who can "diversify" their holdings through buying shares from many different agents with independent income risks. The diversification process drives down the expected return on the shares to the market rate of interest. This mechanism ensures that individuals can finance their educational investments on favorable terms, thereby avoiding an economy-wide underinvestment in education.

Friedman's suggestion is not explicit about the precise way in which loan repayments should be linked to individual incomes. In particular, there is a question whether all students should be offered the same terms of repayment or whether these terms might take into account certain individual characteristics correlated to an agent's future earning prospects. In this chapter, we reconsider this issue. Our aim is to analyze the implications of alternative income-contingent financing schemes for higher education, differing mainly in the degree of risk-pooling that they involve. The Friedman argument suggests that the educational investment process with income-contingent loans finance is more efficient, if individual income risks are pooled more comprehensively. As we shall see, this conjecture is not always true. In general, the process that transforms aggregate investment in education into aggregate human capital can be improved by restricting risk-pooling to certain subgroups of agents.

In the last three decades, some forms of student loans' programs with specific risk sharing elements have been implemented in various countries. Barr and Crawford (1998) evaluate the impact of higher education student loans in the UK. International experience with student loan schemes, repayment, and debt default has also been discussed by Woodhall (1988), Chapman (1997), and Lleras (2004). Chapman (2006) provides a detailed account of the experience in Australia, where the world's first national income-contingent loan scheme was established in 1989.

Building on the general framework developed in Chapter 3, we shall distinguish between three financing regimes that specify the terms of repayment for education loans. Under the first regime, the government guarantees students unrestricted access to competitive credit markets. The government also guarantees enforcement of debt collection. The second regime links the repayment of a loan to an agent's future income in a way that allows risk pooling across all members in the same generation. The third regime also links the terms of repayment to future income, but in a "narrower" sense that supports pooling of income risks only among individuals in the same signal group. By restricting risks being pooled only within signal groups and, hence, among individuals with the same future income prospects, educational investment becomes less vulnerable to moral hazard type distortions. As a consequence, we find that the third regime performs best in terms of economic growth and welfare.

Based on this result, we consider the third regime most suitable for funding higher education. In a second step, we ask how, under this preferred regime, economic growth and welfare are affected when the screening mechanisms in higher education are improved so as to produce more reliable information about individual ability.

5.1 BASIC FRAMEWORK WITH MULTIPLE FUNDING SCHEMES

We build on the overlapping-generations framework of Chapter 4. The economy has a single commodity, say physical capital, which can be consumed or invested in production. Individuals live for three periods. In the "young period," each individual is supported by his parents. At this stage, the agent takes out a loan and makes a capital investment in education in order to acquire skills. In the "middle period," individuals work, earn labor income, consume, and save. Labor income depends on each agent's skills, or human capital, which is assumed to be observable. Part of the labor income is earmarked for the repayment of the loan. Finally, in the "retirement period," individuals consume their total savings. There is no population growth and each generation G_t (i.e., all individuals born at date $t-1$) consists of a continuum of agents, say the interval $[0, 1]$.

Heterogeneity among individuals is generated by random innate ability. While nature assigns abilities to individuals at birth, no individual knows exactly his own ability when, at young age, he invests privately in education. Therefore, the investment decision, x, is made under uncertainty. In the next period, the agent learns his ability $A \in \mathbb{R}_{++}$. The time-invariant density of agents with ability A is denoted $\nu(A)$.

The level of human capital, or skills, of an individual $i \in G_t$, denoted by h_t^i, depends on the (random) innate ability A^i, the private investment in education $x^i \in \mathbb{R}_+$, and the *average* human capital of the older generation H_{t-1} (which may represent the human capital of "teachers" and parents), that is,

$$h^i = A^i g(x^i, H_{t-1}). \tag{5.1}$$

Public investment in individual education, which is assumed to be the same for all agents, is included in the accumulation function g. We make the following assumption about this process:

Assumption 5.1. *$g(x,H)$ is twice differentiable, strictly increasing and concave in the first argument, and satisfies* $\lim_{x\to 0} g_1'(x,H) = \infty$ *for* $H > 0$. *Also, $g_1'(x,H)$ is nondecreasing in H. Furthermore,*

$$K(x,H) := -\frac{g_{11}''(x,H)}{g_1'(x,H)}$$

is nonincreasing in x, that is, $K_1'(x,H) \leq 0$ for all x, H.

$K(x,H)$ is a measure of concavity (with respect to x) of the accumulation function g. By Assumption 5.1, this measure of concavity is decreasing in x, which implies that $g_1'(x,H)$ is convex in x. Thus, the marginal product of investment in education decreases at a declining rate. This restriction is satisfied by most functional forms commonly used in the literature to describe the transformation of educational investment into human capital formation.

Each agent chooses private investment in education after he has learned a publicly observable signal $y \in Y \subset \mathbb{R}$ of his ability A. Students receive such signals before they enter higher education. Examples include personality tests and matriculation examinations used by universities to screen the field of applicants. The test results are noisy but they are correlated with the characteristics that have been tested. Within the group of agents with ability A, the signals are distributed according to the density $\nu_A(y)$. The signal assigned to an agent is used as a screening device for his unknown ability.

Based on the screening information conveyed by the signal, the agent forms expectations about his ability in a Bayesian way. The average ability of an agent who has received signal y is

$$\bar{A}_y := E\left[\tilde{A}|y\right] = \int_{\mathbb{R}_+} A\nu_y(A)\, \mathrm{d}A,$$

where $\nu_y(A)$ denotes the density of the conditional distribution of A given the signal y.

We assume that the Monotone likelihood ratio property (MLRP) holds, that is, the signals are ordered in such a way that $y' \geq y$ implies that the posterior distribution of ability conditional on y' dominates the posterior distribution of ability conditional on y in the first-degree stochastic dominance. In this sense, higher signals are "good news": a student with a higher signal faces a better (in the sense of first-degree stochastic dominance) posterior distribution of ability. In particular, he will perform better *on average* than students with lower signals. This does not rule out, of course, that an individual with an excellent test result may perform poorly, or that a poorly tested student may perform excellently. The MLRP imposes a restriction on the joint distribution of signals and abilities. Most of our results do not rely on this restriction. Only the welfare analysis in Section 5.3 makes explicit use of it.

Each young individual needs a loan in order to finance his investment in education. The terms of repayment are subject to government intervention. We consider three different forms of government intervention in the market for education loans:

1. *Regime I (unrestricted access to credit markets).* Under this regime, the government guarantees each student unrestricted access to credit markets for funds needed to finance higher education. The government also guarantees enforcement of debt collection, for example, through levies on wages.
2. *Regime II (unrestricted insurance of loans).* Under this regime, the terms of repayment of a loan are linked to the realization of an individual's future income (hence linked to the realization of his human capital). This insurance arrangement pools the risks of *all* young agents in the same cohort who choose to invest in education. The governmental intervention includes releasing information about individual incomes, as well as guaranteeing the collection of debt.
3. *Regime III (restricted insurance of loans).* Again, the terms of repayment are linked to random individual future incomes. Yet the insurance arrangement pools the risks within each signal group (group of agents who have received the same signal) separately.

We study these three financing regimes separately, assuming that the *same* regime applies to all agents. Thus in our economy only one regime prevails; in particular, students cannot choose between a loan in the credit markets with uncontingent terms of repayment (Regime I) and a loan with contingent repayment (Regime II or III). This assumption seems reasonable because the implementation of any regime requires some government intervention. This holds true even for Regime I, given the evidence about borrowing constraints that students face in the financial markets (e.g., Galor and Zeira, 1993; Carneiro and Heckman, 2002). The prevailing regime should be viewed as a political choice variable. The implications of this political choice for the time path of aggregate human capital and welfare are analyzed in the sequel.

Regime II serves as a benchmark in our analysis. In some European countries (e.g., Germany), funding concepts for higher education in the spirit of Regime II were discussed in the 1970s. While this regime may have some appeal from the viewpoint of an egalitarian income distribution, it has major drawbacks in terms of inefficiencies for the human capital formation process. In addition, Regime II must be enforced by the state; it cannot be sustained as a market equilibrium, because banks would ask to see people's signals and offer individuals with high signals loans on better terms than individuals with low signals. Therefore, we treat Regime II mainly as a standard of comparison for the other two regimes. Nevertheless, the financing scheme under Regime II does have practical relevance, as it is equivalent to a public debt funding scheme where interest payments are linked to future tax revenues (Huber, 1990; De Fraja, 2002).

The agents are expected utility maximizers with von Neumann-Morgenstern lifetime utility function

$$U(c_1, c_2) = u_1(c_1) + u_2(c_2).$$

c_1 and c_2 denote consumption in the second and third periods of life, respectively. In his first period of life, each agent makes a capital investment in education, but he does not consume. The utility functions u_i: $\mathbb{R}_+ \to \mathbb{R}$, $i = 1, 2$ are strictly increasing and strictly concave.

We maintain our technological assumptions of Chapter 4: competitive firms use capital K and human capital H to produce a single commodity that can be used either for consumption or for production. The production process is described by an aggregate production function $F(K, H)$, which satisfies Assumption 4.1. In his "working period," each agent i inelastically supplies l units of labor, hence his supply of human capital is lh^i. Without loss of generality, we set $l = 1$.

Physical capital is internationally mobile, while human capital is assumed to be immobile. This implies that the interest rate $\bar{r}_t$ is exogenously given at each date (small country assumption). Physical capital fully depreciates in each period, hence marginal productivity of aggregate physical capital equals $1 + \bar{r}_t$. Thus, given H_t, the stock of physical capital, K_t, adjusts such that

$$R_t := 1 + \bar{r}_t = F_K(K_t, H_t), \quad t = 1, 2, 3, \ldots,$$

is satisfied. This implies that K_t/H_t is determined by the international rate of interest $\bar{r}_t$. Hence, the wage rate (price of one unit of human capital) $w_t = F_L(K_t/H_t, 1)$ is also determined once $\bar{r}_t$ is given.

5.1.1 Regime I: Unrestricted Access to Credit Markets

Suppose the government guarantees all agents unrestricted access to competitive credit markets. At date $t-1$, when "young," individual $i \in G_t$ chooses investment in education, x^i, while his ability is still unknown. The investment decision will be based on the noisy information about the agent's ability that is conveyed by his signal y^i. The investment x^i is financed through a standard loan contract that is signed at date $t-1$ and involves the obligation to pay back $R_t x^i$ in period t.

An optimal decision is taken in two consecutive steps. At date $t-1$, after the signal y^i has been observed, our agent $i \in G_t$, chooses an optimal level of investment in education, x^i, and signs the associated loan contract. When choosing the investment level, the agent perceives his ability to be randomly distributed according to $\nu_{y^i}(\cdot)$. Optimal savings s^i are chosen at date t *after* ability A^i has been observed. At this time, x^i (which has been chosen at date $t-1$) is predetermined.

For given levels of h^i, x^i, w_t, R_t, and R_{t+1}, the optimal consumption and saving decision is determined by

$$\max_{c_1^i, c_2^i, s^i} u_1(c_1^i) + u_2(c_2^i) \tag{5.2}$$

$$\text{s.t. } c_1^i = w_t h^i - R_t x^i - s^i, \tag{5.3}$$

$$c_2^i = R_{t+1} s^i. \tag{5.4}$$

Optimal savings satisfy the necessary and sufficient first-order condition:

$$u_1'\left(w_t h^i - R_t x^i - s^i\right) = R_{t+1} u_2'(R_{t+1} s^i) \quad \text{for all } A^i. \tag{5.5}$$

The optimal level of investment in education is determined by:

$$\max_{x^i} E\left[u_1\left(\tilde{c}_1^i\right) + u_2\left(\tilde{c}_2^i\right)\middle| y^i\right] \tag{5.6}$$

$$\text{s.t. } \tilde{c}_1^i = w_t \tilde{h}^i - R_t x^i - \tilde{s}^i, \tag{5.7}$$

$$\tilde{c}_2^i = R_{t+1} \tilde{s}^i, \tag{5.8}$$

where $\tilde{h}^i$ is given by Eq. 5.1 and $\tilde{s}^i$ satisfies Eq. 5.5. By the envelope theorem and the strict concavity of the utility functions, this optimization problem has a unique solution determined by the first-order condition

$$E\left\{\left[w_t \tilde{A} g_1'(x^i, H_{t-1}) - R_t\right] u_1'\left(\tilde{c}_1^i\right)\middle| y^i\right\} = 0. \tag{5.9}$$

At date $t-1$, the members of G_t differ only by the signals that they have received. Therefore, all individuals in the same signal group, $G_t(y)$, choose the same investment level denoted $x_t(y)$. The *net* income (gross income net of loan repayment) in the working period of individuals in $G_t(y)$ is

$$I_t(A, y) = w_t A\, g(x_t(y), H_{t-1}) - R_t x_t(y). \tag{5.10}$$

Finally, the aggregate stock of human capital at date t can be expressed as

$$H_t = \int_Y \bar{A}_y g(x_t(y), H_{t-1}) \mu(y)\, dy. \tag{5.11}$$

For notational convenience, we have chosen not to include H_{t-1} as an argument in the investment function $x_t(y)$. Throughout this chapter, we shall apply this convention to all behavioral functions.

From the above first-order equations we derive optimal saving and optimal consumption as a function of income $I_t(A, y)$. In particular, using Eqs. 5.10 and 5.5 we may write optimal savings as $s_t(I_t(A, y))$. Optimal consumption in the second and third period of life are denoted by $c_t^1(I_t(A, y))$ and $c_t^2(I_t(A, y))$, respectively. Moreover, from Eqs. 5.3, 5.4, and 5.5, we get:

$$s_t'(I) \in (0, 1); \quad c_t^{1\prime}(I) \in (0, 1), \text{ and } \quad c_t^{2\prime}(I) \in (0, R_{t+1}).$$

Our economy starts at date 0 with given initial stocks of physical capital, K_0, and human capital, H_0. The dynamic equilibrium describes the time path of factor prices, savings, and consumption profiles, as well as the evolution of the individual human capital stocks that depend on the investments in education of the younger generations.

Definition 5.1. *Given the international interest rates* $(\bar{r}_t)$ *and the initial stocks of human and physical capital* H_0 *and* K_0*, a competitive equilibrium consists of a sequence* $\{(c_1^i, c_2^i, s^i, x^i)_{i \in G_t}\}_{t=1}^{\infty}$ *and a sequence of wages* $(w_t)_{t=1}^{\infty}$*, such that at each date t, for* $t = 1, 2, \ldots$*:*

- **(i)** *Given* $\bar{r}_t$*,* H_{t-1}*, and* w_t*, the optimum for each* $i \in G_t$ *in Problems 5.2–5.4 and 5.6–5.8 is given by* (c_1^i, c_2^i, s^i, x^i)*.*
- **(ii)** *The aggregate stocks of human capital,* H_t*, satisfy Eq. 5.11.*
- **(iii)** *The factor prices satisfy* $w_t = F_L(K_t/H_t, 1)$ *and* $1 + \bar{r}_t = F_K(K_t/H_t, 1)$*.*

Our comparative dynamics analysis assumes that competitive equilibria (under various regimes) start from the same initial stocks K_0, H_0, and compares the allocations along these dynamic paths period by period. The above definition of equilibrium also applies (with minor and obvious modification), if the economy operates under one of the two financing schemes outlined below.

5.1.2 Regime II: Unrestricted Insurance of Loans

Suppose that the funds needed to finance investment in higher education take the form of "insured loans." More precisely, the loan payback obligations are linked to the individuals' future (gross) incomes, such that agents with higher incomes have higher payback obligations. Clearly, such loan contracts provide insurance against uncertain income prospects that are due to random income realizations. We consider a nonsubsidized risk-pooling program of education loans that includes all young individuals of a given generation. In particular, by assumption, the regular credit markets cannot be used for funding educational expenditures.

Let $\bar{A} := E\tilde{A} = \int_{\mathbb{R}_+} A\nu(A)\,dA$, define (gross) income of agent $i \in G_t$ as $I_g^i := w_t h^i$, and let $\bar{I}_g$ be the agent's unconditionally expected income. For each dollar loaned, agent i in G_t is obliged to pay back $R_t I_g^i / \bar{I}_g = R_t A^i / \bar{A}$ dollars in his working period, if his income turns out to be I_g^i (and hence his ability is A^i). Note that the repayment per dollar loaned does not depend on the agent's investment decision, hence no moral hazard problem arises. Instead, agent i's *expected* payback, $R_t x^i \bar{A}_{y^i} / \bar{A}$, is increasing in the signal, that is, the scheme "penalizes" agents with high income prospects.

This financing scheme does not take into account the heterogeneity in ability prospects that is already revealed through the individual signals when investment and borrowing decisions are made. Thus the scheme does not just provide insurance. Effectively, it combines insurance against the unrealized part of ability with cross-subsidization between classes of people in different signal groups.

Proceeding as in the previous section, the necessary and sufficient conditions for optimal savings and investment decisions are

$$u_1'\left(w_t h^i - R_t x^i \frac{A^i}{\bar{A}} - s^i\right) = R_{t+1} u_2'(R_{t+1} s^i) \quad \text{for all } A^i, \tag{5.12}$$

$$\bar{A} g_1'(x^i, H_{t-1}) = \frac{R_t}{w_t}. \tag{5.13}$$

Under the current regime, the conditional repayment amount is $R_t A^i/\bar{A}$. Replacing R_t with $R_t\tilde{A}/\bar{A}$ in Eq. 5.9 yields

$$0 = E\left\{\frac{w_t\tilde{A}}{\bar{A}}\left[\bar{A} g_1'(x^i, H_{t-1}) - \frac{R_t}{w_t}\right]\right\},$$

from which Eq. 5.13 follows immediately.

Equation 5.13 implies that all individuals will invest the same amount, regardless of the signal they have received, that is, $x^i = \hat{x}_t$ for all $i \in G_t$. The investment decision is independent of the signal because as the signal changes, the expected marginal gain from investing changes by exactly the same amount as the expected marginal cost of investing. This parallelism eliminates any incentive to adjust the investment level. To see why, observe that the expected marginal gain from investing is $w_t g_1'(x^i, H_{t-1})\bar{A}_{y^i}$, and the expected marginal cost of investing is $R_t\bar{A}_{y^i}/\bar{A}$. By Eq. 5.13, the signal does not affect the difference between these expressions, so at the optimum, the incentives to invest are independent of the signal.

By Eq. 5.13, $\hat{x}_t$ also depends on H_{t-1}, and by our assumptions $\hat{x}_t$ is nondecreasing in H_{t-1}. Due to the pooling of predictable future income differences across agents with different signals, coupled with the risk-aversion assumption, the optimal investment in education $\hat{x}_t$ maximizes the expected lifetime net income prior to the revelation of the signal; that is $\hat{x}_t$ solves

$$\max_x E\left\{w_t\tilde{A}\, g(x, H_{t-1}) - R_t x \frac{\tilde{A}}{\bar{A}}\right\} \tag{5.14}$$

and is thus independent of y.

This finding is not really surprising, because one can think of Regime II as an insurance scheme from the ex ante point of view, that is, prior to any information being revealed. Since ex ante all agents are identical, the scheme leads to everyone investing the same amount.

Net income in the working period of an agent in G_t with ability A is given by

$$\hat{I}_t(A) = w_t A\, g(\hat{x}_t, H_{t-1}) - R_t\hat{x}_t\frac{A}{\bar{A}}, \tag{5.15}$$

and the aggregate stock of human capital at date t is

$$\hat{H}_t = \bar{A}\, g(\hat{x}_t, H_{t-1}). \tag{5.16}$$

Using Eq. 5.15 in Eq. 5.12, we may write optimal savings as $\hat{s}_t(\hat{I}_t(A))$.

5.1.3 Regime III: Restricted Insurance of Loans

A weakness of Regime II is that it may be difficult to implement unless participation in the funding scheme is mandatory. We now consider a regime that functions easily on a voluntary basis. The regime consist of a class of "insured" loan contracts that specify different terms of repayment for individuals in different signal groups. Again, the payback obligation of a loan is linked to an agent's future income, but the implied risk pooling is restricted to individuals in the same signal group. There exist real-world examples where private funding is based on grouping students either by universities (e.g., at Yale, Harvard, etc.) or by fields of career. Lleras (2004, p. 66) argues that such practice is justified because "grouping students by fields reflects similarity in the risks and the expected returns within the same group."

An agent i in G_t with signal y^i who receives a loan to finance investment in education x^i is obliged to pay back $R_t x^i I_g^i / E[\tilde{I}_g^i | y^i] = R_t x^i A^i / \bar{A}_{y^i}$ in his working period if his income turns out to be I_g^i and, hence, his ability is A^i. This program of education loans allows risk sharing on fair terms within each signal group, but does not provide risk sharing or cross-subsidization among different signal groups. In particular, an agent's *expected* payback does not depend on his signal, so agents with high signals are not "penalized."

This loan program does not require any funding from the government. Indeed, the agency providing the loans pays a gross interest rate R_t in the capital market equal to the rate realized on total loans within each signal group,

$$\int_{\mathbb{R}_+} R_t \frac{A}{\bar{A}_y} \nu_y(A)\, \mathrm{d}A = R_t.$$

Under this loan program, the necessary and sufficient conditions for optimal savings and investment decisions are

$$u_1'\left(w_t h^i - R_t x^i \frac{A^i}{\bar{A}_{y^i}} - s^i\right) = R_{t+1} u_2'(R_{t+1} s^i) \quad \text{for all } A^i, \tag{5.17}$$

$$\bar{A}_{y^i} g_1'(x^i, H_{t-1}) = \frac{R_t}{w_t} \quad \text{for all } y^i. \tag{5.18}$$

According to Eq. 5.18, optimal investment in education of agents in the signal group $G_t(y)$ depends on the signal only via the term $\bar{A}_y$. We may therefore express individual investment as $\check{x}_t(\bar{A}_y)$. Again, our notation suppresses the dependence of investment on H_{t-1}. From Eq. 5.18, we see that $\check{x}_t(\bar{A}_y)$ maximizes the expected conditional net income $\bar{A}_y w_t g(x, H_{t-1}) - R_t x$.

Since $g(x, H)$ is concave in x and $\bar{A}_y$ is increasing in y (due to MLRP), Equation 5.18 implies the following lemma.

Lemma 5.1. *Optimal investment in education under Regime III, $\check{x}_t(\cdot)$, is increasing in the signal y, and nondecreasing in H_{t-1}.*

Thus good news (higher signal) stimulates investment in education. Net income in the working period of an agent in G_t with ability A is given by

$$\check{I}_t(A, \bar{A}_y) = w_t A\, g(\check{x}_t(\bar{A}_y), H_{t-1}) - R_t \check{x}_t(\bar{A}_y) \frac{A}{\bar{A}_y}, \tag{5.19}$$

and the aggregate stock of human capital at date t is

$$\check{H}_t = \int_Y \bar{A}_y g(\check{x}_t(\bar{A}_y), H_{t-1}) \mu(y)\, \mathrm{d}y. \tag{5.20}$$

Using Eq. 5.19 in Eq. 5.17, we may write optimal savings as $\check{s}_t(\check{I}_t(A, \bar{A}_y))$.

5.1.4 Remarks on the Implementation of the Regimes

The implementation of income-contingent loans programs that entail risk pooling within cohorts of students, such as Regimes I and II, can be difficult due to adverse selection problems. Individuals with good income prospects have an incentive to avoid the risk pooling scheme, if part of their repayments will be used to subsidize individuals with poor future prospects. Unless participation is mandatory, the cohort of students willing to borrow under the scheme will, on average, be made up of individuals expecting their future earnings to be low. This is particularly troublesome, if a university acts as creditor and provides income-contingent loans to its own students. Such loans are highly attractive to students who expect to perform below average in the labor market, and may thus be in conflict with the university's (presumed) goal to attract the highest quality students (see Jacobs and van der Ploeg, 2006).

The stylized design of our Regime III avoids this problem of adverse selection by restricting risk pooling to cohorts of students with identical income prospects. Therefore, as a theoretical abstraction, this scheme could be operated outside the public sector by private institutions. Yet, since the scheme requires the setup of a continuum of groups to which individuals will be assigned based on their income prospects, it cannot be implemented one to one in practice. Any practical implementation will have to allow for some heterogeneity within student cohorts, that is, students with similar, but different, future prospects (signals) will be grouped together. As a consequence, the adverse selection problem and, hence, the scope for government intervention does not completely disappear. In order to further minimize adverse selection in such circumstances, eligibility for a specific income-contingent loan contract may be determined not only by test outcomes (signals) but also through academic merit (see Chapman, 2006).

Our analysis is based on the assumption that only one financing regime is operative at a time. In practice, though, regimes may compete against each other endogenously, and students who differ with regard to their income prospects may choose to borrow under different schemes. If, for example, there is competition between Regimes I and II, individuals with high signals will borrow in the credit market (Regime I) while individuals with low signals prefer income-contingent loans under Regime II. In particular, the cohort of students who borrow under Regime II will be adversely selected. The same pattern arises if Regime II competes against Regime III. By contrast, competition between Regime I and Regime III does not lead to adverse selection. Under both regimes, the expected repayment of an education loan is the same, but Regime III provides some risk pooling while Regime I does not. Therefore, all students shun the credit market and borrow under Regime III.

In addition to system competition, also competition within a given system may emerge. Universities will possibly respond to the implementation of a regime through modifications of their education programs and fee structures. Some universities may try to obtain "high-signal market positions" by charging high fees and offering high quality. Others may try to position themselves in the medium or lower quality segment. Even though our analysis abstracts from possible interactions between the supply side of the education sector and the specifics of a financing regime, these aspects certainly deserve attention and may be studied in future work.

The literature also considers some forms of information asymmetry regarding the unknown ability of students entering the higher education institutions. For example, Gary-Bobo and Trannoy (2008) use an education framework in which both universities and students receive private signals about some aspects of ability. Focusing mainly on the supply side of the education sector, they characterize an optimal policy of admission of students to universities that applies both tuition fees as well as certain admission standards.

5.2 HUMAN CAPITAL ACCUMULATION

In exploring the economic implications of the three financing regimes of investment in higher education, we first concentrate on the accumulation of human capital. The financing schemes provide different degrees of risk sharing in the economy. It is well known that an investor may invest more funds into a risky project if, due to effective risk sharing arrangements, he can insure part of the project risk on easy terms. On the other hand, risk sharing mechanisms also have the potential of destroying the incentives for some agents to properly invest in education. The role of the various financing schemes for investment in education and human capital accumulation therefore deserves close scrutiny.

Proposition 5.1. *In equilibrium,*

(i) *each agent chooses higher investment in education under financing Regime III compared with financing Regime I:* $x_t(y) < \check{x}_t(\bar{A}_y)$ *for all signals* y*;*

(ii) *the stock of human capital under financing Regime III is larger than that under financing Regime I:* $\check{H}_t > H_t$ *for* $t = 1, 2, \ldots$.

Risk pooling, even if restricted to signal groups, has a significant impact on the growth path of the economy. Indeed, if such risk pooling takes place on conditionally fair terms, it enhances individual investment in education and stimulates the formation of human capital, compared to noninsured funding via credit markets. The intuition for this finding is rather straightforward. Under Regime III, the agents invest more because their exposure to residual ability uncertainty is reduced through risk pooling.

It is worth pointing out, however, that a positive link between reduced uncertainty through risk pooling and investment activity is not a universal result. Sandmo (1971) shows in a different context that the *marginal* impact of uncertainty on a firm's investment decision, that is, the effect of making a given distribution "slightly more risky," is generally ambiguous. By contrast, the *overall* effect, which is the difference between the investment level under uncertainty and the investment level under certainty, is positive under standard assumptions.

The comparison between Regime II (unconditional risk pooling) and Regime III (conditional risk pooling) is more intricate. While average investment in education may (but need not) be higher under Regime II than under Regime III, the latter regime always generates higher levels of aggregate human capital. To derive these results, we introduce the concepts of "moderately decreasing concavity" and "strongly decreasing concavity." Let

$$\hat{K}(x,H) := -\frac{g''_{11}(x,H)}{(g'_1(x,H))^2} = [K(x,H)/g'_1(x,H)].$$

$K(\cdot)$ and $\hat{K}(\cdot)$ are both (different) measures of concavity of the accumulation function $g(\cdot)$.

Definition 5.2. *Given the restrictions formulated in Assumption 5.1, the accumulation function $g(x;H)$ exhibits*

(i) *moderately decreasing concavity if $\hat{K}(x,H)$ is increasing in x and*
(ii) *strongly decreasing concavity if $\hat{K}(x,H)$ is decreasing in x.*

In order to illustrate these concepts, let us focus for a moment on two classes of accumulation functions to which we will refer occasionally later on. The first class is the family of constant relative risk aversion (CRRA) functions, and the second class is the family of constant absolute risk aversion (CARA) functions.

Case 1. Let $g(x,H) : \mathbb{R}^2_+ \to \mathbb{R}$ belong to the CRRA family, that is,

$$g(x,H) = \frac{x^{1-\gamma}}{1-\gamma}H, \quad 0 < \gamma < 1. \tag{5.21}$$

Straightforward calculation shows that $K'_1(x,H) \leq 0$ for all x, H, that is, the accumulation functions exhibit decreasing concavity. Furthermore,

$\hat{K}(x,H) = \gamma x^{\gamma-1}/H$ is strictly decreasing in x, hence the accumulation function exhibits strongly decreasing concavity.

Case 2. Let $g(x,H)$ belong to the CARA family, that is,

$$g(x,H) = (1 - \mathrm{e}^{-\gamma x})H, \quad \gamma > 0. \tag{5.22}$$

In this case, $\hat{K}(x,H) = \mathrm{e}^{\gamma x}/H$, $K(x) = \gamma$, hence $g(x,H)$ exhibits moderately decreasing concavity.

Note that "moderately decreasing concavity" and "strongly decreasing concavity" are mutually exclusive properties. These properties are important because of their implications for the curvature of the investment function $\check{x}_t(\cdot)$.

Lemma 5.2. *The investment function $\check{x}(\bar{A}_y)$ under Regime III is concave (convex) in $\bar{A}_y$, if $g(x,H)$ exhibits moderately (strongly) decreasing concavity in x.*

Lemma 5.2 links the curvature of the accumulation function $g(\cdot)$ to the curvature of the investment function $\check{x}_t(\cdot)$. For the purpose of illustration, assume that $g(\cdot)$ exhibits moderately decreasing concavity. Such curvature implies, as compared to the case of strongly decreasing concavity, that the marginal return to investment decreases more rapidly. As a consequence, $\check{x}_t(\cdot)$ responds increasingly less sensitively to higher signals, and therefore investment is concave.

Let aggregate investment in education at time t under Regime I be $X_t := E[x_t(\tilde{y})]$. For Regimes II and III, aggregate investments $\hat{X}_t$ and $\check{X}_t$ are defined analogously.

Proposition 5.2. *In equilibrium,*

(i) *aggregate investment in education is higher under Regime III than under Regime II, that is, $\check{X}_t \geq \hat{X}_t$ for all t, if the accumulation function $g(x,H)$ exhibits strongly decreasing concavity;*
(ii) *$\hat{X}_t \geq \check{X}_t$ holds for all t, if $g(x,H)$ is independent of H and exhibits moderately decreasing concavity.*

This result is quite surprising because the better talented agents subsidize the less talented ones more heavily under Regime II, where *all* risks are pooled, than under Regime III, where risks are pooled conditional on the signals. Yet, in the absence of adverse incentive effects, this sort of cross-subsidization affects the aggregate investment level only through the curvature of $\check{x}_t(\cdot)$. If the investment function is concave (convex), then investment chosen at the average signal—which is the investment level under Regime II—is higher (lower) than average investment under Regime III.

As we show in the next proposition, the financing Regimes II and III can unambiguously be ranked with regard to their impact on human capital formation. Thus, in view of Proposition 5.1, higher investment in education is neither necessary nor sufficient for higher economic growth.

Proposition 5.3. *The equilibrium aggregate human capital levels under Regime III are higher than those under Regime II at all dates: $\check{H}_t \geq \hat{H}_t$ for all t.*

Thus, the financing Regime III is more efficient than Regime II in terms of generating economic growth. It is to be expected, of course, that *the same amount* of aggregate investment transforms into more aggregate human capital under Regime III than under Regime II. After all, agents use the signal information under the former regime, while they discard the information under the latter regime. Yet, Proposition 5.2 makes the stronger (and less obvious) claim that this effect always dominates the higher level of aggregate investment that obtains under Regime II, if the concavity of $g(\cdot)$ is moderately decreasing.

The result in Proposition 5.1 is based on a simple economic mechanism. Since marginal returns to investment depend on individual abilities, the distribution of individual investments across agents with different abilities affects the formation of human capital in the economy. In particular, a financing regime that encourages investments of highly talented agents and discourages investments of poorly talented agents may achieve high levels of aggregate human capital with relatively low levels of aggregate investment in education. In fact, this happens as we switch from Regime II to Regime III, if $g(\cdot)$ is independent of H and exhibits moderately decreasing concavity. Under Regime II, investment in education is high but uncorrelated to individual ability. Under Regime III, by contrast, the better talented agents tend to invest more aggressively than the poorly talented agents. Since individual investments and abilities are better aligned under Regime III than under Regime II, aggregate human capital levels are higher even though the economy as a whole may invest less in education.

5.3 WELFARE COMPARISON

Our welfare analysis of the three financing regimes will be based on an ex ante welfare concept. We define economic welfare, W_t, of generation G_t as the ex ante expected utility of members of G_t. Financing Regime j will be ranked higher than financing Regime k ($j, k = \text{I, II, III}$) if *all* generations attain higher welfare under Regime j than under Regime k.

Welfare of generation G_t under Regime I is given by

$$W_t := \int_Y V_t(y, H_{t-1})\mu(y)\,\mathrm{d}y,$$

where, for each y, the value function of generation G_t is defined by

$$V_t(y, H_{t-1}) := E\left[u_1\left(c_t^1\left(\tilde{A}, y\right)\right) + u_2\left(c_t^2\left(I_t\left(\tilde{A}, y\right)\right)\right)\Big|\, y\right].$$

The value function of generation G_t represents the conditional expected utility of each member of G_t with signal y. Since $g(x, H_{t-1})$ is increasing in H_{t-1}, the value function is also increasing in H_{t-1}. The value functions and welfare levels of generation G_t under Regimes II and III—denoted, respectively, $\hat{V}_t(y, \hat{H}_{t-1})$, $\check{V}_t(y, \check{H}_{t-1})$ and $\hat{W}_t, \check{W}_t$—are defined symmetrically. We say, for example, that welfare is higher under Regime III than under Regime II, if $\check{W}_t \geq \hat{W}_t$ holds for all $t \geq 1$.

Proposition 5.4. *In equilibrium, economic welfare is higher under Regime III than under Regime I.*

Thus, under any political voting process conducted prior to the revelation of signals, the arrangement of conditionally insured financing of private investment in education under Regime III will prevail against a regime of pure credit markets. Regime III leads to higher welfare, because the individuals benefit from partial risk pooling. This positive impact on welfare is not counteracted by adverse incentive effects that might result from risk sharing. The reason is that risks are only shared within signal groups and, hence, the signal risk remains uninsured. Therefore, the incentive structure remains intact and all agents continue to take their signals into account when choosing investment in education.

Next we turn to a comparison of economic welfare under Regimes II and III. Under Regime III, aggregate human capital is accumulated more efficiently because agents take their signals into account when deciding about investment in education. That is, agents with good signals who are, on average, better talented invest more than agents with bad signals. Under Regime II, by contrast, everybody invests the same amount regardless of the signal. On the other hand, Regime II provides better pooling of individual income risks than Regime III. To illustrate this interaction between economic efficiency and risk sharing, we specialize our economy by choosing the following functional forms:

$$u_1(c) = \frac{c^{1-\beta}}{1-\beta}, \quad u_2(c) = \delta\frac{c^{1-\beta}}{1-\beta}, \quad g(x) = \frac{x^{1-\gamma}}{1-\gamma}, \tag{5.23}$$

where $\gamma \in (0, \frac{1}{2})$ and $1 \neq \beta > 0$. The specification in Eq. 5.23 implies that $g(\cdot)$ depends only on investment in education and is independent of the human capital stock of the previous generation. The purpose of this simplification is to separate the trade-off between economic efficiency and risk sharing in a given period from the externalities of the growth effects that have been characterized in Proposition 5.3. In view of that proposition, the growth externalities under Regime III are stronger than those under Regime II. Therefore, by choosing $g(\cdot)$ to be independent of H_{t-1}, we reduce the welfare gap between Regime III and Regime II.

Under the above specifications, the saving propensity out of net income is constant and will be denoted by m, where $0 < m < 1$. Optimal consumption under Regime III can then be written as follows:

$$\check{c}_t^1 = \frac{A\gamma(1-m)}{1-\gamma} w_t^{1/\gamma} \left(\frac{\bar{A}_y}{R_t}\right)^{(1-\gamma)/\gamma}, \tag{5.24}$$

$$\check{c}_t^2 = \frac{AR_{t+1}\gamma m}{1-\gamma} w_t^{1/\gamma} \left(\frac{\bar{A}_y}{R_t}\right)^{(1-\gamma)/\gamma}. \tag{5.25}$$

From Eqs. 5.24 and 5.25 we derive the value function $\check{V}_t(\cdot)$, which satisfies

$$\frac{1-\beta}{M_t}\check{V}_t(y) = E\left[\tilde{A}^{1-\beta}\middle| y\right]\left(\frac{\bar{A}_y}{R_t}\right)^{(1-\gamma)(1-\beta)/\gamma}, \tag{5.26}$$

where $M_t := [\gamma w_t^{1/\gamma}/(1-\gamma)]^{1-\beta}[(1-m)^{1-\beta} + \delta(R_{t+1}m)^{1-\beta}]$ is a positive constant. Similarly, the value function for Regime II satisfies

$$\frac{1-\beta}{M_t}\hat{V}_t(y) = E\left[\tilde{A}^{1-\beta}\middle| y\right]\left(\frac{\bar{A}}{R_t}\right)^{(1-\gamma)(1-\beta)/\gamma}. \tag{5.27}$$

Proposition 5.5. *Assume that the utility functions and the human capital formation function are of the type specified in Eq. 5.23.*

(i) *If the measure of relative risk aversion β is larger than 1, then economic welfare under Regime II is higher than under Regime III.*
(ii) *If $\beta \leq (1-2\gamma)/(1-\gamma)$, then economic welfare under Regime II is lower than under Regime III.*

We saw earlier that individual investments and individual abilities are better aligned, and therefore the allocation of investment in education is more efficient, under Regime III than under Regime II. Nevertheless, according to Proposition 5.5(i), all agents may be better off under Regime II. This result can be reconciled with economic intuition once we realize that economic welfare depends not only on the efficiency of the human capital accumulation process but also on the equilibrium risk allocation. Under Regime II, individual ability risks are better insured while under Regime III, investments are more efficiently transformed into human capital. According to Proposition 5.5, the former effect is dominant in terms of economic welfare if the individuals are highly risk-averse; and the latter effect is dominant if individuals are moderately risk-averse, that is, if the measure of relative risk aversion is sufficiently small.

Proposition 5.5 was derived under the assumption that the capital formation function $g(\cdot)$ is independent of H. If, under a more general specification, $g(\cdot)$ is an increasing function of H, the welfare comparison between Regimes II and III shifts in favor of Regime III. In view of Proposition 5.3, aggregate human capital levels are higher under Regime III than under Regime II. Therefore, since under any regime the value function of generation G_t is increasing in the human capital stock of G_{t-1}, the second part of Proposition 5.5 remains valid (and is even strengthened). By contrast, the first part of Proposition 5.5, which claims that welfare under Regime II can be higher than welfare under Regime III, may no longer hold if the previous generation's capital stock exerts a strong externality on capital formation in the current period.

We conclude the above analysis with a review of the main results. The incentives for individuals to invest in higher education are affected by the financing scheme under which educational loans are available to them. We have analyzed and compared the implications of three different funding regimes.

The regimes differ with regard to the terms of repayment of educational loans. In particular, the extent to which the payback obligations are contingent on the individuals' future incomes plays a critical role. While all regimes are self-financing, that is, they do not require government subsidies, some government intervention is necessary in order to make the funding mechanism operative. The first regime works via competitive credit markets. The role of the government is to ensure that students have unrestricted access to those markets and to enforce debt collection. The second regime pools the income risks of all agents in the same generation and treats them equally, that is, it imposes the same income-dependent payback obligations on all individuals. This regime cannot be decentralized but must be implemented by the government. The third regime pools income risks within each signal group (partial risk pooling). All agents in the same signal group are treated equally, but individuals with good signals receive loans on more favorable (income-contingent) terms than agents with bad signals.

We have studied these three financing regimes under the assumption that the *same* regime applies to all agents. In particular, agents are not free to choose the repayment scheme that looks most attractive to them. In a more general setting, several financing schemes might coexist at the same time so that in equilibrium agents self-select into different groups according to the repayment schemes they prefer. This possibility was excluded in the above analysis but will be considered in Chapter 6.

We found that aggregate investments in education and human capital stocks are higher under Regime III than under Regime I. Thus, partial pooling of income risks stimulates economic growth. By contrast, *unrestricted* risk pooling causes efficiency losses. Investments in education are more efficiently transformed into human capital under Regime III than under Regime II. Finally, Regime III leads to higher welfare than Regime I. And the welfare comparison between Regime II and Regime III depends on the individuals' attitudes toward risk. Regime III generates higher (lower) welfare than Regime II, if the measure of relative risk-aversion is sufficiently small (high). This result reflects the interaction of two mechanisms resulting from the fact that income risks are better pooled under Regime II, while the process that transforms educational investment into human capital is more efficient under Regime III.

The main purpose of our study was to compare Regime I (competitive credit markets) with Regime III (partial risk pooling), because these regimes are implementable in a decentralized setting. Our analysis yields a clear and unambiguous policy recommendation in favor of Regime III, which generates higher growth as well as higher welfare than Regime I.

5.4 THE EFFECT OF BETTER SCREENING

So far we have assumed in this chapter that the information system that determines the reliability of the test outcomes in the screening process is exogenously given. And we found that restricted insurance of loans works best from the perspective of human capital accumulation and economic welfare. We now change the focus of our analysis. Assuming that a Students Loans Institution (SLI) provides loans with restricted insurance, that is, the economy operates under the optimal financing Regime III, we investigate the role of the underlying screening mechanism.

From the viewpoint of transforming investment in education efficiently into human capital it would be appropriate, if agents with high ability prospects invest more aggressively in education than agents with poor ability prospects. This observation begs the question whether a better screening mechanism that produces more reliable test outcomes is desirable in the sense that it leads to a better alignment of individual ability prospects and investment levels. We shall investigate this question with regard to both the efficiency of the human capital formation process and economic welfare. In doing so, we shed some light on the intricate interaction between improved investment decisions and (possibly counteracting) risk effects under more reliable screening.

We simplify our earlier framework in order to ease the technical analysis. The human capital production process satisfies

$$\tilde{h}^i = A^i g(x^i). \tag{5.28}$$

In particular, the human capital accumulation function, $g(x)$, no longer depends on the average human capital level of the preceding generation.

Since the economy operates under financing Regime III (cf. Section 5.1.3), the terms of repayment differ for agents in different signal groups. Each dollar borrowed and invested in education by individual i in G_t with signal y^i and income $I^i := w_t h^i = w_t A^i g(x^i)$ involves an obligation to pay back $R_t I^i / \bar{I}_{y^i}$ dollars in the working period, where $\bar{I}_{y^i} := w_t \bar{A}_{y^i} g(x^i)$ denotes the average income in the group of all agents with signal y^i. Thus, the SLI uses the publicly observable signals as a screening device. It provides loans that allow individual income risks to be shared on fair terms within the various signal groups. In particular, the SLI makes zero profit on the loans extended to all agents in the same signal group. Indeed, the SLI pays a gross interest rate, R_t, in the capital market which is just equal to the rate realized on total loans within each signal group, that is, $E[R_t \tilde{I} / \bar{I}_y | y] = R_t$.

The type of education loans provided by the SLI restricts income risk sharing to classes of agents with the same signal. Within a given signal group, incomes differ only due to the randomness of individual ability. Since the ability risks are idiosyncratic, they can be pooled and shared costlessly by agents in the same signal group. In particular, all agents in the group voluntarily participate in the risk sharing arrangement since they pay no risk premium. Note that it is not necessarily in the interest of the agents to extend risk sharing beyond signal groups. Members of a high signal group generally do not want to be pooled with members of a low signal group, because this would worsen the terms of repayment for their education loans. The financing regime we have chosen is therefore a natural candidate as it provides the maximum amount of risk sharing all agents are happy to accept after their signals have become known. More comprehensive risk sharing arrangements cannot be implemented on a voluntary basis.

The optimal decisions each consumer takes are done in two consecutive steps. At date $t-1$, after the signal y^i has been observed, agent $i \in G_t$ chooses an optimal level of investment in education, x^i. At this time, the agent perceives his ability to be randomly distributed according to $\nu_{y^i}(\cdot)$. Optimal saving, s^i, is chosen at date t after income and, hence, ability A^i has been observed.

For any given levels of A^i, h^i, x^i, w_t, R_t, and R_{t+1} the optimal *saving* decision satisfies the necessary and sufficient first-order condition:

$$u_1'\left[w_t h^i - x^i \frac{R_t A^i}{\bar{A}_{y^i}} - s^i\right] = R_{t+1} u_2'(R_{t+1} s^i), \quad \forall A^i. \tag{5.29}$$

Thus, the optimal level of investment in education x^i is determined by

$$\max_{x^i} E\left[u_1\left(\tilde{c}_1^i\right) + u_2\left(\tilde{c}_2^i\right) \middle| y^i\right]$$

$$\text{s.t. } \tilde{c}_1^i = w_t \tilde{h}^i - x^i \frac{R_t \tilde{A}^i}{\bar{A}_{y^i}} - \tilde{s}^i,$$

$$\tilde{c}_2^i = R_{t+1} \tilde{s}^i,$$

where $\tilde{h}^i$ is given by Eq. 5.28 and $\tilde{s}^i$ satisfies Eq. 5.29. Due to the Envelope theorem and the strict concavity of the utility functions, we obtain a unique solution determined by the first-order condition

$$w_t g'(x^i) = R_t / \bar{A}_{y^i}. \tag{5.30}$$

At date $t-1$, the members of G_t differ only by the signals they have received. Therefore, all individuals in the same signal group, $G_t(y)$, choose the same investment level, denoted by $x_t(\bar{A}_y)$. Similarly, at date t the members of G_t differ by their abilities and by the signals they have received one period earlier. All agents in the same ability/signal group $G_t(A, y)$ make the same savings and consumption decisions, denoted by $s_t(A, \bar{A}_y)$, $c_t^1(A, \bar{A}_y)$, $c_t^2(A, \bar{A}_y)$.

According to Eq. 5.30, optimal investment in education is a strictly increasing function of $\bar{A}_y$,

$$\frac{\partial x_t(\bar{A}_y)}{\partial \bar{A}_y} = -\frac{R_t}{w_t(\bar{A}_y)^2 g''(x_t)} > 0.$$

Differentiating Eq. 5.29 and using Eq. 5.30 we find that optimal saving, $s_t(A, \bar{A}_y)$, is strictly increasing in both arguments:

$$\frac{\partial s_t(\cdot)}{\partial A} = \frac{u_1''\left[w_t g(x_t) - x_t(R_t/\bar{A}_y)\right]}{u_1'' + R_{t+1}^2 u_2''} > 0, \tag{5.31}$$

$$\frac{\partial s_t(\cdot)}{\partial \bar{A}_y} = \frac{u_1'' x_t R_t A / (\bar{A}_y)^2}{u_1'' + R_{t+1}^2 u_2''} > 0. \tag{5.32}$$

Similarly, it can be verified that consumption in the second period of life, $c_t^1(A, \bar{A}_y)$ and in the third period of life, $c_t^2(A, \bar{A}_y)$, are both strictly increasing in $\bar{A}_y$.

Aggregate investment in education, X_t, and the aggregate stock of human capital at date t, H_t, can be represented as

$$X_t = E\left[x_t\left(\bar{A}_{\tilde{y}}\right)\right] = \int_Y x_t(\bar{A}_y)\mu(y)\,\mathrm{d}y, \tag{5.33}$$

$$H_t = E\left[\bar{A}_{\tilde{y}}g\left(x_t\left(\bar{A}_{\tilde{y}}\right)\right)\right] = \int_Y \bar{A}_y g(x_t(\bar{A}_y))\mu(y)\,\mathrm{d}y. \tag{5.34}$$

Our economy starts at date 0 with given initial stocks of physical capital, K_0, and human capital, H_0. In accordance with Definition 5.1, the dynamic equilibrium describes the time path of factor prices, savings, investments, and consumption profiles.

5.4.1 Screening and Human Capital Formation

We analyze the implications of better screening for the level of aggregate investment in education and for aggregate human capital formation. Since agents differ with regard to their abilities, they realize different ex post returns on their investments in education. For the economy as a whole, the transformation process of aggregate investment into aggregate human capital can be expected to be more efficient the better individual investments are aligned with the agents' true abilities. In the sequel, we investigate whether this goal can be achieved through more efficient screening, that is, via a better information system in the sense of Blackwell (cf. Definition 1.6).

As it turns out, the curvature of the accumulation function, $g(x)$, is again of critical importance. We maintain Assumption 5.1 (now with $g(\cdot)$ being independent of H) and the concepts of strongly/moderately decreasing concavity in Definition 5.2 with

$$\hat{K}(x) := -g''(x)/(g'(x))^2 = [K(x)/g'(x)].$$

Depending on the curvature of the accumulation function, better screening may lead to higher or lower aggregate investment in education.

Proposition 5.6. *Aggregate investment in education increases (decreases) with better screening, if the accumulation function $g(\cdot)$ exhibits strongly (moderately) decreasing concavity.*

The link between uncertainty and investment decisions has been studied extensively in the literature. It is well known that under standard assumptions a reduction of uncertainty raises the level of investment (Sandmo, 1971). At first sight, our result in Proposition 5.6 may appear inconsistent with this literature. Better screening reduces the risk exposure of the decision makers and, therefore, should unambiguously raise investment. Note, however, that the mechanism which links screening to investment in our model is quite different from the above line of argument. In particular, this mechanism is not based on an individual's residual ability uncertainty. The reason is that, conditional on the signal, individual ability risks are pooled; hence, they do not affect investment decisions. According to Eq. 5.30, investment in education depends only on the conditional mean, but not on the variability of random ability.

To understand the critical role of the curvature of $g(\cdot)$ in Proposition 5.6, observe that according to Eq. 5.30 agents choose investment in education such that the marginal return (per unit of ability), $w_t g'(x)$, equals the marginal cost (per unit of ability), $R_t/\bar{A}_y$. This implies that a change in marginal cost has a bigger impact on investment when the accumulation function is flatter, that is, less concave. Therefore, since $g(\cdot)$ exhibits decreasing concavity, a cost change induces large adjustment in investment when the received signal is high, and small adjustment in investment when the received signal is low. Both effects work in opposite directions since under better screening investment costs (per unit of ability) decrease for agents with high signals and increase for agents with low signals. The faster (local) concavity of $g(\cdot)$ declines, the stronger is the first effect relative to the second effect. Proposition 5.6 tells us that, in the aggregate, the first effect is dominant if $g(\cdot)$ exhibits strongly decreasing concavity, while the second effect is dominant if $g(\cdot)$ exhibits moderately decreasing concavity.

While aggregate investment in education may either be higher or lower under better screening, aggregate human capital always increases.

Proposition 5.7. *Aggregate human capital increases with better screening.*

With better screening, highly talented agents invest more in their education, and poorly talented agents invest less. Thus, the economy-wide process which transforms investments in education into aggregate human capital becomes more efficient because individual investments and individual abilities are better aligned. As a consequence of this "efficiency-effect," aggregate human capital accumulates faster. On the other hand, aggregate investment in education may increase or decrease with better screening according to Proposition 5.6. This "investment-effect" on the formation of aggregate human capital can therefore be positive or negative. Both effects work in the same direction and stimulate aggregate human capital formation, if the accumulation function exhibits strongly decreasing concavity. If the accumulation function exhibits moderately decreasing concavity, then the two effects counteract because aggregate investment in education declines. Nevertheless, the net effect of better screening on aggregate human capital formation is positive according to Proposition 5.7. Thus, the positive efficiency-effect outweighs the negative investment-effect.

5.4.2 Screening and Welfare

Better screening may reduce risk sharing opportunities and thereby impose welfare costs on risk-averse agents (Hirshleifer, 1971; Schlee, 2001). On the other hand, we have just seen that better screening enhances the efficiency of the aggregate human capital formation process by providing incentives for better talented individuals to invest more, and for poorly talented individuals to invest less. Better screening may therefore raise the welfare of the economy even if it destroys some risk sharing opportunities. We now analyze the interaction of these two information-induced welfare effects in greater detail.

Again, we define the welfare of generation G_t as the common ex ante expected utility level of each member of G_t. A welfare improvement for the economy implies higher welfare levels for all generations.

Welfare of generation G_t is then defined by:

$$W_t(\nu_A) = E\left[V_t\left(\nu_{\tilde{y}}\right)\right] = \int_Y V_t(\nu_y)\mu(y)\,\mathrm{d}y, \tag{5.35}$$

where

$$\begin{aligned} V_t(\nu_y) = \int_{\mathbb{R}_+} \Bigg[u_1 \left(w_t A g(x_t(\bar{A}_y)) - x_t(\bar{A}_y)\frac{R_t A}{\bar{A}_y} - s_t(A, \bar{A}_y) \right) \\ + u_2(R_{t+1} s_t(A, \bar{A}_y)) \Bigg] \nu_y(A)\,\mathrm{d}A. \end{aligned} \tag{5.36}$$

$V_t(\nu_y)$, the value function for generation G_t, represents the conditionally expected utility of a member of G_t who has received the signal y.

How is the welfare of generation G_t affected by the reliability of the screening process? In our model, only part of the diversifiable educational investment risk is insured. Nevertheless, the overall investment process is free from distortions. Indeed, all individuals make socially optimal investment decisions, that is, they choose investment profiles which are consistent with the maximization of ex ante welfare in Eq. 5.35. To see this, note that at a social optimum aggregate income

$$\int_Y [w_t \bar{A}_y g(x_t(y)) - x_t(y) R_t]\mu(y)\,\mathrm{d}y$$

is maximized. Thus, the socially optimal investment level of agents with signal y satisfies

$$w_t g'(x_t(y)) = R_t/\bar{A}_y$$

and, hence, coincides with the individually optimal investment choice in Eq. 5.30.

In this economic setting, there are two channels through which better screening can affect welfare: (i) better screening enhances the efficiency of the human capital accumulation process and (ii) better screening may adversely affect risk sharing from an ex ante perspective. Our next proposition confirms the intuition that the second transmission channel becomes negligible, if the agents are (almost) risk-neutral in their youth period.

Proposition 5.8. *Let $\bar{\nu}_A$ and $\hat{\nu}_A$ be two information systems satisfying $\bar{\nu}_A \succ_{\text{inf}} \hat{\nu}_A$. If $u_1'' = 0$, that is, agents are risk-neutral in the working period of life, then all agents are better-off (or at least nobody is worse-off) under $\bar{\nu}_A$ than $\hat{\nu}_A$.*

By a continuity argument, the claim in the proposition remains valid if risk aversion is positive but sufficiently small, that is, $|u_1''(\cdot)| \leq \epsilon$ (uniformly) for sufficiently small $\epsilon > 0$.

In the absence of risk aversion in the first period of life, better screening raises welfare. This result is not surprising because the risk sharing implications of better screening do not affect welfare if the agents are risk-neutral. Yet, if the agents' preferences exhibit strong risk aversion, then better screening may result in lower economic welfare. We demonstrate this possibility for an economy with CRRA preferences. For this purpose, our further analysis will be based on the following functional forms:

$$u_1(c_1) = \frac{c_1^{1-\gamma}}{1-\gamma}; \quad u_2(c_2) = \beta \frac{c_2^{1-\gamma}}{1-\gamma}; \quad g(x) = \frac{1}{1-\alpha}(x^{1-\alpha} - \underline{x}^{1-\alpha}), \tag{5.37}$$

where $0 \leq \gamma \neq 1 \neq \alpha > 0$ and $\underline{x}$ is a lower bound for investment in education which satisfies

$$0 < \underline{x} < \alpha^{1/(1-\alpha)} \left(\frac{w_t \underline{A}}{R_t} \right)^{1/\alpha} \quad \text{for all } t. \tag{5.38}$$

The restriction in Eq. 5.38 makes sure that optimal savings are strictly positive and that optimal investment is strictly larger than $\underline{x}$. We think of $\underline{x}$ as a positive number which is close to zero. Note that $g(\cdot)$ exhibits moderately decreasing concavity if $\alpha > 1$, and strongly decreasing concavity if $\alpha \in (0, 1)$.

Solving the first-order conditions for s, x, c_1, and c_2 yields

$$x(\bar{A}_y) = \left(\frac{R_t}{w_t \bar{A}_y} \right)^{-1/\alpha}, \tag{5.39}$$

$$s(A, \bar{A}_y) = \frac{w_t A \left[\alpha \left(\frac{R_t}{w_t \bar{A}_y} \right)^{(\alpha-1)/\alpha} - \underline{x}^{1-\alpha} \right]}{(1-\alpha)[1 + \beta^{-1/\gamma} R_{t+1}^{(\gamma-1)/\gamma}]}, \tag{5.40}$$

$$c_1(A, \bar{A}_y) = \beta^{-1/\gamma} R_{t+1}^{(\gamma-1/\gamma)} \frac{w_t A \left[\alpha \left(\frac{R_t}{w_t \bar{A}_y} \right)^{(\alpha-1)/\alpha} - \underline{x}^{1-\alpha} \right]}{(1-\alpha) \left[1 + \beta^{-1/\gamma} R_{t+1}^{(\gamma-1)/\gamma} \right]}, \tag{5.41}$$

$$c_2(A, \bar{A}_y) = R_{t+1} \frac{w_t A \left[\alpha \left(\frac{R_t}{w_t \bar{A}_y} \right)^{(\alpha-1)/\alpha} - \underline{x}^{1-\alpha} \right]}{(1-\alpha) \left[1 + \beta^{-1/\gamma} R_{t+1}^{(\gamma-1)/\gamma} \right]}. \tag{5.42}$$

The value function can then be written as

$$V(\nu_y) = \left(1 + \beta^{-1/\gamma} R_{t+1}^{(\gamma-1)/\gamma}\right)^{\gamma} \frac{\beta (w_t R_{t+1})^{1-\gamma}}{(1-\gamma)} \rho(\bar{A}_y) \int_{\mathbb{R}_+} A^{1-\gamma} \nu_y(A)\, \mathrm{d}A, \tag{5.43}$$

where

$$\rho(\bar{A}_y) := \left[\frac{\alpha \left(\frac{w_t \bar{A}_y}{R_t}\right)^{(1-\alpha)/\alpha} - \underline{x}^{1-\alpha}}{1-\alpha} \right]^{1-\gamma}. \tag{5.44}$$

We remark that the term in brackets on the RHS of Eq. 5.44 is positive and increasing in $\bar{A}_y$ for all $\alpha \neq 1$.

Lemma 5.3. *Let $\hat{\rho} : \mathbb{R}_+ \to \mathbb{R}_+$. The function*

$$\hat{V}(\nu_y) := \hat{\rho}(\bar{A}_y) \int_{\mathbb{R}_+} A^{(1-\gamma)} \nu_y(A)\, dA$$

is convex in the posterior belief ν_y under each of the following conditions:

(i) $\gamma \leq 1$ *and $\hat{\rho}(\cdot)$ is increasing and convex.*
(ii) $\gamma \geq 1$ *and $\hat{\rho}(\cdot)$ is decreasing and convex.*

By Lemma 5.3 and Eq. 5.44, $V(\nu_y)$ is convex in the posterior belief ν_y for $\gamma < 1$ and concave for $\gamma > 1$, as long as ρ is a convex function. Thus, we can apply Theorem 1.3 to obtain the following result.

Proposition 5.9. *Assume that $\gamma < 1$. Then, if $\rho(\cdot)$ is a convex function, better screening results in higher economic welfare.*

We note that for $\alpha \in (0, \frac{1}{2})$ and $0 \leq \gamma < 1 - \alpha/(1-\alpha)$, the convexity condition in Proposition 5.9 is satisfied, if the lower bound $\underline{x} \in \mathbb{R}_{++}$ is sufficiently small such

$$\underline{x} \leq \left(\frac{w_t \underline{A}}{R_t}\right)^{1/\alpha} \left[\alpha \left(1 - \gamma \frac{1-\alpha}{1-2\alpha}\right)\right]^{1/(1-\alpha)}$$

is satisfied.

In our model, better screening adversely affects risk sharing from an ex ante point of view. At the same time, better screening improves the efficiency of the process which transforms aggregate investment in education into aggregate human capital. Therefore, the screening-induced welfare gains (or losses) depend on both the risk aversion parameter γ and the technological parameter α. If $\underline{x}$ tends to zero, then the sign of $((1-\alpha)(1-\gamma)/\alpha) - 1$ determines whether $\rho(\cdot)$ is convex or concave: with higher α, a smaller degree of risk aversion is needed in order for $\rho(\cdot)$ to be convex.

In high risk aversion economies, better screening reduces economic welfare.

Proposition 5.10. *If the economy is highly risk-averse in the sense that $\gamma > 1$ is satisfied, then better screening results in lower economic welfare.*

The concavity of the accumulation function declines more rapidly, that is, $\hat{K}(x)$ decreases at a higher rate, if α assumes smaller values. Therefore, the screening-induced efficiency gains in the transformation process are larger for smaller values of α. Yet, even for α close to zero, the efficiency gains are not big enough to outweigh the deterioration of the risk allocation, if the measure of relative risk aversion, γ, is larger than 1. As a consequence, better screening reduces economic welfare.

In this section, we have considered a loan market for educational investment where individual payback obligations differ across signal groups. Agents with better signals are able to sign loan contracts on more favorable terms. As a consequence, risk sharing is incomplete because individual ability risks are pooled only among agents in the same signal group. From an ex ante point of view, the uncertainty associated with an agent's assignment to a signal group remains uninsured. As was pointed out earlier, this signal risk cannot be pooled on a voluntary basis because nobody wants to be grouped together with another agent who has received a lower signal than himself. If the government *enforces* an arrangement which pools the signal risks, the process of aggregate human capital formation becomes inefficient. If, for instance, the signal risks are perfectly pooled, then $\bar{A}$ replaces $\bar{A}_{y^i}$ in the investment Eq. 5.30. As a consequence, all agents invest the same amount even though individuals with high signals have higher marginal returns to investment in education than individuals with low signals.

Our model nevertheless mimics the case of unrestricted risk pooling, if it is endowed with the null-information system. If the signals are uninformative, then $\bar{A}_{y^i} = \bar{A}_{y^j}$ for all $i, j \in G_t$ and, hence, the terms of repayment do not differ across signal groups. All agents in G_t sign the same contract and ability risks are pooled across the entire generation. We may therefore conclude from Proposition 5.7 that aggregate human capital accumulates faster if risk pooling is restricted to signal groups. In other words, unrestricted risk pooling implemented through some government regulation slows down the human capital formation process. On the other hand, in view of Propositions 5.9 and 5.10, unrestricted risk pooling leads to higher economic welfare in a highly risk-averse economy, but may reduce economic welfare if the economy is moderately risk-averse.

Our analysis puts Friedman's suggestion of equity financing of investment in higher education on a firmer footing. Friedman's idea has been used in various countries as the basis of operating programs of student loans with income-contingent repayment. Since rating human beings with respect to their potential future incomes is extremely difficult and costly, these plans use certain types of screening information in order to group individuals in rather broadly defined repayment cohorts. We have analyzed how the precision of such screening information affects investment in education, human capital formation, and economic welfare.

To date, the nature of the educational transformation process is still elusive and poorly understood. In this area, more empirical and theoretical work is necessary, all the more so since our results clearly demonstrate that the curvature of the human capital formation function is of critical importance for the efficiency of the transformation process as well as for the contribution to overall welfare created in the higher education sector.

We have excluded moral hazard and adverse selection problems from our analysis. Yet, in a more general setting which allows for informational asymmetries, individual decisions may be subject to moral hazard phenomena if the returns to human capital accumulation contain noneconomic components. Since such components cannot be captured in a loan-repayment scheme, they may affect the agents' ex post incentives to choose remunerative jobs. Moreover, in the presence of informational asymmetries, the cohort of agents who are willing to participate in an income-contingent loan-repayment scheme can be adversely selected. This is because individuals with poor income prospects are more likely to borrow under such a program than those with favorable income prospects. An extension of our approach that would allow for the existence of informational asymmetries between the students and the financial institution might yield further insights into the role of screening in higher education.

APPENDIX TO CHAPTER 5

Proof of Proposition 5.1.

(i) Under Regime I, individuals have access to loans provided by the banks at the market interest rates R_t. For each given y and fixed H_{t-1}, we have

$$\mathrm{Cov}\left[\tilde{A}, u_1'\left(c_t^1\left(\tilde{A}, y\right)\right)\Big|y\right] \leq 0. \tag{A.5.1}$$

The covariance in Eq. A.5.1 is nonpositive, since $c_t^1(A, y)$ is increasing in A. Equation 5.9 can be written as

$$E\left[w_t g_1'(x_t(y), H_{t-1})\tilde{A} - R_t\Big|y\right] E\left[u_1'\left(c_t^1\left(\tilde{A}, y\right)\right)\Big|y\right]$$
$$= -\mathrm{Cov}\left[\tilde{A}, u_1'\left(c_t^1\left(\tilde{A}, y\right)\right)\Big|y\right].$$

Combining this equality with Eq. A.5.1 yields

$$E\left[w_t g_1'\left(x_t(y), H_{t-1}\right)\tilde{A} - R_t\Big|y\right] \geq 0,$$

which implies that

$$g_1'(x_t(y), H_{t-1})\bar{A}_y \geq \frac{R_t}{w_t}. \tag{A.5.2}$$

Combining Eqs. 5.18 and A.5.2, and making use of the concavity of $g(x, H)$ in x, we conclude that $x_t(y) \leq \check{x}_t(\bar{A}_y)$.

(ii) The proof is by induction over time periods $t = 1, 2, \ldots$. Since K_0, H_0 are given at the outset, part (i) implies that $\check{H}_1 \geq H_1$. Assume that $\check{H}_{t'} \geq H_{t'}$ for all $t' \leq t$. Since, by assumption, $g_1'(x, H)$ is nondecreasing in H,

$$g_1'(x_{t+1}(y), \check{H}_t)\bar{A}_y \geq g_1'(x_{t+1}(y), H_t)\bar{A}_y \geq \frac{R_{t+1}}{w_{t+1}}$$

and

$$g_1'(\check{x}_{t+1}(\bar{A}_y), \check{H}_t)\bar{A}_y = \frac{R_{t+1}}{w_{t+1}}$$

are satisfied. Thus $x_{t+1}(y) \leq \check{x}_{t+1}(\bar{A}_y)$ holds for each individual in generation G_{t+1} with signal y. Integrating over all signals yields $H_{t+1} \leq \check{H}_{t+1}$. □

Proof of Lemma 5.2. Differentiating Eq. 5.18, we obtain

$$\frac{\partial \check{x}_t(\bar{A}_y)}{\partial \bar{A}_y} = \frac{w_t}{\check{K}(\check{x}_t(\cdot), \check{H}_{t-1})R_t}.$$

$\check{x}_t(\cdot)$ is increasing in $\bar{A}_y$ according to Eq. 5.18. Therefore, $\check{x}_t(\cdot)$ is concave (convex) in $\bar{A}_y$ if $g(x, H)$ exhibits moderately (strongly) decreasing concavity in x. □

Proof of Proposition 5.2.

(i) Since $g(\cdot)$ exhibits strongly decreasing concavity, $\hat{x}_t(\cdot)$ is convex in $\bar{A}_y$ according to Lemma 5.2. Then Eqs. 5.13 and 5.18 imply that $\hat{x}_t = \check{x}_t(\bar{A})$. Proposition 5.3 claims (and proves independently of this proposition) that $\check{H}_{t-1} \geq \hat{H}_{t-1}$. Using this fact along with monotonicity of $\check{x}_t$ in $\check{H}_{t-1}$ and convexity in $\bar{A}_y$, we conclude that

$$\begin{aligned} x_t &= E\left[\hat{x}_t\left(\bar{A}_{\tilde{y}}, \hat{H}_{t-1}\right)\right] \geq \hat{x}_t(\bar{A}, H_{t-1}) \geq \hat{x}_t\left(\bar{A}, \hat{H}_{t-1}\right) \\ &= \hat{x}_t\left(\hat{H}_{t-1}\right) = \hat{X}_t. \end{aligned} \tag{A.5.3}$$

(ii) Under this restriction on the functional form of $g(\cdot), \hat{x}_t(\cdot)$ is independent of $\check{H}_{t-1}$ and concave in $\bar{A}_y$. The inequality signs in Eq. A.5.3 are thus all reversed, which proves the claim. □

Proof of Proposition 5.3. The proof consists of two steps.

(i) Let $\bar{h}(z, H_{t-1}) := z\,g(\check{x}_t(z), H_{t-1})$. In a first step, we show than $\bar{h}(z, H_{t-1})$ is convex in z. Differentiating $\bar{h}(\cdot)$ with respect to z and using Eq. 5.18 we obtain

$$\bar{h}_{11}''(z, H_{t-1}) = \frac{R_t \check{x}_t'(z)}{w_t z}\left[1 + \frac{\check{x}_t''(z)z}{\check{x}_t'(z)}\right].$$

From Eq. 5.18 we calculate the elasticity of the investment function as

$$\frac{\check{x}_t''(z)z}{\check{x}_t'(z)} = -\left(1 + \frac{K_1'(\check{x}_t(z), H_{t-1})}{[K(\check{x}_t(z), H_{t-1})]^2}\right).$$

Combining the last two equations, we obtain

$$\bar{h}_{11}''(z, H_{t-1}) = -\frac{K_1'(\check{x}_t(z), H_{t-1})/z}{[K(\check{x}_t(z), H_{t-1})]^2 \hat{K}(\check{x}_t(z), H_{t-1})}.$$

By Assumption 5.1, $K_1'(\cdot)$ is nonpositive, hence $\bar{h}(\cdot)$ is convex in z.

(ii) Now we prove the claim of the proposition by an induction argument. Assume that $\check{H}_{t'-1} \geq \hat{H}_{t'-1}$ for $t' \leq t$. We conclude that

$$\begin{aligned}\check{H}_t &= E\left[\bar{h}\left(\bar{A}_{\tilde{y}}, \check{H}_{t-1}\right)\right] \geq \bar{h}\left(\bar{A}, \check{H}_{t-1}\right) = \bar{A}\, g\left(\check{x}_t\left(\bar{A}\right), \check{H}_{t-1}\right) \\ &\geq \bar{A}\, g\left(\hat{x}_t, \hat{H}_{t-1}\right) = \hat{H}_t,\end{aligned}$$

where the first inequality follows from step (i), and the second inequality follows from the induction hypotheses in conjunction with Lemma 5.1. □

Proof of Proposition 5.4. We show that $\check{V}_t(y, \check{H}_{t-1}) \geq V_t(y, H_{t-1})$ holds for all y and any fixed t from which the claim in the proposition follows immediately. From Proposition 5.1 we know that $\check{H}_{t-1} \geq H_{t-1}$. Therefore, since $\check{V}(\cdot)$ is increasing in the second argument, it is sufficient to show that $\check{V}_t(y, H_{t-1}) \geq V_t(y, H_{t-1})$ is satisfied for all y. Optimal consumption decisions under Regime I are given by

$$c_t^1(A, y) = [w_t g(x_t(y), H_{t-1})A - s_t(I_t(A, y))] - R_t x_t(y), \tag{A.5.4}$$

$$c_t^2(I_t(A, y)) = R_{t+1} s_t(I_t(A, y)), \tag{A.5.5}$$

where net income $I_t(\cdot)$ was defined in Eq. 5.10. The value function is

$$V_t(y, H_{t-1}) = E\left[u_1\left(c_t^1\left(\tilde{A}, y\right)\right) + u_2\left(c_t^2\left(I_t\left(\tilde{A}, y\right)\right)\right) \middle| y\right].$$

If we set $\hat{H}_{t-1} = H_{t-1}$ (as argued above) and denote by $\bar{s}_t(y) := E[s_t(I_t(\bar{A}, y))]$ average savings conditional on the signal y, then under Regime III the following ˘-allocation is admissible (but not necessarily optimal):

$$\check{x}_t(y) = x_t(y), \tag{A.5.6}$$

$$\check{s}_t(A; y) = s_t(I_t(A, y))\left[1 - \frac{R_t x_t(y)}{w_t \bar{A}_y g(x_t(y), H_{t-1})}\right] + R_t x_t(y)\frac{\bar{s}_t(y)}{w_t \bar{A}_y g(x_t(y), H_{t-1})}, \tag{A.5.7}$$

$$\breve{c}_t^1(A,y) = \left[1 - \frac{R_t x_t(y)}{w_t \bar{A}_y g(x_t(y), H_{t-1})}\right][w_t g(x_t(y), H_{t-1})A - s_t(I_t(A,y))]$$
$$- R_t x_t(y) \frac{\bar{s}_t(y)}{w_t g(x_t(y), H_{t-1})\bar{A}_y}, \tag{A.5.8}$$
$$\breve{c}_t^2(A,y) = R_{t+1}\breve{s}_t(A,y). \tag{A.5.9}$$

To complete the proof we show that the $\breve{}$-decision leads to higher expected utility conditional on y than the optimal decision under Regime I. From Eqs. A.5.4 and A.5.8, it is immediate that $E[\breve{c}_t^1(\tilde{A},y)|y] = E[c_t^1(\tilde{A},y)|y]$. Also, $[w_t g(x_t(y), H_{t-1})A - s_t(I_t(A,y))]$ is increasing in A (see Eq. 5.5). Thus, $c_t^1(\tilde{A},y)$ differs from $\breve{c}_t^1(\tilde{A},y)$ by a mean preserving spread implying $E[u_1(\breve{c}_t^1(\tilde{A},y))] \geq E[u_1(c_t^1(\tilde{A},y))|y]$. Similarly, $E[u_2(\breve{c}_t^2(\tilde{A},y))|y] \geq E[u_2(c_t^2(I_t(\tilde{A},y)))|y]$ because $s_t(I_t(\tilde{A},y))$ is a mean preserving spread of $\breve{s}_t(\tilde{A},y)$. We have shown that $\breve{V}_t(y,H_{t-1}) \geq V_t(y,H_{t-1})$. □

Proof of Proposition 5.5.

(i) For $\beta > 1$, $(\bar{A}_y/R_t)^{(1-\gamma)(1-\beta)/\gamma}$ is a convex function of $\bar{A}_y$, which is positively correlated with $E[\tilde{A}^{1-\beta}|y]$. The representations in Eqs. 5.26 and 5.27 therefore imply the following assessment.

$$\begin{aligned}
\frac{1-\beta}{M_t}\breve{W}_t &= \frac{1-\beta}{M_t}E\left[\breve{V}_t(\tilde{y})\right] \\
&> E\left[\tilde{A}^{1-\beta}\right]E\left[\left(\frac{\bar{A}_{\tilde{y}}}{R_t}\right)^{(1-\gamma)(1-\beta)/\gamma}\right] \\
&> E\left[\tilde{A}^{1-\beta}\right]\left(\frac{\bar{A}}{R_t}\right)^{(1-\gamma)(1-\beta)/\gamma} \\
&= \frac{1-\beta}{M_t}E\left[\hat{V}_t(\tilde{y})\right] \\
&= \frac{1-\beta}{M_t}\hat{W}_t
\end{aligned}$$

Since $(1-\beta)$ is negative, $\breve{W}_t < \hat{W}_t$, for $t \geq 1$, follows.

(ii) Under this specification, $(\bar{A}_y/R_t)^{(1-\gamma)(1-\beta)/\gamma}$ is again a convex function of $\bar{A}_y$ that is positively correlated with $E[\tilde{A}^{1-\beta}|y]$. The same assessment as under (i) therefore yields $\breve{W}_t > \hat{W}_t$ since now $(1-\beta)$ is positive. □

Proof of Proposition 5.6. Using Eq. 5.30, the derivative of $x_t(\bar{A}_y)$ can be written as

$$\frac{\partial x_t(\bar{A}_y)}{\partial \bar{A}_y} = \frac{w_t}{\hat{K}(x_t(\cdot))R_t}.$$

Since $x_t(\cdot)$ is increasing in $\bar{A}_y$ according to Eq. 5.30, $x_t(\cdot)$ is convex (concave) in $\bar{A}_y$ if $g(\cdot)$ exhibits strongly (moderately) decreasing concavity. The claim then follows from Eq. 5.33 in combination with Kihlstrom's Theorem 1.4. □

Proof of Proposition 5.7. Aggregate human capital can be written as

$$H_t = \int_Y \bar{h}_t(\bar{A}_y)\mu(y)\,dy,$$

where

$$\bar{h}_t(z) := zg(x_t(z)), \quad z \in \mathbb{R}_+.$$

$\bar{A}_y$ is linear in the posterior probabilities. Therefore, in view of Kihlstrom's Theorem 1.4, we need to show that $\bar{h}_t(\cdot)$ is convex. Differentiating $\bar{h}_t(\cdot)$ and using Eq. 5.30 we get

$$\bar{h}_t''(z) = \frac{Rx_t'(z)}{w_t z}\left[1 + \frac{x_t''(z)z}{x_t'(z)}\right]. \tag{A.5.10}$$

Differentiating Eq. 5.30 twice and rearranging yields

$$\frac{x_t''(z)z}{x_t'(z)} = -\left(1 + \frac{K'(x_t(z))}{[K(x_t(z))]^2}\right). \tag{A.5.11}$$

Combining Eqs. A.5.10 and A.5.11 we obtain:

$$\bar{h}_t''(z) = -\frac{K'(x_t(z))/z}{[K(x_t(z))]^2\hat{K}(x_t(z))}.$$

Since $K'(\cdot)$ is nonpositive, $\bar{h}_t(\cdot)$ is a convex function. □

Proof of Proposition 5.8. With $u_1'' = 0$ the value function can be written as

$$V(\nu_y) = \int_{\mathbb{R}_+} U(A,\bar{A}_y)\nu_y(A)\,dA, \tag{A.5.12}$$

where

$$U(A,\bar{A}_y) := u_1(w_t A g(x_t(\bar{A}_y)) - R_t x_t(\bar{A}_y) - s_t(A,\bar{A}_y)) + u_2(R_{t+1}s_t(A,\bar{A}_y)). \tag{A.5.13}$$

We show that the value function in Eq. A.5.12 is convex in the posterior belief ν_y. Assume $\nu_y = \alpha\bar{\nu}_y + (1-\beta)\hat{\nu}_y, \alpha \in [0,1]$, and denote average ability under the beliefs $\bar{\nu}_y$ and $\hat{\nu}_y$ by $\bar{\bar{A}}_y$ and $\hat{\bar{A}}_y$.

$$\begin{aligned}
V(\nu_y) &= \int_{\mathbb{R}_+} U(A,\bar{A}_y)[\alpha\bar{\nu}_y(A) + (1-\alpha)\hat{\nu}_y(A)]\,dA \\
&= \alpha\left[\int_{\mathbb{R}_+} U(A,\bar{A}_y)\bar{\nu}_y(A)\,dA\right] + (1-\alpha)\left[\int_{\mathbb{R}_+} U(A,\bar{A}_y)\hat{\nu}_y(A)\,dA\right] \\
&\le \alpha\left[\int_{\mathbb{R}_+} U(A,\bar{\bar{A}}_y)\bar{\nu}_y(A)\,dA\right] + (1-\alpha)\left[\int_{\mathbb{R}_+} U(A,\hat{\bar{A}}_y)\hat{\nu}_y(A)\,dA\right] \\
&= \alpha V(\bar{\nu}_y) + (1-\alpha)V(\hat{\nu}_y).
\end{aligned}$$

The inequality holds because $[x_t(\bar{\bar{A}}_y), s_t(A, \bar{\bar{A}}_y)]$ and $[x_t(\hat{\hat{A}}_y), s_t(A, \hat{\hat{A}}_y)]$ maximize expected utility, if the posterior belief is given by $\bar{\nu}_y$ and $\hat{\nu}_y$, respectively. In view of Kihlstrom's Theorem 1.4, convexity of the value function implies the claim in Proposition 5.8. □

Proof of Lemma 5.3.

(i) Let $\bar{y}$ and $\hat{y}$ be two signals with $\bar{y} \geq \hat{y}$ and choose $\lambda \in [0, 1]$ arbitrarily.

$$\hat{V}(\lambda \nu_{\bar{y}} + (1-\lambda)\nu_{\hat{y}}) = \hat{\rho}(\lambda \bar{A}_{\bar{y}}$$
$$+ (1-\lambda)\bar{A}_{\hat{y}})\left[\lambda \int_{\mathbb{R}_+} A^{1-\gamma}\nu_{\bar{y}}(A)\,\mathrm{d}A + (1-\lambda)\int_{\mathbb{R}_+} A^{1-\gamma}\nu_{\hat{y}}(A)\,\mathrm{d}A\right]$$
$$\overset{(\hat{\rho}\text{ convex})}{\leq} \lambda\hat{\rho}(\bar{A}_{\bar{y}})\left[\lambda \int_{\mathbb{R}_+} A^{1-\gamma}\nu_{\bar{y}}(A)\,\mathrm{d}A + (1-\lambda)\int_{\mathbb{R}_+} A^{1-\gamma}\nu_{\hat{y}}(A)\,\mathrm{d}A\right]$$
$$+ (1-\lambda)\hat{\rho}(\bar{A}_{\hat{y}})\left[\lambda \int_{\mathbb{R}_+} A^{1-\gamma}\nu_{\bar{y}}(A)\,\mathrm{d}A + (1-\lambda)\int_{\mathbb{R}_+} A^{1-\gamma}\nu_{\hat{y}}(A)\,\mathrm{d}A\right]$$
$$= \lambda\hat{V}(\nu_{\bar{y}}) + (1-\lambda)\hat{V}(\nu_{\hat{y}}) - \lambda(1-\lambda)\left[\int_{\mathbb{R}_+} A^{1-\gamma}\nu_{\bar{y}}(A)\,\mathrm{d}A\right.$$
$$\left. - \int_{\mathbb{R}_+} A^{1-\gamma}\nu_{\hat{y}}(A)\,\mathrm{d}A\right][\hat{\rho}(\bar{A}_{\hat{y}}) - \hat{\rho}(\bar{A}_{\bar{y}})] \leq \lambda\hat{V}(\nu_{\bar{y}}) + (1-\lambda)\hat{V}(\nu_{\hat{y}}) \tag{A.5.14}$$

The second inequality follows from $\bar{y} \geq \hat{y}$ and the MLRP, which imply that the two terms in brackets are both nonnegative.

(ii) Since $\hat{\rho}$ is convex, the first inequality in (ii) remains valid. The second inequality also remains intact: since $\bar{A}_{\bar{y}} \geq \bar{A}_{\hat{y}}$ and $\hat{\rho}(\cdot)$ is decreasing, the term in the last bracket in Eq. A.5.14 is nonpositive. The term in the second to last bracket is also nonpositive, because $\gamma \geq 1$ and MLRP hold. This proves the convexity of $\hat{V}(\cdot)$ in the posterior belief ν_y. □

The proof of Proposition 5.10 makes use of the following two lemmas:

Lemma A.5.1. *Let* $\hat{\underline{x}} \in \mathbb{R}_+, z > (\hat{\underline{x}})^{1/\alpha}, h : [z, \infty) \to \mathbb{R}$,

$$h(x) = (x^a - \hat{\underline{x}})^b, \quad b < 0;\; a > 0.$$

$h(\cdot)$ is a convex function.

Proof. Differentiating $h(\cdot)$ twice yields

$$h''(x) = ab[x^a - \hat{\underline{x}}]^{b-2}x^{2a-2}\left[(ab-1) + (1-a)\frac{\hat{x}}{x^a}\right].$$

Thus, $h(\cdot)$ is convex if

$$(ab-1) + (1-a)\frac{\hat{\underline{x}}}{x^a} \leq 0, \quad \forall x \geq z,$$

or

$$(1-a)\frac{\hat{\underline{x}}}{x^a} \leq (1-ab), \quad \forall x \geq z.$$

Since $\hat{\underline{x}}/x^a < 1$, the above inequality is always satisfied. □

Lemma A.5.2. *Let* $\hat{\underline{x}} \in \mathbb{R}_+, z > (\hat{\underline{x}})^{1/\alpha}, \theta : [z,\infty) \to \mathbb{R}$,

$$\theta(x) = (\hat{\underline{x}} - x^a)^b, \quad b < 0; \quad a < 0.$$

$\theta(\cdot)$ *is convex for any* $\hat{\underline{x}} > 0$.

Proof. Differentiating $\theta(\cdot)$ yields

$$\theta'(x) = -b[\hat{\underline{x}} - x^a]^{b-1} a x^{a-1}.$$

Obviously, $\theta'(x)$ is increasing in x. □

Proof of Proposition 5.10. In view of Kihlstrom's Theorem 1.4, we need to show that for $\gamma > 1$ the function $\rho(\cdot)$ in Eq. 5.44 is convex for all $\alpha \neq 1$.

(i) For $\alpha > 1$, $\rho(\bar{A}_y)$ can be written as

$$\rho(\bar{A}_y) = \left(\frac{1}{\alpha-1}\right)^{1-\gamma}\left[\alpha\left(\frac{w_t}{R_t}\right)^{(1-\alpha)/\alpha}\right]^{1-\gamma} \times \left\{\frac{\underline{x}^{1-\alpha}}{\alpha\left(\frac{w_t}{R_t}\right)^{(1-\alpha)/\alpha}} - \bar{A}_y^{(1-\alpha)/\alpha}\right\}^{1-\gamma}.$$

According to Lemma A.5.2, $\rho(\cdot)$ is a convex function.

(ii) For $\alpha < 1$, the convexity of $\rho(\cdot)$ follows from Lemma A.5.1. □

Chapter 6

The Role of Government in Financing Higher Education

Chapter Outline

6.1 Subsidizing Tuition Versus Subsidizing Student Loans 102
- 6.1.1 The Model 104
  - 6.1.1.1 The Social Investment Optimum 107
  - 6.1.1.2 Individual Behavior and Equilibrium 108
- 6.1.2 Exogenous Subsidization Policies 110
  - 6.1.2.1 Subsidizing Student Loans (SL-Subsidy) 111
  - 6.1.2.2 Subsidizing Tuition Fees (T-Subsidy) 114
  - 6.1.2.3 Comparing the Subsidization Policies 116
- 6.1.3 Endogenous Subsidization Policies 117
- 6.1.4 Tax-Deductible Investment 117
- 6.1.5 Policy Implications 118

6.2 Should Diverse Funding Schemes Coexist in Higher Education? 119
- 6.2.1 The Model 121
  - Funding Structure and Individual Behavior 122
  - 6.2.1.1 Credit Funding Equilibrium (CRE) 123
  - 6.2.1.2 Equilibrium with Funding Diversity (FDE) 124
- 6.2.2 Funding Structure and Social Welfare 128
- 6.2.3 Access Restriction to Higher Education 129
  - 6.2.3.1 Restricted Participation FDE (RP/FDE) 129
  - 6.2.3.2 Restricted Participation and Social Welfare 130
- 6.2.4 A Generalization 131
- 6.2.5 Policy Implications and Conclusion 132

Appendix to Chapter 6 133

While funding schemes with income-contingent repayment characteristics generally improve the process of human capital formation, they do not eliminate *all* inefficiencies in the higher education sector. Moreover, the economy may settle on an equilibrium path with unsatisfactory income distribution. In this

© 2015 Elsevier Inc. All rights reserved.

chapter, we analyze some government options to further improve the performance of the higher education system. These options include various forms of subsidies in a system of income-contingent education finance as well as access restrictions to higher education when income-contingent finance coexists alongside competitive credit markets.

This chapter is related to two strands of literature dealing with optimal allocation of public funds in the education sector. The first strand discusses the financing of higher education in the presence of capital market failures and the role of government herein. One of the earlier contributions is Loury (1981) who analyzes imperfections in the form of exogenous borrowing constraints for education funding. Since then, a number of papers have integrated similar constraints into more extended equilibrium models of higher education. For example, De Gregorio and Kim (2000) and De Fraja (2002) develop models in which students from better off households are less affected by borrowing constraints which leads to an elitist education provision in equilibrium. Using a Kehoe and Levine (1993) framework, Andolfatto and Gervais (2006) and De La Croix and Michel (2007) have analyzed the role of endogenous liquidity constraints for educational decisions and human capital formation. They show that, under endogenous constraints, the welfare properties of some usually beneficial policy schemes can get reversed if the schemes make the constraints more binding. The other strand of this literature studies the role of government policy in the presence of education or funding externalities (e.g., Hare and Ulph, 1979; Johnson, 1984; Bevia and Iturbe-Ormaetxe, 2002). Specifically, Garrat and Marshall (1994) and Jacobs (2007) analyze tax and education policies when markets for education finance are imperfect. Kane (1995) examines the role of subsidies in rectifying underinvestment and promoting college enrollment in the United States. Garcia-Penalosa and Wälde (2000) compare the efficiency of three tax-subsidies financing schemes for higher education. Caucutt and Kumar (2003) study the implications of higher education subsidies in the United States for income inequality, welfare, and efficiency. Hanushek et al. (2003) compare education to other tax-transfer schemes designed to achieve more income equality. Blankenau (2005) studies the role of college subsidies for economic growth. Yet, with the exception of De Fraja (2002), to our knowledge the literature does not contain a systematic analysis of education and funding externalities in the presence of income-contingent education finance.

We will begin with an analysis of two subsidy policies that are commonly used in parts of Europe and North America. Our focus will be on the implications of such policies for the formation of human capital and for income inequality within a system of income-contingent education finance.

6.1 SUBSIDIZING TUITION VERSUS SUBSIDIZING STUDENT LOANS

Higher education is costly and increasingly faces fiscal pressures for public spending in many countries. To the extent that these costs are financed out of general tax revenues, there may be regressive effects on the distribution of incomes, because most students enrolled in higher education belong to wealthier socioeconomic classes (for empirical evidence, see Chapman, 1997; Carneiro and Heckman, 2002). Governments have therefore sought to shift part of the financial burden to the students who are the direct beneficiaries of the system. Yet, such policy is known to have severe side-effects and, in fact, is likely to result in economy-wide underinvestment in higher education. The reasons for this are twofold.

First, since human capital cannot easily be used as collateral, banks tend to be reluctant in granting loans for higher education investment. In particular, prospective students from poor backgrounds may face binding credit constraints. Hence, underinvestment is likely to occur due to capital market failures. This problem can be tackled by making resources available to students through an income-contingent loans program (ICLP) which is operated by the government. We have seen in Chapter 5 that an ICLP, if properly designed, can in fact remedy inefficiencies in the human capital investment process caused by capital market failures. Under such program, in a first step, students are screened for their (unknown) abilities. Then, in a second step, all students are offered education loans. Each loan specifies terms of repayment which are linked to a student's screening result as well as to his future income. In this section, we assume that students have access to this kind of ICLP. Hence, inefficiencies in the investment process, should they arise, do not originate from failures in financial markets.

Second, the social value of investment in human capital may be higher than the private return on education so that students underinvest in human capital. In this case, government subsidies to education may be justified, if they restore investment incentives thereby lifting human capital investment to more efficient levels. This section focuses on this issue, that is, we analyze how tax-financed subsidies in higher education should be designed when underinvestment in human capital is due to externalities of education rather than failures in financial markets.

It turns out that the design of the subsidy scheme is important for its suitability to mitigate the underinvestment problem and to promote a less unequal income distribution. Our analysis compares an egalitarian subsidy scheme with a merit-based subsidy policy. The egalitarian subsidy scheme reduces by a uniform amount the tuition of individuals who acquire higher education. By contrast, the merit-based subsidy is proportional to the repayment obligation of the education loan. Under the ICLP, this repayment obligation is higher for students with high abilities. These two schemes are called "Tuition Subsidy" (T-subsidy) and "Student Loan Subsidy" (SL-subsidy), respectively. We find that the choice of subsidization method has important implications for the formation of human capital and for income inequality.[1]

---

1. See some related discussions in Garrat and Marshall (1994), De Meulemeester and Rochat (1995), Garcia-Penalosa and Wälde (2000), Caucutt and Kumar (2003), Dynarski (2003), and Blankenau (2005).

Our analysis uses the following framework. Individuals live for two periods. In the "youth" period, agents obtain education and in the "working" period, they generate incomes based on their human capital and skills. At birth, each individual is randomly endowed with some innate ability which becomes fully known only in the working period. Following compulsory schooling, each individual receives a (publicly observed) signal which is correlated to his/her true ability. The decision whether to acquire higher education will be based on the information conveyed by the signal as well as the financial terms of student loans. Agents with different signals differ in their posterior distributions of ability and, hence, they have different income prospects. Students finance the costs of higher education through an ICLP under which loan repayments are linked to future incomes. Due to an externality in the production of education, in equilibrium individuals underinvest in human capital.

We consider two tax-financed subsidization regimes. Under the SL-subsidy regime, the government bears a certain percentage of each student's outstanding education loan. By contrast, under the T-subsidy regime each individual who acquires higher education receives as subsidy a fixed amount which does not depend on the incurred costs or on the signal. If the total amount of subsidy funds is fixed (or predetermined), we find that both subsidization schemes reduce underinvestment as well as income inequality. Nevertheless, the SL-subsidy regime dominates the T-subsidy regime according to some social desirability criterion. Things are very different, if total subsidy funds constitute a decision variable of the government and can be chosen flexibly under each regime. In that case, the T-subsidy regime is socially more desirable than the SL-subsidy regime. Thus, the ranking of the two regimes depends on the flexibility that governments have with regard to the size of the subsidy funds.

6.1.1 The Model

We consider a two-period model with a *continuum of individuals* and a single commodity (capital good). In the first period, following compulsory education, an individual may take out a loan and make a capital investment in higher education in order to acquire additional skills. The capital investment increases the agent's human capital in the second period when the agent works and earns labor income. Labor income depends on each agent's skills, or human capital, which is assumed to be observable. In the second period, each individual consumes his net wealth which is the difference between his labor income and the repayment obligation of the loan.

Diversity within the population, denoted by G, is generated by random innate ability, a, which affects an agent's productivity level if the agent is "skilled." Abilities are assigned to individuals by nature at birth, that is, at the outset of the first period. At this time, however, individual ability is not observable, and is not even known to the agent himself.[2] Therefore, the investment decision in period 1 is made under uncertainty.

For convenience we shall choose a simple process of human capital formation. An agent may either invest one unit of capital in higher education or he may not invest at all. If an individual does not invest, he remains unskilled and attains a basic productivity level $A > 0$ in period 1. The basic productivity level A is independent of the agent's ability but *does depend* on the level of aggregate human capital H, that is, $A = A(H)$, as will be specified below.

Formally, there is a continuum of individuals, $G = [0, 1]$, with abilities determined by a random variable a distributed according to a density function $\nu(\cdot)$ on an interval $\mathcal{A} := [a^1, a^2] \subset \mathbb{R}_{++}$. The strategy set of an individual is $\{0, 1\}$ where 0 represents the choice of "do not invest" and 1 represents the choice of "invest." A strategy profile is a function x from G to $\{0, 1\}$.

Given strategy profile x, in period 2 the human capital of individual i is given by[3]

$$h^i(x) = A(H) + a^i x^i, \tag{6.1}$$

where $x^i = 1$, if the individual chooses to invest in period 1, and $x^i = 0$ otherwise; and where $H = \int_{i \in G} A(H) + a^i x^i \, \mathrm{d}i$.

Assumption 6.1. *The basic productivity level of unskilled workers depends on the aggregate stock of human capital and satisfies* $A'(H) \in (0, 1)$ *and* $A''(H) \leq 0$.

This assumption introduces an externality through which the aggregate stock of human capital affects individual human capital formation: unskilled workers are more productive if, in the aggregate, the economy is endowed with more human capital.[4]

Each agent receives a publicly observable signal $y \in Y := [\underline{y}, \bar{y}] \subset \mathbb{R}$ of his ability, a, before he makes the investment decision. The signal might be interpreted as a noisy test result which is correlated with the agent's ability. Real world examples include high school grades and the matriculation examinations used by many universities to screen the field of applicants. Since the tests are noisy, individuals with the same ability, a, typically receive different signals. We denote by $\nu_a(y)$ the density according to which signals are distributed across agents with ability a. Each individual uses the signal as a screening device and forms expectations about his unknown ability in a Bayesian way. The signals are distributed across the entire population according to $\mu(y) = \int_{\mathcal{A}} \nu_a(y)\nu(a) \, \mathrm{d}a$.

2. Alternatively, a might be interpreted as reflecting the uncertain future labor market condition for a skilled individual.

3. For convenience, we assume that agents are ex ante identical; in particular, family background will not affect the human capital formation.

4. The size of social returns to higher education is a controversial issue in the empirical literature. While there are differences in detail, many empirical studies have found that the social returns to higher education are significant and positive (see Moretti, 2004; Canton, 2007).

With $\nu_y(a)$ denoting the density of the conditional distribution of $\tilde{a}$ given the signal y, average ability of all agents in the signal group y is $\bar{a}_y := \int_A a\nu_y(a)\,da$.

We assume that signals are monotone, that is, $y' > y$ implies that the posterior distribution of ability conditional on y' dominates the posterior distribution of ability conditional on y in terms of first-degree stochastic dominance. Referring to our discussion in Section 1.3.3, we assume without loss of generality that $Y = [0, 1]$ and that the signals are uniformly distributed, that is, $\mu(y) = 1$ $\forall y \in [0, 1]$.

We also assume that higher signals are more precise in the following sense.

Assumption 6.2. *For any two signals $y > y'$,*

$$\frac{(\tilde{a}|y)}{\bar{a}_y} \succsim_{sd} \frac{(\tilde{a}|y')}{\bar{a}_{y'}},$$

that is, the rate of return on investment in education conditional on y is ranked ahead of the rate of return conditional on y' in the sense of second-order stochastic dominance.

In economic terms, this assumption means that the (normalized) abilities of agents with high signals are less dispersed in the sense of a mean preserving spread (MPS) than the abilities of agents with low signals. In this sense, high signals contain more precise information than low signals. We will see later that under Assumption 6.2 investment decisions are monotone in the signal. While this property is not essential to our analysis, it is nevertheless helpful to overcome obstacles in some technical derivations in Section 6.1.2.

All agents are risk-averse expected utility maximizers with von-Neumann Morgenstern (vNM)-utility function $u(\cdot)$. As it turns out, however, our results are largely independent of individual preferences. At this stage, therefore, there is no need to specify the vNM-utility functions beyond assuming that marginal utility is strictly positive and nonincreasing.

Production is carried out by competitive firms in period 2 according to a constant returns to scale production technology which uses physical capital, K, and human capital, H, as factors of production. The aggregate production function $F(K, H)$ is concave, homogeneous of degree 1, and satisfies $F_K > 0, F_H > 0, F_{KK} < 0, F_{HH} < 0$. Each individual i inelastically supplies 1 unit of labor. The agent's supply of effective labor units is given by h^i. His labor income in period 2 is wh^i, where w denotes the wage rate (price of one efficiency unit of labor).

Our economy represents a small country in a world where physical capital is internationally mobile while human capital is immobile. By and large, this specification is in line with the empirical observation that the globalization process has promoted international mobility of physical capital far more than international mobility of labor. International capital mobility in combination with the small country assumption implies that the interest rate, r, is exogenously given. Physical capital fully depreciates in the production process. Hence, marginal productivity of aggregate physical capital equals $R := 1 + r$. Given the aggregate stock of human capital, H, the stock of physical capital K adjusts such that

$$F_K(K, H) = R \tag{6.2}$$

is satisfied. Equation 6.2 in combination with the properties of the aggregate production function implies that K/H is determined by the gross international rate of interest R. The wage rate which equals the marginal product of effective labor, $w = F_L(K/H, 1)$, is also determined once R is given.

6.1.1.1 The Social Investment Optimum

Before turning to the agents' decision problems we characterize the socially optimal aggregate investment allocation in this economy. The socially optimal investment allocation maximizes aggregate net output or, equivalently, aggregate consumption. At the time when investment decisions are made, agents differ only by their signals. We refer to the set of all agents with the same signal y as "signal group y." At the social investment optimum, aggregate consumption, C, is maximized,

$$C_{\max} = \max_{y'} C(y'), \quad C(y') := A(H)w + \int_{y'}^{1} (\bar{a}_y w - R)\, \mathrm{d}y. \tag{6.3}$$

Here, y' is the cutoff signal, that is, investment takes place in all signal groups $y \geq y'$. Note that the net return to investment in signal group y is $\bar{a}_y w - R$, which is strictly increasing in y by signal monotonicity. Therefore, if at the social investment optimum signal group y invests in higher education, then any signal group $y'' \geq y$ also invests. This means that the set of all signals for which investment occurs in the corresponding signal groups is of the type $[y', 1]$. This observation justifies the representation in Eq. 6.3.

Lemma 6.1. *The function $C : [0, 1] \to \mathbb{R}$ is concave.*

The socially optimal cutoff signal y^* satisfies the necessary and sufficient first-order condition for the problem in Eq. 6.3,

$$A'(H)w\left.\frac{\partial H}{\partial y'}\right|_{y'=y^*} - \bar{a}_{y^*}w + R = 0. \tag{6.4}$$

Combining Eqs. A.6.3 and 6.4 yields

$$\bar{a}_{y^*} = \left(1 - A'(H)\right)\frac{R}{w} < \frac{R}{w}. \tag{6.5}$$

Due to the externality, $A'(H)$, the average marginal return to education in signal group y^*, given by $w\bar{a}_{y^*}$, is less than R.

Finally, from the concavity of $C(y')$ we conclude

$$C'(y') \leq 0, \quad \text{for all } y' \in [y^*, 1]. \tag{6.6}$$

The property in Eq. 6.6 will simplify some technical assessments in Section 6.1.2.

6.1.1.2 *Individual Behavior and Equilibrium*

We now turn to the decision problem that each agent $i \in G$ faces, given R and w. In period 1, the individual decides whether or not to invest in higher education while his ability is still unknown. This decision is based on the noisy information about the agent's ability conveyed by his signal y^i, and on the specifics of the available ICLP. The ICLP considered here was analyzed in Chapter 5, and it has the important property that it would restore investment efficiency, if there were no externalities. This set up allows us to focus on possible remedies for the externality in the absence of any initial distortions caused by capital market failures.

While the various ICLPs that are currently operative worldwide differ in many details, they all share two common features. First, the ICLPs mitigate the risks involved in future incomes. This goal is achieved by linking the loan repayments to uncertain future incomes. And second, income risks are only *partially* insured. Full insurance is normally deemed inappropriate as it may give rise to moral hazard problems in the process of education and job selection.[5]

In accordance with these stylized facts of existing ICLPs, we assume that a financial institution (Student Loans Institution, or SLI) offers income-contingent loan contracts to all individuals who are willing to invest in higher education. In doing so, the SLI uses the publicly observable signals as a screening device, that is, different terms of repayment apply to individuals in different signal groups. In the literature, this sort of screening has been called "merit based," as it links the funding of higher education to individual test outcomes (Caucutt and Kumar, 2003).

If agent i decides to invest 1 unit of capital in period 1, he receives a loan of 1 unit with repayment obligation $Ra^i/\bar{a}_{y^i}$ in period 2. The net income from this investment in period 2 is

$$a^i\left[w - \frac{R}{\bar{a}_{y^i}}\right].$$

Thus, agent i invests in higher education if and only if his signal satisfies

$$\bar{a}_{y^i} \geq \frac{R}{w}. \tag{6.7}$$

5. Since in our model, informational asymmetries are ruled out, full insurance is, in principle, achievable through a suitably designed signal-contingent repayment scheme. Yet, such a scheme would lack robustness as its effectiveness breaks down under more general information and incentive structures.

Observe that the SLI makes no profits. It just breaks even as it provides loans that share income risks on fair terms within each signal group.

In Chapter 5, we found that this type of income-contingent repayment scheme for student loans is superior to other more common schemes, mainly because it avoids distortions due to adverse selection problems. The scheme has the additional advantage that it is implementable without government regulation, that is, all agents *voluntarily* participate in the ICLP because individual ability/income risks are pooled within signal groups rather than across the entire population. Risk pooling beyond signal groups inevitably creates adverse selection problems as agents in high signal groups are required to subsidize agents in low signal groups. Such cross subsidization creates incentives for agents in high signal groups to quit the ICLP and seek funding in the credit market.

We denote the signal for which Eq. 6.7 holds with equality by $\hat{y}$,

$$\bar{a}_{\hat{y}} = \frac{R}{w}. \tag{6.8}$$

In order to exclude the trivial case where no investment takes place we assume $\hat{y} < 1$. The aggregate stock of human capital can then be represented as

$$H = A(H) + \int_{\hat{y}}^{1} \bar{a}_y \, \mathrm{d}y, \tag{6.9}$$

and aggregate consumption is

$$C = A(H)w + \int_{\hat{y}}^{1} (\bar{a}_y w - R) \, \mathrm{d}y. \tag{6.10}$$

In equilibrium, each agent chooses investment in education according to Eq. 6.7, factor markets clear, and aggregate human capital follows the accumulation Eq. 6.9.

Definition 6.1. *Given the international gross interest rate $R = 1 + r$, an equilibrium consists of a vector $(\hat{y}, w, K, H) \in \mathbb{R}^4_+$ such that:*

(i) *The cutoff signal, $\hat{y}$, satisfies Eq. 6.8.*
(ii) *The aggregate stock of human capital, H, satisfies Eq. 6.9.*
(iii) *The factor prices satisfy $w = F_L(K/H, 1)$ and $R = F_K(K/H, 1)$.*

The equilibrium in Definition 6.1 always exists and it is unique: for given $R > 0$, the second equality in (iii) uniquely determines K/H. For given K/H, the first equality in (iii) uniquely determines the wage rate w. Equation 6.8 then yields the cutoff signal $\hat{y}$ which is independent of H. Finally, aggregate human capital, H, is determined by Eq. 6.9. Since the integral in Eq. 6.9 does not depend on H, and since $A'(H)$ is bounded away from 1 by Assumption 6.1, Eq. 6.9 has a unique solution in H.

In equilibrium, the process of aggregate human capital formation is inefficient. Indeed, comparing Eqs. 6.5 and 6.8 reveals that $\hat{y} > y^*$, that is, the economy *underinvests* in higher education.

6.1.2 Exogenous Subsidization Policies

The welfare losses resulting from underinvestment in higher education raise the question whether, and how, the government should subsidize individual educational investment in order to stimulate human capital formation. When addressing this question, we need to bear in mind that a subsidy not only affects investment decisions but may also have implications for the distribution of incomes across signal groups. This section treats the subsidy level as an exogenous parameter. In Section 6.1.3, we will endogenize the subsidization policy by making the subsidy level a choice variable of the government. This modification will have significant consequences for educational investment, human capital formation, and the distribution of incomes.

In the absence of further restrictions, the set of admissible subsidization policies will be large because, in principle, subsidies can be made contingent on all observable characteristics such as individual signals and abilities. Clearly, in such an unrestricted environment, the government can achieve a first best outcome. Yet, as a matter of practicality, policy rules ought to be simple. In the sequel, we will therefore restrict the government to a narrow set of two policy options, both of which are easy to implement. Given this restriction, first-best is no longer attainable. We analyze and compare the two subsidization regimes with regard to their effectiveness in raising aggregate investment and with regard to the implied consequences for the distribution of incomes.

The government earmarks a *fixed* subsidy amount Rs for each signal group y. The subsidy will be paid out to the members of a signal group only if they invest in higher education. Under the first policy regime, the government supports investment in education by subsidizing a fixed fraction of interest payments on each student loan. We shall call this policy "Student Loan Subsidy" (SL-subsidy). Under the second policy regime, the government subsidizes the tuition fee by a flat payment, that is, all individuals who invest in higher education receive the same support. This policy will be called "Tuition Subsidy" (T-subsidy). In our model, the subsidy is financed through a higher education tax which is levied on those individuals who have obtained higher education. We assume that higher education costs are tax-deductible and show in Section 6.1.4 that our qualitative results prevail when the tax authorities do not allow for such deduction.[6]

Since abilities (and incomes) are observable, the government can, in principle, achieve a first-best allocation through the implementation of a suitably

---

6. In the United States, for instance, interest paid on student loans is tax-deductible.

designed individualized tax schedule. Here, we follow a different and more practical line. In our study, the tax schedule is fixed, that is, it does not constitute a policy instrument. Instead, the sole purpose of the higher education tax is to finance the subsidy, and only the latter is under the control of the government.

6.1.2.1 *Subsidizing Student Loans (SL-Subsidy)*

Under this regime, the government supports each student who invests in higher education with a subsidy in amount of a fixed fraction $s > 0$ of the individual's *repayment obligation*. Since we normalized the cost of higher education to 1, an agent in signal group y pays back, net of the subsidy, $R\frac{a}{\bar{a}_y}(1-s)$ if his ability turns out to be a. The government also levies a tax, τ_p, on the net extra income earned from the investment. The tax rate is endogenous and will be chosen in such a manner that overall tax receipts match the total of all subsidy payments. The subscript "p" hints at the "proportional" nature of the SL-subsidy. Tax rates and subsidies are related through the government budget constraint. Our analysis proceeds on the assumption that the subsidy has been predetermined in the political process. Alternatively, the tax rate could be taken as predetermined in which case the subsidy would adjust endogenously. Our analysis is thus motivated by the belief that it makes more intuitive sense to compare subsidy regimes with predetermined subsidies rather than predetermined taxes.

An agent of signal group y invests in higher education, if his net return from investing

$$(1-\tau_\mathrm{p})\left[aw - R\frac{a}{\bar{a}_y}(1-s)\right]$$

is nonnegative, that is, iff

$$\bar{a}_y \geq \frac{R}{w}(1-s). \tag{6.11}$$

The tax rate applies only to the *extra* income earned from education. This is an important feature of the proposed tax schedule as it implies that the tax has no distortionary effects on the education decision and that only individuals are taxed who benefit from the subsidy. In this regard, our approach differs from earlier work that has considered alternative tax bases (e.g., Johnson, 1984; Fender and Wang, 2003).

If $s \geq 1 - \frac{w\bar{a}_0}{R}$, all individuals invest in higher education. It therefore does not make sense to raise the subsidy beyond that level. If $s < 1 - \frac{w\bar{a}_0}{R}$, we denote by $\hat{y}_\mathrm{p}$ the cutoff signal for which Eq. 6.11 holds with equality. By signal monotonicity, Eq. 6.11 is satisfied for all $y \in Y_\mathrm{p} := [\hat{y}_\mathrm{p}, 1]$. For later reference, we note that the set Y_p is independent of individual preferences. Comparing Eqs. 6.8 and 6.11 shows that $\hat{y}_\mathrm{p} < \hat{y}$. In particular, $\hat{y}_\mathrm{p} < 1$ is satisfied.

For $s = A'(H)$, the economy achieves the social investment optimum, that is, $\hat{y}_{\mathrm{p}} = y^*$. This follows from Eqs. 6.5 and 6.11.

The tax rate, τ_{p} is determined by the government budget constraint which requires that total tax revenues equal total subsidy payments:

$$\tau_{\mathrm{p}} \int_{Y_{\mathrm{p}}} \left[w\bar{a}_y - R(1-s)\right] \mathrm{d}y = Rs\,(1-\hat{y}_{\mathrm{p}})$$

$$\Longleftrightarrow \frac{\tau_{\mathrm{p}}}{1-\tau_{\mathrm{p}}} \int_{Y_{\mathrm{p}}} \left[w\bar{a}_y - R\right] \mathrm{d}y = Rs\,(1-\hat{y}_{\mathrm{p}})) \tag{6.12}$$

The subsidization policy (s, τ_{p}) is said to be *feasible* if it satisfies the budget constraint in Eq. 6.12. Comparing Eqs. 6.8 and 6.11, we find that an SL-subsidy increases investment in higher education and human capital formation.

Proposition 6.1. *The introduction of a tax-financed SL-subsidy, (s, τ_{p}), $s > 0$, induces more individuals to invest in higher education and thereby leads to a higher stock of aggregate human capital. Formally, $\hat{y}_{\mathrm{p}} < \hat{y}$ and $H_{\mathrm{p}} > H$.*

The cutoff signal $\hat{y}_{\mathrm{p}}$ is determined such that the net extra income earned from investment in education is zero. The net extra income depends on the subsidy which affects an individual's repayment obligation, but not on the tax rate which is levied on the extra income. The cutoff signal $\hat{y}_{\mathrm{p}}$ is therefore independent of the tax rate τ_{p}, and independent of the preferences as well. In the absence of a tax effect, the subsidy stimulates investment by raising its net return before taxes.

According to Proposition 6.1, the SL-subsidy reduces the economy-wide underinvestment in higher education. Large subsidies may even result in overinvestment. We denote by $S_{\mathrm{p}} \subset (0, 1)$ the set of all subsidies that *do not lead* to overinvestment, that is, $\hat{y}_{\mathrm{p}} \geq y^*\ \forall s \in S_{\mathrm{p}}$. In particular, any policy $s \in S_{\mathrm{p}}$ increases aggregate consumption C in Eq. 6.10.

Next we study the impact of the SL-subsidy on the inequality of the income distribution across signal groups. Our analysis focuses on the distribution of the *mean income* in the various signal groups. This distribution matches the distribution of expected incomes conditional on the signals ex interim, that is, after the signals are observed but before individual incomes are known. Indeed, by the Law of Large Numbers ex post average income in signal group y is equal to ex interim conditionally expected income of an agent with signal y. We will call the distribution of mean incomes conditional on the signals "interim income distribution." If the government does not subsidize higher education, average income, $I(y)$, in signal group y is

$$I(y) = \begin{cases} A(H)w; & y < \hat{y} \\ \left(A(H) + \bar{a}_y\right) w - R; & y \geq \hat{y} \end{cases}. \tag{6.13}$$

Under SL-subsidization, (s, τ_{p}), average income, $I_{\text{p}}(y)$, in signal group y is

$$I_{\text{p}}(y) = \begin{cases} A(H_{\text{p}})w; & y < \hat{y}_{\text{p}} \\ A(H_{\text{p}})w + (1-\tau_{\text{p}})\left[\bar{a}_y w - R(1-s)\right]; & y \geq \hat{y}_{\text{p}} \end{cases}. \tag{6.14}$$

Note that $I(y)$ and $I_{\text{p}}(y)$ are both monotone increasing in y.

We say that an interim-income distribution $\hat{I}(y)$ is socially *more desirable* than another income distribution $\bar{I}(y)$, if the former distribution dominates the latter one in the *Generalized Lorenz* sense (see Shorrocks, 1983). Ramos et al. (2000) have shown that two income distributions can be ordered in the Generalized Lorenz sense, if they differ by a mean-decreasing spread. Our subsequent analysis will therefore be based on the following criterion which implies the Generalized Lorenz order (see Theorem 2.1 in Ramos et al., 2000).

Definition 6.2. *Let $\hat{I}(y)$ and $\bar{I}(y)$, $y \in Y$, be two distributions of average incomes across signal groups. We say that $\hat{I}(\cdot)$ is socially more desirable than $\bar{I}(\cdot)$, if*

(i) *the inequality*

$$\int_Y \hat{I}(y)\,\mathrm{d}y \geq \int_Y \bar{I}(y)\,\mathrm{d}y \tag{6.15}$$

holds, and

(ii) *there is some $\hat{y}$ in Y such that*

$$\hat{I}(y) \geq \bar{I}(y) \text{ for } y \in [\underline{y}, \hat{y}] \quad \text{and} \quad \hat{I}(y) \leq \bar{I}(y) \text{ for } y \in (\hat{y}, \bar{y}] \tag{6.16}$$

is satisfied.

According to Definition 6.2, the transition from an interim income distribution, $\bar{I}(y)$, to a socially more desirable interim income distribution, $\hat{I}(y)$, implies an increase of aggregate income (and therefore higher aggregate consumption) as well as a redistribution of expected incomes from the top to the bottom in a special sense: all signal groups which achieve income gains under the transition from $\bar{I}(y)$ to $\hat{I}(y)$ have uniformly lower incomes than signal groups which suffer income losses (if any).

An SL-subsidy improves the equilibrium income distribution in the sense of social desirability.

Proposition 6.2. *The introduction of an SL-subsidy, (s, τ_{p}), $s \in S_{\text{p}}$, leads to a socially more desirable income distribution.*

The SL-subsidy reduces the extent of underinvestment in education thereby raising aggregate income. Moreover, since the subsidy is financed through a tax system that places a larger burden on high-income earners than on low-income earners, income inequality declines. These two effects in combination improve the level of social desirability in equilibrium.

6.1.2.2 *Subsidizing Tuition Fees (T-Subsidy)*

Next we consider a regime where the government subsidy is distributed *uniformly* across all agents who invest in higher education. Each agent who invests receives Rs, $s > 0$, as a subsidy. This policy can be interpreted as a *tuition fee subsidy*. Note that for fixed s, total subsidies paid to members of signal group y are the same as under the SL-subsidy regime as long as the members of signal group y invest under either regime. We will see in Section 6.1.2.3, however, that some signal groups which invest under an SL-subsidy, refrain from investing under a T-subsidy. Denote by τ_u the tax rate imposed on net gains from education under the T-subsidy regime. The subscript "u" hints at the "uniform" nature of the T-subsidy.

An agent in signal group y who invests in higher education realizes a net return

$$(1-\tau_u)\left[Rs + a\left(w - \frac{R}{\bar{a}_y}\right)\right] \tag{6.17}$$

on his investment, if his ability turns out to be a. As the agent is an expected utility maximizer, a necessary condition for choosing $x = 1$ is that the *expected* net return from investing, $(1-\tau_u)\left[\bar{a}_y w - R(1-s)\right]$, is nonnegative, that is,

$$\bar{a}_y \geq \frac{R}{w}(1-s). \tag{6.18}$$

Under risk neutrality, Eq. 6.18 is also a sufficient condition for investment in education. Thus, since Eq. 6.18 is identical to Eq. 6.11, under risk neutrality individual investment decisions and, hence, human capital formation are the same under both subsidy regimes. Under risk aversion, however, an agent with signal y will not invest in education unless Eq. 6.18 is satisfied with strict inequality.[7]

To overcome some technical problems in the further analysis, we show that the set $Y_u := \{y \in Y | x(y) = 1\}$ of all signals that lead to investment in education is an interval.

Lemma 6.2. *The set Y_u is an interval, that is, if an agent with signal y decides to invest in higher education, then all agents with signals higher than y also invest.*

According to Lemma 6.2, there exists a unique cutoff signal for investment in higher education under a T-subsidization policy. Let us denote this cutoff signal

---

7. A necessary and sufficient condition for investment in education under a T-subsidy is

$$\bar{a}_y w - (1-s)R \geq \frac{-\mathrm{Cov}\left(\tilde{a}\left[w - \frac{R}{\bar{a}_y}\right], u'\left(Aw + Rs + \tilde{a}\left[w - \frac{R}{\bar{a}_y}\right]\right)\right)}{Eu'(\cdot)}.$$

In particular, under a T-subsidy the cutoff signal, $\hat{y}_u$, is no longer independent of individual preferences. Note that the RHS of the above inequality is strictly positive unless u' is constant. This implies that the investment efficiency-restoring Pigouvian subsidy satisfies $s \geq A'(H)$.

by $\hat{y}_u$ such that $Y_u = [\hat{y}_u, 1]$. As was mentioned earlier, this cutoff signal will in general depend on the preferences.

Again, the tax rate is determined by the government budget constraint

$$\frac{\tau_u}{1-\tau_u}\int_{Y_u}[w\bar{a}_y - R]\,dy = Rs\,(1-\hat{y}_u). \tag{6.19}$$

Comparing Eqs. 6.7 and 6.18 shows that a T-subsidy stimulates investment in education and human capital formation.

Proposition 6.3. *The introduction of a tax-financed T-subsidy,* (s, τ_u), $s > 0$, *induces more individuals to invest in higher education and thereby leads to a higher stock of aggregate human capital. Formally,* $\hat{y}_u \leq \hat{y}$ *and* $H_u > H$.

Thus, the T-subsidy reduces the economy-wide underinvestment just as the SL-subsidy does. We denote by S_u the set of all T-subsidies that do not lead to overinvestment, that is, $\hat{y}_u \geq y^* \; \forall s \in S_u$. Then, any policy (s, τ_u) with $s \in S_u$ stimulates human capital formation where τ_u satisfies Eq. 6.19.

We now turn to an analysis of the inequality of the income distribution under a T-subsidization policy. As in Section 6.1.2.1, we focus on the distribution of average incomes across signal groups. Average income, $I_u(y)$, in signal group y is

$$I_u(y) = \begin{cases} A(H_u)w; & y \notin Y_u \\ A(H_u)w + (1-\tau_u)\left[\bar{a}_y w - R(1-s)\right]; & y \in Y_u \end{cases}. \tag{6.20}$$

Proposition 6.3 implies $I_u(y) > I(y)$ for all $y \in [0, \hat{y})$. Since $[\hat{y}, 1] \subset Y_u$, we conclude from Eqs. 6.13 and 6.20 that

$$\frac{\partial}{\partial y}(I(y)) = \frac{1}{1-\tau_u}\quad\frac{\partial}{\partial y}(I_u(y)) > \frac{\partial}{\partial y}(I_u(y)) \quad \forall y \in [\hat{y}, 1]. \tag{6.21}$$

Thus, the income curve $I(y)$ intersects the income curve $I_u(y)$ at most once and, if so, from below. The same reasoning as in the proof of Proposition 6.2 can therefore be applied to yield the following result.

Proposition 6.4. *The introduction of a T-subsidy,* $(s, \tau_u), s \in S_u$, *leads to a socially more desirable income distribution.*

The results in Propositions 6.3 and 6.4 appear to be fairly robust with regard to modifications of the theoretical framework. Indeed, Hanushek et al. (2003) have demonstrated in a different model that subsidization of tuition fees (financed by tax income) raises GDP and creates more equal income distribution.

Comparing Propositions 6.1 and 6.2 with Propositions 6.3 and 6.4, we conclude that the effects of a T-subsidy are similar to those of an SL-subsidy. Under both policies underinvestment in education declines, aggregate human capital accumulation increases, and the income distribution across signal groups becomes socially more desirable. Below we will compare the two policies with regard to their effectiveness, that is, we will analyze which policy generates stronger effects on investment, human capital stocks, and the income distribution for a given subsidy level.

6.1.2.3 Comparing the Subsidization Policies

How do the tax rates, the levels of aggregate human capital formation and the income distributions compare under the two subsidization policies? The following lemma will facilitate our analysis.

Lemma 6.3. *Let $\gamma : Y \to \mathbb{R}$ be a differentiable and increasing function. Then $\Gamma : Y \to \mathbb{R}$,*

$$\Gamma(y^f) := \frac{\int_{y^f}^{1} \gamma(y)\,dy}{1 - y^f},$$

is an increasing function.

Let $S := S_p \cap S_u$ and consider the policies (s, τ_p) and (s, τ_u), $s \in S$. We have seen earlier that both policies reduce the economy-wide underinvestment in education. Our next proposition states that the policy of SL-subsidization is more effective in reducing aggregate underinvestment and results in a higher tax rate than the T-subsidization policy.

Proposition 6.5. *For any $s \in S$, under SL-subsidization aggregate investment, aggregate human capital, and the tax rate are all higher than under T-subsidization. Formally: $Y_u \subset Y_p$, $H_p \geq H_u$, and $\tau_p \geq \tau_u$.*

Under SL-subsidization, the after tax net return from investment per unit of ability, $w - R(1 - s)/\bar{a}_y$, is nonrandom. Since each individual maximizes this after tax net return, his decision is not affected by uncertainty. Under T-subsidization, by contrast, the after tax net return per unit of ability is random because the subsidy is fixed rather than proportional to ability. Each individual therefore makes a choice under uncertainty which leads to a more cautious investment behavior than under SL-subsidization, that is, $Y_u \subset Y_p$.

The higher tax rate under SL-subsidization has an intuitive economic interpretation. While all signal groups are equally costly in terms of the subsidies they can claim, the contribution to the tax base differs across signal groups. Agents in higher signal groups pay more taxes than agents in lower signal groups. As we switch from a T-subsidy to an SL-subsidy, some additional agents with signals less than $\hat{y}_u$ invests in higher education. Since these agents earn below average expected incomes, their contribution to the tax revenue falls short of the subsidies paid to them. Therefore, the tax rate must increase in order to keep the government budget balanced.

The social desirability criterion also ranks SL-subsidization ahead of T-subsidization.

Proposition 6.6. *The income distribution under a policy of SL-subsidization $s \in S$ is socially more desirable than under a policy of T-subsidization.*

Under SL-subsidization, more individuals invest in higher education and, therefore, aggregate income is higher than under T-subsidization. In addition, under the SL-subsidy there is less income inequality due to a higher tax rate. Both effects together imply that SL-subsidization is socially more desirable than T-subsidization as long as the average per capita subsidy, Rs, is fixed.

6.1.3 Endogenous Subsidization Policies

So far we have analyzed the implications of the two subsidization policies under the restriction that the subsidy amount earmarked for each signal group is fixed. In particular, if a signal group y invests under both subsidy regimes, the same total subsidy amount, Rs, will be distributed among its members under either regime. As a main result, we found that for all *fixed* $s \in S$, SL-subsidization dominates T-subsidization according to the criterion of social desirability of the induced income distributions.

We now extend our analysis by allowing the government to choose s freely under each regime. Thus, while the comparison of subsidization policies will again be based on the criterion of social desirability, the involved equilibrium income distributions may now include different average per capita subsidies, Rs_{p} and Rs_{u}, under the two regimes.

Definition 6.3. *Under the endogenous policy regime, we say that T-subsidization dominates SL-subsidization if for any feasible* $(s_{\mathrm{p}}, \tau_{\mathrm{p}})$, $s_{\mathrm{p}} \in S_{\mathrm{p}}$, *there exists a feasible* $(s_{\mathrm{u}}, \tau_{\mathrm{u}})$, $s_{\mathrm{u}} \in S_{\mathrm{u}}$, *such that the policy* $(s_{\mathrm{u}}, \tau_{\mathrm{u}})$ *leads to a socially more desirable income distribution than the policy* $(s_{\mathrm{p}}, \tau_{\mathrm{p}})$.

Switching from an exogenous to an endogenous policy regime constitutes no minor modification. In fact, such shift reverses the ranking of the subsidization policies.

Proposition 6.7. *Under the endogenous policy regime, T-subsidization dominates SL-subsidization.*

With the subsidy level exogenously fixed, our model suggested a policy recommendation in favor of SL-subsidies rather than T-subsidies. According to Proposition 6.7, this recommendation reverses in favor of T-subsidization, if the subsidy level s is a choice variable of the government. Which policy should be chosen therefore depends on the strategy space of the government. If the extent of subsidization is predetermined, for example, by budgetary constraints or earlier policy decisions, then higher subsidies should be paid to individuals with higher repayment obligations. Yet, if the extent of subsidization can be chosen contingent on the subsidy scheme, then the economy performs better in the sense of our social desirability criterion if all agents who invest receive the same subsidy payment.

6.1.4 Tax-Deductible Investment

Our analysis so far assumed that educational investment costs are fully tax-deductible. While tax authorities in many countries allow for the deduction of tuition and other expenditures related to higher education, there exist notable exceptions like Germany or Israel where the major part of these costs is not tax-deductible. If investment in higher education is not tax-deductible, then the underinvestment problem studied in this chapter is even more severe.

Under SL-subsidization, for instance, all agents with signals such that

$$\bar{a}_y \geq \frac{R(1-s)}{(1-\tau)w}$$

holds, acquire higher education if the government taxes gross incomes.

Taxing net incomes, by contrast, induces investment in all signal groups for which Eq. 6.11 is satisfied. Since $\tau > 0$, aggregate investment is higher if the government taxes net incomes rather than gross incomes. Thus, making investment in higher education tax-deductible helps mitigate the underinvestment problem, but does not eliminate it.

Below we argue that the implications of the two subsidization policies studied in this chapter are largely independent of the extent to which investments in higher education reduce individual tax liabilities. In particular, we demonstrate that our comparison of SL-subsidization versus T-subsidization remains qualitatively unchanged if costs of higher education are not tax-deductible at all.

If the government taxes the gross return from investment in higher education, $w\tilde{a}$, then the net return from this investment for an agent with signal y is

$$\tilde{a}\left[(1-\tau_{\mathrm{p}}^{\mathrm{n}})w - \frac{R(1-s)}{\bar{a}_y}\right]$$

under SL-subsidization, and

$$\tilde{a}\left[(1-\tau_{\mathrm{u}}^{\mathrm{n}})w - \frac{R)}{\bar{a}_y}\right] + Rs$$

under T-subsidization. The superscript "n" indicates "nondeductibility." A similar reasoning as in Section 6.1.2 shows that for fixed s the tax rates, the cutoff signals, and the levels of aggregate human capital satisfy $\tau_{\mathrm{u}}^{\mathrm{n}} \leq \tau_{\mathrm{p}}^{\mathrm{n}}, \hat{y}_{\mathrm{p}}^{\mathrm{n}} \leq \hat{y}_{\mathrm{u}}^{\mathrm{n}} < \hat{y}$, and $H_{\mathrm{p}}^{\mathrm{n}} \geq H_{\mathrm{u}}^{\mathrm{n}}$. Hence, while both subsidization policies stimulate investment in education and human capital formation, the SL-subsidy is more effective than the T-subsidy. Furthermore, under the SL-subsidy there is less income inequality due to the higher tax rate. The arguments in the proof of Proposition 6.6 therefore remain valid if investment in education is not tax-deductible showing that, again, the income distribution under a policy of SL-subsidization is socially more desirable than under a policy of T-subsidization.

6.1.5 Policy Implications

Our analysis suggests that the economy-wide underinvestment in education which is caused by an externality of aggregate human capital on the basic productivity level of unskilled workers can be reduced effectively through a tax-financed policy of subsidizing investment in higher education. Yet, the design of the subsidy poses a delicate policy problem. If the policy is exogenous in the sense that the per capita subsidy, s, earmarked for individuals who invest in higher education is predetermined, then subsidizing student loans leads to higher aggregate consumption and human capital as well as to less income inequality than a policy of tuition subsidization. In this sense, a student loans subsidy is socially more desirable than a tuition subsidy. However, if the policy is endogenous in the sense that the government can choose s along with the subsidization scheme, then the economy achieves a socially more desirable equilibrium under tuition subsidization. Due to predetermined budgets and inflexibilities in the political decision processes, the political realities in many countries seem to be better described by the exogenous policy regime where the per capita subsidy, s, is fixed. Even so, in principle, a policy regime of endogenous subsidization is advantageous from a well-being point of view. Under this regime, however, a scheme of tuition subsidization is the better option.

Finally, the comparison in Proposition 6.7 of student loans subsidization versus tuition subsidization under the endogenous policy regime also carries over to the nontax-deductible case. For any admissible student loans subsidy policy $(s_{\mathrm{p}}^{\mathrm{n}}, \tau_{\mathrm{p}}^{\mathrm{n}})$ one can construct in a straightforward way an admissible tuition subsidy policy which leads to a socially more desirable income distribution. Thus, the policy implications derived in this chapter for subsidizing investments in higher education appear to be reasonably robust with regard to the specific way in which returns from such investments are taxed.

6.2 SHOULD DIVERSE FUNDING SCHEMES COEXIST IN HIGHER EDUCATION?

In this section, we analyze a second set of government options to reduce or eliminate inefficiencies in the higher education system. Our approach is motivated by two observations from Chapter 5. The first observation is that financial markets—and competitive credit markets, in particular—are unlikely to provide adequate pooling or diversification of investment risks in higher education. This failure is due to the existence of moral hazard incentives in an agent's acquisition of human capital and in his performance in the labor market. The second observation refers to the distributional implications and incentive effects of income-contingent loans repayment programs. While income-contingent loans may ease credit constraints and improve the risk allocation, such funding may also imply significant cross-subsidization between subgroups of students with different income prospects leading to excessive investment in higher education. In fact, students with poor income prospects are more likely to take out education loans under such a scheme than students with good income prospects and, hence, the human capital formation process is characterized by both adverse selection and overinvestment in education (Eckwert and Zilcha, 2012).

Yet, pairwise comparison of different funding schemes can be misleading because, typically, these schemes do not exist in isolation. For instance, when an ICLP for higher education is set up, participation in the program is normally voluntary. As a consequence, the program will coexist with other forms of funding including credit markets. The observation that competitive credit markets tend to produce underinvestment in higher education, while income-contingent education loans tend to produce overinvestment suggests that, perhaps, a market structure in which both schemes coexist and compete might produce the efficient level of aggregate investment in human capital formation. Moreover, since a market structure with funding diversity offers students additional options in financing their educational investments, economic welfare may also be higher.

This section concentrates upon the implications of funding diversity, which includes credit markets and income-contingent education loans, for human capital formation and economic welfare. We set up a theoretical framework in which individuals live for two periods. In the "youth" period, agents obtain education and in the "working" period, they generate incomes based on their human capital and skills. At birth, each individual is randomly endowed with some innate ability which becomes fully known only in the working period. Following compulsory schooling in the youth period, each individual receives a (publicly observed) signal which is correlated to his/her true innate ability. To simplify our analysis we take all agents to be ex ante identical. In particular, we ignore family background when decisions about higher education are made. The decision whether to acquire higher education after compulsory schooling will be based on the financing options available to the agent and on the information conveyed by the signal. Agents with different signals differ in their posterior distributions of ability and, hence, they have different income prospects.

We consider two financing regimes. Under the first regime, the government guarantees access to *credit markets* for all students who attend higher education. And under the second regime, which is the main focus of our study, income-contingent education finance coexists with competitive credit markets. The income-contingent education finance is provided by an SLI that offers *income-contingent loan contracts* to all individuals who are willing to invest in higher education. We find that pure credit market funding leads to underinvestment in higher education. By contrast, funding diversity leads to overinvestment and adverse selection: aggregate investment in higher education is suboptimally high, and the pool of students who participate in the ICLP is adversely selected.

In the absence of government intervention, funding diversity in higher education is plagued by adverse selection in two respects. First, the cross-subsidization within the ICLP entices students with negative expected net returns on their investments to participate in the program. This misallocation of educational investment raises the financing costs for all participants, because the program is not subsidized by the government and, hence, must break even in equilibrium. Second, the elevated financing costs within the program provide incentives for students with good income prospects to shun the program and turn to the credit market for funding. This effect pushes the financing costs within the program even higher. Thus, in equilibrium, individuals with poor income prospects tend to pay higher financing costs.

The fact that funding diversity alone does not remedy the misallocation of educational investment suggests a role for government policy. This policy would *restrict access* to higher education to individuals with nonnegative expected net returns on their investments, given the signals attained after compulsory schooling. We find that such policy, if combined with funding diversity in higher education, is quite appropriate as it restores efficiency of the educational investment process and, at the same time, mitigates the adverse selection problem within the ICLP. In particular, under a policy of restricted access, funding diversity leads to higher social welfare compared with pure credit market funding. We conclude that funding diversity in combination with access restrictions constitutes the best feasible regulatory framework for the funding of higher education.

6.2.1 The Model

The basic framework is the same as in Section 6.1. Again, we consider a two-period model with a single commodity (capital good) and a continuum of individuals, say, in the interval [0, 1]. In the first period, following compulsory education, an individual may take out a loan and make a capital investment in higher education in order to acquire additional skills. Labor income depends on each agent's skills, or human capital, which is assumed to be observable by the government (tax authorities), but cannot be observed by private credit institutions.[8] In the second period, each individual consumes his net wealth which is the difference between his labor income and the repayment obligation of the loan.

Diversity within the population is again generated by random innate ability, which affects an agent's productivity level. Abilities are assigned to individuals by nature at birth. That is, at the outset of the first period. At this time, however, individual ability is not observable and is not even known to the agent himself. Human capital of individual i depends on his random innate ability a^i and on his private investment in higher education, x^i. The investment decision is made at date 0 while random innate ability realizes at date 1.

In period 1, the agent faces a binary investment choice: he may either invest one unit of capital in education or he may not invest at all. Following a standard modeling procedure in the growth literature, ability affects productivity of the individual only if he becomes "skilled." More specifically, we assume that if the individual does not invest, $x^i = 0$, he remains unskilled and attains a basic human capital level $A > 0$ in period 1. If the agent invests, $x^i = 1$, then he becomes a skilled worker. In that case, his human capital in period 2 is $A + \tilde{a}^i$, where ability $\tilde{a}^i$ represents the additional productivity due to higher education. The random variable $\tilde{a}^i$ assumes values in some interval $\mathcal{A} := [a^1, a^2] \subset \mathbb{R}_{++}$.

8. This observability assumption differs from, for example, De Fraja (2002) who assumes that ability and, hence, income is private information.

We denote by $\nu(a)$ the density of agents with ability a and adopt the normalization $\int_A \nu(a)\,da = 1$. Each agent receives a publicly observable signal $y \in Y := [\underline{y}, \bar{y}] \subset \mathbb{R}$ of his ability, a, before he makes the investment decision. Again, we assume that signals are monotone (cf. Section 6.1). We denote by $\nu_a(y)$ the density according to which signals are distributed across agents with ability a. The signals are distributed across the entire population according to $\mu(y) = \int_A \nu_a(y)\nu(a)\,da$. If $\tilde{a}_y$ denotes random ability conditional on the signal y, then average ability of all agents in the signal group y is $\bar{a}_y := E[\tilde{a}_y]$.

The human capital of agent i who has received signal y^i, will be[9]

$$\tilde{h}_{y^i} = \begin{cases} A; & \text{if } x^i = 0 \\ A + \tilde{a}_{y^i}; & \text{if } x^i = 1 \end{cases}. \tag{6.22}$$

The production process, described by the linearly homogeneous aggregate production function, $F(K,H)$, is the same as in Section 6.1.1. Our economy represents a small country in a world where physical capital is internationally mobile while human capital is immobile. By and large, this specification is in line with the empirical observation that the globalization process has promoted international mobility of physical capital far more than international mobility of labor.[10] International capital mobility in combination with the small country assumption implies that the interest rate, r, is exogenously given. Physical capital fully depreciates in the production process. Hence, marginal productivity of aggregate physical capital equals $R := 1 + r$. The wage rate equals the marginal product of effective labor, $w = F_L(K/H, 1)$. Throughout the chapter we assume $\bar{a} > R/w$, so that investment in education is profitable for an individual with average ability.

Funding Structure and Individual Behavior

All individuals are risk-averse expected utility maximizers with vNM-utility function $u(\tilde{c})$, where $\tilde{c}$ denotes random second period consumption.

Assumption 6.3. *The utility function $u : \mathbb{R}_+ \to \mathbb{R}$ is twice differentiable, strictly increasing and concave, and exhibits relative risk aversion less than or equal to 1, that is, $-u''(c)c/u'(c) \leq 1$, $\forall c > 0$.*[11]

Consumption is the difference between the agent's labor income and the repayment obligation of his loan. Below we will analyze two different market structures for financing loans: competitive credit market, and a structure with

9. Later we shall extend our analysis to the case where A depends on the average human capital of the older generation, following the type of assumptions used by Lucas (1988).
10. Note, however, that a system of income-contingent loans in higher education is particularly vulnerable to increased international labor mobility. Indeed, without cooperation from foreign tax authorities repayment of such loans by emigrants can hardly be enforced (Poutvaara, 2004).
11. This restriction on individual attitudes toward risk is needed for technical reasons. It ensures that the "cutoff signal" which separates individuals who join the ICLP from those who go to the credit market is uniquely determined.

coexistence of competitive credit market and income-contingent loans market. The second structure, which gives individuals a choice between two funding schemes, is the main focus of our analysis.

The equilibria under both market structures will be evaluated and compared with regard to their social welfare implications. The social planner's welfare index, W, evaluates the distribution of average incomes across the signal groups,

$$W = \int_{\underline{y}}^{\bar{y}} v(\bar{c}_y)\mu(y)\,\mathrm{d}y, \tag{6.23}$$

where $v : \mathbb{R}_+ \to \mathbb{R}$ is a strictly increasing and concave function, $\bar{c}_y := E[\tilde{c}|y]$, and $(\tilde{c}|y)$ represents random consumption of an individual with signal y.[12] Ceteris paribus, higher average consumption in a signal group raises the index; and higher consumption (=income) dispersion across signal groups decreases the index due to the concavity of v. The concavity of v thus reflects the inequality aversion of the social planner. Beyond concavity, the specific choice of v has no bearing on the results in this chapter.

The social welfare criterion uses only *observable* data, namely average incomes in the various signal groups. These data are available to the government and can thus be used for evaluating policy choices. Therefore, our comparison of funding schemes and policy options will be based on the social welfare criterion in Eq. 6.23.

6.2.1.1 Credit Funding Equilibrium (CRE)

Under this funding structure, the government guarantees access to credit markets for all students who attend higher education. Suppose agent i considers to finance his investment via the credit market at the going interest rate r, where $R = 1 + r > 0$. The agent will choose $x^i = 1$, if

$$E\left[u\left(wA + w\tilde{a}_{y^i} - R\right)\right] > u(wA). \tag{6.24}$$

Otherwise he chooses $x^i = 0$. Due to signal monotonicity, the LHS in Eq. 6.24 is strictly monotone increasing in the signal y^i. Hence, there exists a unique cutoff signal $\hat{y}$ such that all individuals with signals larger than or equal to $\hat{y}$ invest in higher education, and individuals with signals lower than $\hat{y}$ do not invest.

The aggregate stock of human capital can then be represented as

$$H = A + \int_{\hat{y}}^{\bar{y}} \bar{a}_y \mu(y)\,\mathrm{d}y. \tag{6.25}$$

In equilibrium, each agent chooses investment in education according to Eq. 6.24, factor markets clear, and aggregate human capital follows the accumulation Eq. 6.25.

12. In our model, all individuals are identical ex ante. Therefore, in equilibrium, agents with the same signal choose identical consumption profiles.

Definition 6.4. *Given the international gross interest rate $R = 1 + r$, an equilibrium with credit funding (CRE) consists of a vector $(\hat{y}, w, K, H) \in \mathbb{R}^4_+$, $\hat{y} \in [\underline{y}, \bar{y}]$, such that:*

(i) *The cutoff signal, $\hat{y}$, satisfies Eq. 6.24 with equality.*
(ii) *The aggregate stock of human capital, H, satisfies Eq. 6.25.*
(iii) *The wage and physical capital satisfy $w = F_L(K/H, 1)$ and $R = F_K(K/H, 1)$.*

A CRE always exists and it is unique: for given $R > 0$, the second equality in (iii) uniquely determines K/H. For given K/H, the first equality in (iii) uniquely determines the wage rate w. Equation 6.24 then yields the cutoff signal $\hat{y}$ which is independent of H. Finally, aggregate human capital, H, is determined by Eq. 6.25.

In a CRE, the economy-wide aggregate investment in education is suboptimally low. To illustrate this fact, we calculate the *efficient* cutoff signal, y_e, which maximizes social welfare. In the social welfare optimum, y_e separates agents who invest in higher education from those who do not invest. y_e maximizes

$$W(y) = \int_{\underline{y}}^{y} v(wA)\mu(y')\,dy' + \int_{y}^{\bar{y}} v(wA + w\bar{a}_{y'} - R)\mu(y')\,dy'$$

and, hence, satisfies

$$0 = W'(y_e) = \mu(y_e)[v(wA) - v(wA + w\bar{a}_{y_e} - R)] \iff \bar{a}_{y_e} = R/w. \quad (6.26)$$

According to Eq. 6.26, in a social optimum investment in education is efficient in the sense that only those signal groups invest in higher education, for which the expected return, $w\bar{a}_y$, exceeds the funding cost R. This investment rule implies that aggregate consumption is maximized.

From $E[wA + w\tilde{a}_{y_e} - R] = wA$ we conclude

$$E[u(wA + w\tilde{a}_{y_e} - R)] < u(wA) \quad (6.27)$$

due to risk aversion. Combining Eqs. 6.24 and 6.27 yields $\hat{y} > y_e$, that is, the cutoff signal beyond which agents invest in higher education in a CRE is suboptimally high and, hence, investment is suboptimally low.

Proposition 6.8. *In the CRE, aggregate investment in education is suboptimally low.*

6.2.1.2 Equilibrium with Funding Diversity (FDE)

The inefficiency of educational investment under the credit funding regime is due to the fact that credit funding does not allow individuals to share idiosyncratic ability and income risks. Yet, as we have seen in Chapter 5, the provision of income-contingent education loans through some government agency or private lending institution can mitigate the problems of underinvestment and inadequate risk pooling in the higher education sector. Therefore, in a next step we allow income-contingent loan contracts to coexist alongside credit markets and analyze how these instruments interact in equilibrium.

Assume that a financial institution (SLI) offers income-contingent loan contracts to all individuals who are willing to invest in higher education. The payback obligation of a loan is linked to an individual's future (gross) income. Agents with higher incomes have higher payback obligations. Clearly, such loan contracts reduce the riskiness of future net incomes as they provide partial insurance against uncertain income prospects that are due to random ability realizations. We consider an income-contingent loans (ICL) program that includes all individuals who voluntarily participate and which requires no subsidization from the government. Thus, if established, the ICL competes against the regular credit market to attract customers willing to invest in higher education.

If agent i decides to invest in higher education and to participate in the ICL, he receives a loan of 1 unit in period 0 with repayment obligation Ra^i/a_0 in period 1.[13] The positive constant a_0 will be determined in equilibrium such that the ICL breaks even. The net income from this investment in period 1 is

$$a^i\left[w - \frac{R}{a_0}\right]. \tag{6.28}$$

Note that agent i's *expected* payback, $R\bar{a}_{y^i}/a_0$, is increasing in the signal, that is, the scheme "penalizes" agents with high signals.

The ICL-program takes no account of the heterogeneity in ability prospects that is already revealed through the individual signals when investment and borrowing decisions are made. Thus the ICL-program does not just provide insurance, but rather it combines insurance against the unrealized part of ability with cross-subsidization between classes of people in different signal groups. Indeed, individuals with high signals "subsidize" those with low signals.

Next we analyze whether income-contingent education finance can coexist with competitive credit markets in the absence of government regulation and, if so, how competition between the two financing schemes affects the efficiency properties of the formation of skilled labor in this economy. Let

$$\bar{a}(y') := E\left[\bar{a}_{\tilde{y}} | \underline{y} \le \tilde{y} \le y'\right] \tag{6.29}$$

denote average ability of agents in the signal groups between $\underline{y}$ and y'. Consider the following arrangement: if all individuals with signals less than or equal to y' participate in the ICL-program and all other individuals do not participate, then

13. Such student loan markets exist in Australia, where repayments are enforced by the tax authorities. Student loan markets also exist in Sweden, the UK, and Chile (for more details see Barr and Crawford, 1998; Lleras, 2004). More recently, the US loan system for students has allowed for Income-based Repayment Plan (see Lewin, 2011).

a_0 in Eq. 6.28 will be set equal to $\bar{a}(y')$. The equality $a_0 = \bar{a}(y')$ ensures that the ICL-program just breaks even, if it attracts all individuals with signals less than or equal to y'.

The net return to investment in education under the ICL-program is then given by

$$\tilde{a}_y \left(w - \frac{R}{\bar{a}(y')} \right) \tag{6.30}$$

for all agents in signal group y. Thus, if the net return in Eq. 6.30 is positive for *some* signal group y, then it is positive for *all* signal groups. Therefore, if the ICL-program does not break down in equilibrium, that is, if it attracts at least one customer, then *all* individuals invest in higher education. Some of these individuals, however, may find it optimal to finance their investments via the credit market.

We now investigate which signal groups participate in the ICL-program and which ones choose the credit market. Let

$$\tilde{c}_1(y) = Aw + \tilde{a}_y w - R \tag{6.31}$$

and

$$\tilde{c}_2(y; y') = Aw + \tilde{a}_y \left(w - \frac{R}{\bar{a}(y')} \right), \tag{6.32}$$

where Eq. 6.31 describes random consumption of an agent with signal y if he invests via the credit market, and Eq. 6.32 describes random consumption under the ICL-program. We denote by

$$V_1(y) = Eu(\tilde{c}_1(y)); \quad V_2(y; y') = Eu(\tilde{c}_2(y, y'))$$

the corresponding expected utilities.

Lemma 6.4. *Suppose y^* satisfies*

$$V_1(y^*) = V_2(y^*; y^*). \tag{6.33}$$

Then

$$V_1(y) - V_2(y; y^*) \tag{6.34}$$

is strictly increasing in y.

Equation 6.33 implies that individuals in signal group y^* are indifferent between investing via the ICL-program and investing via the credit market, if all agents in the signal groups $y \leq y^*$ participate in the ICL-program. It follows immediately from Lemma 6.4 that all agents with signals greater than y^* finance their investments via the credit market and all agents with signals smaller than y^* participate in the ICL-program.

Definition 6.5. *Given the international gross interest rate $R = 1 + r$, an FDE consists of a vector $(y^*, w, K, H) \in \mathbb{R}^4_+$, $y^* \in [\underline{y}, \bar{y}]$, such that:*

(i) *The cutoff signal, y^*, satisfies $u(Aw) \leq V_2(y^*, y^*) = V_1(y^*)$.*[14]
(ii) *The aggregate stock of human capital satisfies $H = A + E\tilde{a}$.*
(iii) *The wage and physical capital satisfy $w = F_L(K/H, 1)$ and $R = F_K(K/H, 1)$.*

The inequality in (i) ensures that the ICL-program does not break down, and the equality implies that the credit market co-exists alongside the ICL-program. In view of Eq. 6.32, the inequality $u(Aw) \leq V_2(y^*, y^*)$ implies $w\bar{a}(y^*) \geq R$, that is, on average investment in education within the ICL-program is profitable. Moreover, the last inequality in combination with Eqs. 6.23 and 6.33 implies $y^* > \hat{y}$. Thus, in the FDE fewer individuals use the credit market than in the CRE. The equality in (ii) holds because in this equilibrium all individuals invest in higher education. In fact, according to Lemma 6.4, agents with signals lower than y^* join the ICL-program, and the remaining agents finance their educational investments via the credit market.

If the agents are risk-neutral, then the equality in (i) of Definition 6.5 is satisfied only for $y^* = \underline{y}$. In that case, no FDE exists, because $\underline{y} < y_e$ has been assumed. Thus, a sufficient amount of risk aversion is necessary for this type of equilibrium to exist.[15]

In an FDE, all individuals are (weakly) better off at the interim stage, that is, after they have received their signals, than in an equilibrium with credit funding. This follows from the observation that expected utility of individuals with signals $y \geq y^*$ stays the same, and expected utility of all other agents increases because they *voluntarily* choose to participate in the ICL-program rather than using the credit market.

Nevertheless, even though competition between the financing schemes has some merits, the FDE is still inefficient. Inefficiencies are caused by two factors. The first factor consists of an externality, which is caused by the competition between the schemes. The externality is imposed on individuals who participate in the ICL-program. The more agents go to the credit market, the less favorable are the terms of repayment for agents participating in the ICL-program. Due to this externality, the cutoff signal y^* is suboptimally low, that is, it lies below the socially optimal level.

Proposition 6.9. *In the FDE, the cutoff signal, y^*, which separates the signal groups that join the ICL-program from the signal groups that use the credit*

---

14. $y^* := \bar{y}$, if $V_2(y, y) > V_1(y)$ for all y.
15. More precisely, let y' be defined by $\bar{a}(y')w = R$ which implies $y' > y_e$. Then a risk sharing equilibrium exists if, as a sufficient condition, individual preferences satisfy the inequalities

$$u(Aw) < Eu(Aw + w\tilde{a}_{y'} - R)$$
$$Eu(Aw + w\tilde{a}_{\bar{y}} - (\tilde{a}_{\bar{y}}/\bar{a})R) > Eu(Aw + w\tilde{a}_{\bar{y}} - R).$$

market, is suboptimally low, that is,

$$\frac{\partial W(y^*)}{\partial y^*} > 0.$$

According to Proposition 6.9, the externality from funding competition could be mitigated and social welfare could be raised if some individuals who finance their investment through the credit market would join the ICL-program. Yet, in the absence of government intervention these individuals have no incentive to change their financing decisions.

Second, in an FDE, individuals with very low signals $y < y_e$ invest in higher education because they are subsidized by other agents in the ICL-program. Investments of these individuals are inefficient for the economy as a whole because, on average, the returns to these investments fall short of the investment costs, that is, $w\bar{a}_y < R$ for $y < y_e$. We summarize this observation in

Proposition 6.10. *In the FDE, aggregate investment in higher education is suboptimally high.*

6.2.2 Funding Structure and Social Welfare

Under the funding structures considered so far the investment allocation process is inefficient. In the CRE, aggregate investment is suboptimally low while in the FDE, aggregate investment is suboptimally high. Moreover, these funding structures lead to different degrees of income inequality across the signal groups. Both income inequality as well as inefficiencies in the investment process have a negative impact on social welfare. In this section, we focus on the combined impact of these two sources of welfare losses and investigate how the funding structures compare from the perspective of social welfare.

Proposition 6.11. *Suppose*

$$w\bar{a} - R \geq \int_{\hat{y}}^{\bar{y}} (w\bar{a}_y - R)\mu(y)\,\mathrm{d}y, \tag{6.35}$$

that is, the aggregate net return to investment in education is higher in the FDE than in the CRE. Then social welfare is higher in the FDE than in the CRE.

The investment inefficiency in the FDE caused by agents with signals less than y_e investing in higher education and, hence, the term on the LHS in Eq. 6.35 is independent of posterior ability risks and of the individuals' attitudes toward those risks. The investment inefficiency in the CRE, by contrast, results from individuals with signals higher than y_e but lower than $\hat{y}$ who refuse to invest in higher education because they shy away from the involved risk. This effect is strengthened by both higher posterior ability risk and higher individual risk aversion. The investment inefficiency in the CRE therefore increases and, hence, the term on the RHS in Eq. 6.35 declines with higher posterior ability risk and with higher individual risk aversion. Thus, Proposition 6.11 suggests that social welfare is higher in the FDE than in the CRE if either individuals are strongly risk-averse or if the screening information is vague such that the posterior ability risks remain high.

Suppose, for instance, that individual preferences exhibit constant absolute risk aversion, $\alpha > 0$, and that the posterior distribution of abilities takes the form $\tilde{a}_y = \bar{a}_y + \tilde{\epsilon}$, where $\tilde{\epsilon}$ is Normally distributed with mean zero and variance σ^2. Here, σ^2 measures the posterior ability risk as well as the vagueness, or noisiness, of the screening information. In that case, $\bar{a}_{\hat{y}} = \frac{1}{2}w\alpha\sigma^2 + \frac{R}{w}$. Thus, if $\alpha\sigma^2 \rightarrow \frac{2}{w^2}(w\bar{a}_{\bar{y}} - R)$ then $\hat{y} \rightarrow \bar{y}$ such that the inequality in Eq. 6.35 is satisfied if the product of risk aversion and posterior ability risk is sufficiently high.

6.2.3 Access Restriction to Higher Education

In the FDE, the economy-wide aggregate investment in education is suboptimally high. This overinvestment worsens the terms of loan repayment for individuals who participate in the ICL-program. The problem is intensified as individuals in the highest signal groups turn to the credit market for funding which further reduces the attractiveness of the ICL-program. These inherent sources of inefficiency are caused by the free entry to the ICL-program. They can possibly be mitigated by a simple government policy which restricts access to higher education to individuals with signals higher than the efficient threshold level y_e.[16] We now investigate how the equilibria with credit funding and with funding diversity compare with regard to social welfare, if such access restriction to higher education is implemented. Note that the access restriction will *not* be binding in the CRE due to $\hat{y} > y_e$ (cf. Proposition 6.8). Thus, the policy regime interferes only with the FDE but leaves the CRE unaffected.

6.2.3.1 *Restricted Participation FDE (RP/FDE)*

Suppose the government restricts access to higher education under a system of funding diversity where individuals can choose between participating in the ICL-program and using the credit market. Such restriction not only prevents agents with poor ability prospects from investing, but also makes the pool of agents who participate in the ICL-program less adversely selected. As a consequence, the ICL-program might become more attractive to individuals with higher signals thereby raising the cutoff signal y^* and mitigating the externality from the coexistence of (and competition between) the two funding schemes. We now analyze whether this intuition is confirmed by our model. For this purpose,

16. In Israel, such policy exists and is based on the matriculation exams grades at the end of high school.

we define

$$\tilde{c}_2(y; y_e, y') := Aw + \tilde{a}_y \left(w - \frac{R}{\bar{a}(y_e, y')} \right); \quad \bar{a}(y_e, y') := E[\bar{a}_{\tilde{y}} | y_e \leq \tilde{y} \leq y']. \tag{6.36}$$

$\tilde{c}_2(y; y_e, y')$ represents consumption of an individual with signal y who participates in the ICL-program, if the ICL-program attracts all individuals with signals in $[y_e, y']$. Note that $\tilde{c}_2(y; y_e, y') > Aw$ for all $y' > y_e$.

Definition 6.6. *Given the international gross interest rate $R = 1 + r$ and the government threshold policy y_e, a restricted participation equilibrium with funding diversity (RP/FDE, for short) consists of a vector $(y^\dagger, w, K, H) \in \mathbb{R}^4_+$, $y^\dagger \in [y_e, \bar{y}]$, such that:*

- **(i)** *The cutoff signal, $y^\dagger$, satisfies $Eu(\tilde{c}_2(y^\dagger; y_e, y^\dagger)) = V_1(y^\dagger)$.*[17]
- **(ii)** *The aggregate stock of human capital satisfies $H = A + \int_{y_e}^{\bar{y}} \bar{a}_y \mu(y)\, dy$.*
- **(iii)** *The wage and physical capital satisfy $w = F_L(K/H, 1)$ and $R = F_K(K/H, 1)$.*

In an RP/FDE with government policy, y_e, only individuals with signals larger than y_e (are allowed to) invest in higher education, hence aggregate consumption is maximized. An agent with signal y participates in the ICL-program if $y \in [y_e, y^\dagger]$, and he uses the credit market if $y > y^\dagger$.

Observe that $y^\dagger$ is strictly larger than y_e, because $Eu(\tilde{c}_2(y_e, y_e, y_e)) > Eu(\tilde{c}_1(y_e)) = V_1(y_e)$. The inequality holds because $\tilde{c}_1(y_e)$ is an MPS of $\tilde{c}_2(y_e, y_e, y_e)$.[18] Thus, in contrast to FDE, a RP/FDE with operative ICL-program always exists. Moreover, Eq. 6.36 implies that $\tilde{c}_2(y^\dagger; y_e, y^\dagger) > Aw$, from which we conclude that $y^\dagger > \hat{y}$.

In the RP/FDE, all individuals are (weakly) better off at the interim stage, that is, after they have received their signals, than in the equilibrium with credit funding. Indeed, expected utilities of individuals with signals $y < y_e$ or $y \geq y^\dagger$ are the same in both equilibria. And expected utilities of individuals with signals between y_e and $y^\dagger$ are (weakly) higher in the RP/FDE, because the agents *voluntarily* invest and *voluntarily* participate in the ICL-program.

6.2.3.2 *Restricted Participation and Social Welfare*

In a next step, we compare the RP/FDE and the CRE with respect to the social welfare criterion in Eq. 6.23. The welfare comparison in Proposition 6.11 between the FDE and the CRE was ambiguous because both equilibria entail different forms of investment inefficiency. The FDE leads to overinvestment while the CRE leads to underinvestment in higher education. As a consequence,

---

17. $y^\dagger := \bar{y}$, if $Eu(\tilde{c}_2(y; y_e, y)) > V_1(y)$ for all $y \in [y_e, \bar{y}]$.

18. Note that $\tilde{c}_1(y_e)$ and $\tilde{c}_2(y_e, y_e, y_e)$ have the same mean and that $\tilde{c}_2(y_e, y_e, y_e) \overset{(<)}{>} \tilde{c}_1(y_e)$ for $\tilde{a}_{y_e} \overset{(>)}{<} \bar{a}_{y_e}$.

the aggregate net return to educational investment in the FDE can be higher or lower than in the CRE. Yet, if the government restricts access to higher education, investment efficiency is restored under funding competition and, hence, the RP/FDE dominates the CRE in terms of social welfare.[19]

Proposition 6.12. *Social welfare is higher in the RP/FDE than in the CRE.*

Table 6.1 summarizes the results of our social welfare comparison. If access to higher education is not restricted, and if the initial funding structure in the higher education sector consists solely of a competitive credit market, then the creation of an ICL-program which coexists alongside credit market funding may enhance economic welfare. In fact, this happens if the condition in Eq. 6.35 is satisfied. Moreover, a policy which restricts access to higher education to signal groups with positive net returns on educational investment eliminates overinvestment under funding diversity. As a consequence, coexistence of credit markets and an ICL-program raises social welfare as well as individual ex ante expected utility.

6.2.4 A Generalization

So far our analysis has proceeded on the assumption that the social value of investment in human capital equals the private return on education. We have thus abstracted from possible higher education externalities on productivity growth. While these externalities are difficult to measure they are believed to be significant (Creedy, 1995; Hanushek and Kimko, 2000; Englebrecht, 2003). Our model can be generalized to include higher education externalities by assuming that the basic productivity level, A, depends on aggregate human capital, H. In

TABLE 6.1 Welfare Comparison

	Funding Structure		
Access Policy	Funding Diversity		Credit Market
		(under the restriction in Eq. 6.35)	
Unrestr. participation	W^{FDE}	>	W^{CRE}
Restr. participation	$W^{RP/FDE}$	>	W^{CRE}

19. The dominance of the RP/FDE relative to the CRE is not limited to the welfare criterion in Eq. 6.23 but holds more generally. In fact, at the end of Section 6.2.3.1 we noticed that at the interim stage the RP/FDE dominates the CRE in the Pareto sense. This implies in particular that ex ante expected utility of each agent is higher in the RP/FDE than in the CRE.

this generalized setting, the human capital of agent i who has received signal y^i is given by Eq. 6.22, where A is replaced with $A(H)$.[20]

Assumption 6.4. *The basic human capital level of unskilled workers, $A(H)$, is an increasing function of the aggregate human capital, H, and satisfies $0 < A'(H) < 1, \forall H > 0$.*

As the externality in Assumption 6.4 makes investment in higher education socially more valuable, an obvious implication is that underinvestment in the CRE becomes more severe while the extent of overinvestment in the FDE declines. Apart from this, the results in Sections 6.2.2 and 6.2.3 which compare the levels of social welfare between both funding structures remain valid. As to Propositions 6.11 and 6.12 observe that social welfare, W, is an increasing function of individual basic human capital, A, in the FDE and in the RP/FDE. This is true because in both equilibria the set of individuals who invest in higher education is fixed, that is, independent of A,[21] and therefore an increase in A raises average consumption in each signal group. But then, due to the higher education externality, individual basic human capital in the RP/FDE and (under the condition in Eq. 6.35) in the FDE exceed the corresponding level in the CRE. Therefore, the social welfare assessments in Propositions 6.11 and 6.12 remain valid.

Proposition 6.13. *Modifying the human capital formation function in Eq. 6.22 to include education externalities such that $A(H)$ satisfies Assumption 6.4 does not affect the results obtained in Propositions 6.8–6.12.*

6.2.5 Policy Implications and Conclusion

Our analysis suggests that government intervention in the higher education sector can be helpful in two ways. First, such intervention may mitigate imperfections in the market for risk bearing which prevent risks on investment in higher education from being pooled in diversified portfolios. In particular, pure credit market funding does not allow individuals to pool their idiosyncratic ability risks which results in aggregate underinvestment in higher education. One important task of the government is therefore the organization of additional higher education finance by means of an ICLP and its implementation. Such program reduces the risks on investments in human capital through pooling, thereby improving the risk allocation in the economy and enhancing accumulation of human capital.

20. This formulation implies that *all* individuals (skilled and unskilled) benefit from the externality. Some authors argue that the external effect should be confined to agents who invest in higher education: bright students generate positive externalities for other students and for teachers but not for unskilled workers (Gary-Bobo and Trannoy, 2008).

21. In the FDE, *all* individuals invest and in the RP/FDE, those individuals with signals larger than y_e invest. According to Eq. 6.26, y_e is independent of A.

Second, a funding structure for investment in higher education under which an ICLP coexists with, and competes against, credit markets has two considerable drawbacks which call for further government intervention. On the one hand, such funding structure leads to aggregate overinvestment in human capital. And on the other hand, the coexistence of the ICL-program and credit market funding creates an externality which leaves the ICL-program adversely selected thereby worsening the terms of repayment for agents participating in the program. The first drawback can be eliminated, and the second drawback can be mitigated, by a policy which restricts access to higher education to individuals with sufficiently promising ability prospects. Under such regulation, the installation of an ICL-program which competes against the credit market for higher education loans raises social welfare in the economy. In order to be effective, government intervention must therefore combine the provision of income-contingent education loans with access restrictions to higher education.

The incentive mechanisms involved when funding systems compete in higher education are relevant in other areas of economic policy as well. In many countries, for instance, health insurance is provided by a public insurance agency as well as by private insurance companies. The public insurance agency pools health risks across the entire population of insures while the private insurance companies pool health risks only across individuals in the same signal group, that is, with similar health reports. The competition between these insurance schemes gives rise to similar mechanisms of risk pooling and adverse selection as those studied here for the higher education sector.

APPENDIX TO CHAPTER 6

Proof of Lemma 6.1. Differentiating $C(y')$ in Eq. 6.3 yields

$$C'(y') = A'(H)w\frac{\partial H}{\partial y'} - \bar{a}_{y'}w + R \qquad \text{(A.6.1)}$$

where

$$H = A(H) + \int_{y'}^{\bar{y}} \bar{a}_y \, \mathrm{d}y \qquad \text{(A.6.2)}$$

and

$$\frac{\partial H}{\partial y'} = \frac{-\bar{a}_{y'}}{1 - A'(H)} < 0. \qquad \text{(A.6.3)}$$

Combining Eqs. A.6.1 and A.6.3 we get

$$C'(y') = -w\bar{a}_{y'}\left[\frac{A'(H)}{1 - A'(H)} + 1\right] + R. \qquad \text{(A.6.4)}$$

By signal monotonicity, $\bar{a}_{y'}$ is increasing in y'. Moreover, by Assumption 6.1, $A'(H)/[1 - A'(H)]$ is increasing in y'. Thus, in view of Eq. A.6.4, $C'(y')$ is decreasing in y'. This shows that $C(y')$ is a concave function. □

Proof of Proposition 6.1. $\hat{y}_p$ satisfies

$$\bar{a}_{\hat{y}_p} = \frac{R}{w}(1 - s).$$

Combining this equality with Eq. 6.8 yields

$$\bar{a}_{\hat{y}_p} < \frac{R}{w} = \bar{a}_{\hat{y}}.$$

Since signals are monotone, $\hat{y}_p < \hat{y}$ and, hence, $H_p > H$ follow. □

Proof of Proposition 6.2. We show that $I_p(y)$ and $I(y)$ satisfy conditions (i) and (ii) in Definition 6.2.

(i) By definition of S_p, any SL-subsidy $s \in S_p$ increases aggregate consumption. Since in our model aggregate consumption is equal to aggregate income, the inequality in Eq. 6.15 holds for $\hat{I}(\cdot) = I_p(\cdot)$ and $\bar{I}(\cdot) = I(\cdot)$.

(ii) We show that

$$I_p(y) - I(y) \geq 0 \implies I_p(\tilde{y}) - I(\tilde{y}) \geq 0 \quad \forall \tilde{y} \in [\underline{y}, y] \tag{A.6.5}$$

holds for any $y \in Y$. Condition (ii) in Definition 6.2 then follows by setting $\hat{y} := \sup\{y \in Y | I_p(y) \geq I(y)\}$. In order to prove Eq. A.6.5, choose $y \in Y$ such that $I_p(y) \geq I(y)$. If $\tilde{y} \in [\underline{y}, \hat{y}]$, then $I(\tilde{y}) = A(H)w < A(H_p)w \leq I_p(\tilde{y})$, where the strict inequality follows from Proposition 6.1. If $\tilde{y} \in [\hat{y}, y]$, then $\tilde{y} > \hat{y}_p$ follows from Proposition 6.1, and we get

$$\begin{aligned} I_p(\tilde{y}) - I(\tilde{y}) &= [A(H_p) - A(H)]w + Rs + \tau_p[R(1 - s) - \bar{a}_{\tilde{y}}w] \\ &\geq [A(H_p) - A(H)]w + Rs + \tau_p[R(1 - s) - \bar{a}_y w] \\ &= I_p(y) - I(y) \geq 0. \end{aligned}$$

The proof is complete. □

Proof of Lemma 6.2. The claim follows immediately, if we can show that the expected utility of an agent who chooses $x = 1$ is monotone increasing in his signal y. The expected utility of this agent is

$$E\left\{u\left(A(H_u)w + (1 - \tau_u)\left[Rs + \tilde{a}\left(w - \frac{R}{\bar{a}_y}\right)\right]\right)\middle| y\right\}. \tag{A.6.6}$$

If $w - \frac{R}{\bar{a}_y} \geq 0$ holds, then signal monotonicity implies that the expected value in Eq. A.6.6 is monotone increasing in y. To complete our argument, let y and y', $y > y'$, be two signals with $w - \frac{R}{\bar{a}_{y'}} < w - \frac{R}{\bar{a}_y} < 0$. Denote by $c(\tilde{a}, y)$ and $c(\tilde{a}, y')$ the consumption of an agent who invests in higher education and has received the signals y and y', respectively. The monotonicity of expected utility follows from the following assessment:

$$E\left\{u\left(c(\tilde{a},y)\right)\middle|y\right\} = E\left\{u\left(A(H_{\rm u}) + (1-\tau_{\rm u})\left[Rs - \frac{\tilde{a}}{\bar{a}_y}(R - \bar{a}_y w)\right]\right)\middle|y\right\}$$

$$\overset{(y'<y)}{>} E\left\{u\left(A(H_{\rm u}) + (1-\tau_{\rm u})\left[Rs - \frac{\tilde{a}}{\bar{a}_y}(R - \bar{a}_{y'} w)\right]\right)\middle|y\right\} \tag{A.6.7}$$

$$\overset{(A.6.1)}{>} E\left\{u\left(A(H_{\rm u}) + (1-\tau_{\rm u})\left[Rs - \frac{\tilde{a}}{\bar{a}_{y'}}(R - \bar{a}_{y'} w)\right]\right)\middle|y'\right\} \tag{A.6.8}$$

$$= E\left\{u\left(c(\tilde{a},y')\right)\mid y'\right\}.$$

The inequality in Eq. A.6.8 follows from Assumption 6.2, because the argument of the utility function in Eq. A.6.8 is an MPS of the argument of the utility function in Eq. A.6.7. □

Proof of Proposition 6.3. For any $y \in [\hat{y}, \bar{y}]$, $w - (R/\bar{a}_y) \geq 0$ is satisfied by Eq. 6.7. This inequality implies that the net return from investing in Eq. 6.17 is strictly positive for all $a \in \mathcal{A}$ and, hence, $y \in Y_{\rm u}$. □

Proof of Lemma 6.3. Differentiating $\Gamma(\cdot)$ yields

$$\Gamma'(y^f)(1-y^f)^2 = -\gamma(y^f)(1-y^f) + \int_{y^f}^{1} \gamma(y)\,dy \geq 0,$$

which proves the claim. □

Proof of Proposition 6.5. $Y_{\rm u} \subset Y_{\rm p}$ and, hence, $H_{\rm p} \geq H_{\rm u}$ follow from our earlier observation that the condition in Eq. 6.18 is necessary for investment under a T-subsidy while it is sufficient for investment under an SL-subsidy. If we combine the inclusion $Y_{\rm u} \subset Y_{\rm p}$ with the government budget constraint and Lemma 6.3, we get

$$\frac{Rs\,(1-\tau_{\rm u})}{\tau_{\rm u}} = \frac{\int_{Y_{\rm u}} [w\bar{a}_y - R]\,dy}{1-\hat{y}_{\rm u}} \overset{\text{(Lemma 6.3)}}{\geq} \frac{\int_{Y_{\rm p}} [w\bar{a}_y - R]\,dy}{1-\hat{y}_{\rm p}} = \frac{Rs\,(1-\tau_{\rm p})}{\tau_{\rm p}},$$

from which we conclude that $\tau_{\rm u} \leq \tau_{\rm p}$. □

Proof of Proposition 6.6. The income distributions $I_{\rm p}(y)$ and $I_{\rm u}(y)$ satisfy the condition in Eq. 6.15 in Definition 6.2, since

$$\int_Y I_{\rm p}(y)\,dy = A(H_{\rm p})w + (1-\tau_{\rm p})\int_{\hat{y}_{\rm p}}^{\bar{y}} \left[w\bar{a}_y - R(1-s)\right] dy$$

$$= A(H_{\rm p})w + \int_{\hat{y}_{\rm p}}^{\bar{y}} [w\bar{a}_y - R]\,dy$$

$$= C(\hat{y}_{\rm p}) \geq C(\hat{y}_{\rm u}) = \int_Y I_{\rm u}(y)\,dy$$

where the inequality follows from Eq. 6.6 and $\hat{y}_u > \hat{y}_p$ (cf. Proposition 6.5).[22]

In order to show that the condition in Eq. 6.16 is satisfied, note that $H_p > H_u, \hat{y}_u > \hat{y}_p$, and $\tau_p > \tau_u$ imply that the following conditions hold.

$$I_p(y) > I_u(y) \quad \text{for } y < \hat{y}_u \tag{A.6.9}$$

$$\frac{\partial I_p(y)}{\partial y} < \frac{\partial I_u(y)}{\partial y} \quad \text{for } y \geq \hat{y}_u. \tag{A.6.10}$$

If $I_p(y) > I_u(y)\ \forall y \in Y$, then $\hat{y} = \bar{y}$ can be chosen in Eq. 6.16. Otherwise, due to Eq. A.6.10, there exists a unique signal $\hat{y}$ such that $I_p(y) \overset{(<)}{>} I_u(y)$ for $y \overset{(>)}{<} \hat{y}$ Clearly, this property implies Eq. 6.16. □

Proof of Proposition 6.7. Let (s_p, τ_p), $s_p \in S_p$, be a feasible SL-subsidization policy with cutoff signal $\hat{y}_p =: y^0$. Choose a feasible T-subsidization policy (s_u, τ_u), $s_u \in S_u$, such that $\hat{y}_u = y^0$. Equation 6.9 then implies $H_p = H_u =: H^0$. From Eqs. 6.11 and 6.18 we conclude that $s_u \geq s_p$. Let $Y^0 := [y^0, 1]$. The government budget constraints in Eqs. 6.12 and 6.19 can then be written as

$$\frac{\tau_p}{1-\tau_p}\int_{Y^0}\left[w\bar{a}_y - R\right] \mathrm{d}y = Rs_p(1-y^0)$$

$$\frac{\tau_u}{1-\tau_u}\int_{Y^0}\left[w\bar{a}_y - R\right] \mathrm{d}y = Rs_u(1-y^0).$$

Since $s_u \geq s_p$, the above equalities imply $\tau_u \geq \tau_p$. We now show that the income distribution $I_u(y)$ under the policy (s_u, τ_u) is socially more desirable than the income distribution $I_p(y)$ under the policy (s_p, τ_p). Since the signal groups that invest in higher education are the same under both policies, condition (i) in Definition 6.2 is satisfied (with equality). In order to check condition (ii) in Definition 6.2, we compare the distributions of average incomes across signal groups under both policies:

$$I_p(y) = \begin{cases} A(H^0)w; & y \notin Y^0 \\ A(H^0)w - (1-\tau_p)R(1-s_p) + (1-\tau_p)w\bar{a}_y; & y \in Y^0 \end{cases}$$

$$I_u(y) = \begin{cases} A(H^0)w; & y \notin Y^0 \\ A(H^0)w - (1-\tau_u)R(1-s_u) + (1-\tau_u)w\bar{a}_y; & y \in Y^0 \end{cases}.$$

$\tau_u \geq \tau_s$ implies $I'_u(y) \leq I'_s(y)$ for $y \in Y^0$. Therefore, since $\int_Y I_p(y)\,\mathrm{d}y = \int_Y I_u(y)\,\mathrm{d}y$, there exists $\hat{y}_0 \in Y$, such that $I_u(y) \geq I_p(y)$ for $y \leq \hat{y}_0$ and $I_u(y) \leq I_p(y)$ for $y \geq \hat{y}_0$.[23] This yields condition (ii) in Definition 6.2. □

Proof of Lemma 6.4. By signal monotonicity, the term in Eq. 6.34 is strictly increasing in y, if

$$\rho(a) := u(c_1(a)) - u(c_2(a, y^*))$$

22. Note that the inequality in Eq. 6.6 holds for $\hat{y} \in [\hat{y}_p, \hat{y}_u]$ because $s \in S$ implies $\hat{y}_p \geq y^*$.
23. Note that $I_u(y)$ exhibits a discontinuous jump at $y = \hat{y}_0$.

is strictly increasing in a, where

$$c_1(a) := Aw + aw - R; \quad c_2(a, y^*) := Aw + a\left[w - \frac{R}{\bar{a}(y^*)}\right].$$

Differentiating $\rho(\cdot)$ we get

$$\rho'(a) = wu'(c_1(a)) - \left[w - \frac{R}{\bar{a}(y^*)}\right]u'(c_2(a, y^*)).$$

The RHS of the above equality is trivially positive if $c_2(a, y^*) \geq c_1(a)$. Let us therefore consider the case $c_2(a, y^*) < c_1(a)$. The RHS of the last equality can be written as

$$\frac{1}{a}\left[c_1(a)u'(c_1(a)) - c_2(a, y^*)u'(c_2(a, y^*)) + Ru'(c_1(a)) \right.$$
$$\left. + wA\left(u'(c_2(a, y^*)) - u'(c_1(a))\right)\right].$$

This expression is positive because $c_1(a) > c_2(a, y^*)$ and $cu'(c)$ is increasing in c by Assumption 6.3. □

Proof of Proposition 6.9. We need to show that $\partial W(y^*)/\partial y^* > 0$. Define

$$c(y, y^*) := Aw + \bar{a}_y\left[w - \frac{R}{\bar{a}(y^*)}\right]$$
$$c(y) := Aw + \bar{a}_y - R.$$

By signal monotonicity, $c(y, y^*)$ and $c(y)$ are both strictly increasing in y. Note that

$$\int_{\underline{y}}^{y^*}\left(wA + \bar{a}_y\left[w - \frac{R}{\bar{a}(y^*)}\right]\right)\mu(y)\,\mathrm{d}y + \int_{y^*}^{\bar{y}}[wA + \bar{a}_y w - R]\mu(y)\,\mathrm{d}y$$
$$= \int_{\underline{y}}^{\bar{y}}[w(A + \bar{a}_y) - R]\mu(y)\,\mathrm{d}y + \underbrace{\int_{\underline{y}}^{y^*}\left[R - \bar{a}_y\frac{R}{\bar{a}(y^*)}\right]\mu(y)\,\mathrm{d}y}_{=0}.$$

Since the RHS of the above equality is independent of y^*, differentiation with respect to y^* yields

$$\frac{R\bar{a}'(y^*)}{(\bar{a}(y^*))^2}\int_{\underline{y}}^{y^*}\bar{a}_y\mu(y)\,\mathrm{d}y = \mu(y^*)[c(y^*) - c(y^*, y^*)]. \tag{A.6.11}$$

Moreover, differentiating

$$W(y^*) = \int_{\underline{y}}^{y^*}v(c(y, y^*))\mu(y)\,\mathrm{d}y + \int_{y^*}^{\bar{y}}v(c(y))\mu(y)\,\mathrm{d}y$$

yields

$$\frac{\partial W(y^*)}{\partial y^*} = \left[v\left(c(y^*, y^*) - v(c(y^*))\right]\mu(y^*) + \frac{R\bar{a}'(y^*)}{(\bar{a}(y^*))^2}\int_{\underline{y}}^{y^*}v'\left(c(y, y^*)\right)\bar{a}_y\mu(y)\,\mathrm{d}y$$

$$
\begin{aligned}
&> \left[v\left(c(y^*, y^*) - v(c(y^*))\right]\mu(y^*) + v'\left(c(y^*, y^*)\right)\frac{R\bar{a}'(y^*)}{(\bar{a}(y^*))^2}\int_{\underline{y}}^{y^*}\bar{a}_y\mu(y)\,\mathrm{d}y\right. \\
&\overset{(A.6.11)}{=} \mu(y^*)\Big\{\left[v\left(c(y^*, y^*) - v(c(y^*))\right]\right. \\
&\qquad\qquad + v'\left(c(y^*, y^*)\right)\left[c(y^*) - c(y^*, y^*)\right]\Big\} \\
&> 0.
\end{aligned}
$$

The last inequality follows from the concavity of $v(\cdot)$. □

Proof of Proposition 6.11. We prove the proposition by showing that $\bar{c}_{\tilde{y}}^{\mathrm{CRE}}$ is a mean decreasing spread of $\bar{c}_{\tilde{y}}^{\mathrm{FDE}}$. Average consumption in signal group y is

$$
\bar{c}_y^{\mathrm{CRE}} = \begin{cases} wA; & \text{if } y < \hat{y} \\ w(A + \bar{a}_y) - R; & \text{if } y \geq \hat{y} \end{cases} \tag{A.6.12}
$$

in the CRE, and

$$
\bar{c}_y^{\mathrm{FDE}} = \begin{cases} wA + \bar{a}_y\left(w - \frac{R}{\bar{a}(y^*)}\right); & \text{if } y < y^* \\ w(A + \bar{a}_y) - R; & \text{if } y \geq y^* \end{cases} \tag{A.6.13}
$$

in the FDE, where $y^* > \hat{y}$. From Eqs. A.6.12 and A.6.13 it follows immediately that

$$
\bar{c}_y^{\mathrm{FDE}} \overset{(\leq)}{>} \bar{c}_y^{\mathrm{CRE}} \iff y \overset{(\geq)}{<} \hat{y}, \tag{A.6.14}
$$

that is, consumption is more dispersed across signal groups in the CRE than in the FDE. In addition, from Eq. 6.35 we conclude

$$
E\left[\bar{c}_{\tilde{y}}^{\mathrm{FDE}}\right] - E\left[\bar{c}_{\tilde{y}}^{\mathrm{CRE}}\right] = (w\bar{a} - R) - \int_{\hat{y}}^{\bar{y}}(w\bar{a}_y - R)\mu(y)\,\mathrm{d}y \geq 0. \tag{A.6.15}
$$

Thus, aggregate consumption is higher in the FDE than in the CRE. Equations A.6.14 and A.6.15 together imply that $\bar{c}_{\tilde{y}}^{\mathrm{CRE}}$ is a mean decreasing spread of $\bar{c}_{\tilde{y}}^{\mathrm{FDE}}$. □

Proof of Proposition 6.12. We prove the proposition by showing that $\bar{c}_{\tilde{y}}^{\mathrm{CRE}}$ is a mean-decreasing spread of $\bar{c}_{\tilde{y}}^{\mathrm{RP/FDE}}$.

Since in the RP/FDE aggregate consumption is maximized, we conclude

$$
E\left[\bar{c}_{\tilde{y}}^{\mathrm{RP/FDE}}\right] \geq E\left[\bar{c}_{\tilde{y}}^{\mathrm{CRE}}\right]. \tag{A.6.16}
$$

Average consumption in signal group y is given by Eq. A.6.12 in the CRE and by

$$
\bar{c}_y^{\mathrm{RP/FDE}} = \begin{cases} Aw; & \text{if } y < y_e \\ Aw + \bar{a}_y\left(w - \frac{R}{\bar{a}(y_e, y^\dagger)}\right); & \text{if } y \in [y_e, y^\dagger] \\ Aw + \bar{a}_y w - R; & \text{if } y > y^\dagger \end{cases} \tag{A.6.17}
$$

in the RP/FDE. Since $\bar{a}_{y^\dagger} > \bar{a}(y_e, y^\dagger)$ and $\bar{c}_y^{\text{RP/FDE}}$ is flatter than $\bar{c}_y^{\text{CRE}}$ for $y \in (\hat{y}, y^\dagger)$, Eqs. A.6.12 and A.6.17 imply the existence of $\breve{y} \in [\hat{y}, y^\dagger]$ such that

$$\bar{c}_{\tilde{y}}^{\text{RP/FDE}} \overset{(\leq)}{(\geq)} \bar{c}_{\tilde{y}}^{\text{CRE}}, \quad \text{if } y \overset{(\geq)}{\leq} \breve{y}. \tag{A.6.18}$$

In view of Eqs. A.6.16 and A.6.18, $\bar{c}_{\tilde{y}}^{\text{CRE}}$ is a mean-decreasing spread of $\bar{c}_{\tilde{y}}^{\text{RP/FDE}}$.

□

Chapter 7

Screening and Income Inequality

Chapter Outline

7.1 **Inequality of Income Opportunities** **142**
- 7.1.1 Theoretical Framework 143
- 7.1.2 Screening and Inequality Without Risk Sharing 148
- 7.1.3 Screening and Inequality with Risk Sharing 152

7.2 **Inequality of Income Distribution** **154**
- 7.2.1 The Framework and Assumptions 155
- 7.2.2 Formation of Human Capital and Income Inequality 158
- 7.2.3 The Case of CEIS Preferences 162
- 7.2.4 Discussion and Policy Implications 164

Appendix to Chapter 7 **164**

This chapter explores the importance of screening information about individual skills for understanding the mechanisms that may lead to an unequal distribution of incomes in a society. A proper understanding of these mechanisms is crucial, because it has been shown in the theoretical literature that better public and/or private education systems per se do not necessarily lead to less income inequality (e.g., Glomm and Ravikumar, 1992; Sylwester, 2002a,b). And other macroeconomic policies, too, often have complex and ambiguous implications for the distribution of incomes in equilibrium (Loury, 1981; Galor and Zeira, 1993; Benabou, 1996; Orazem and Tesfatsion, 1997; Aghion, 2002).

The endogenous growth literature has investigated the causes of inequality in income distribution, concentrating on four main transmission channels. First, differences in unobservable individual talent may generate income inequality (e.g., Juhn et al., 1993). Second, based on subjective assessments of individual talent, agents may choose different levels of investment in education (e.g., Galor and Tsiddon, 1997; Viaene and Zilcha, 2002). Third, the stock of human capital of parents may affect their children's learning. If this linkage is specific to the household, it will contribute to income inequality (e.g., Hassler and Mora, 2000). Fourth, the rate of technological change may affect the return to investment in education. Rubinstein and Tsiddon (2004) show that this mechanism accounts

© 2015 Elsevier Inc. All rights reserved.

for a significant part of the inequality between different education groups. Our analysis focuses on the first two channels.

We develop an approach which embeds the social mechanism of selecting individual education levels in an endogenous growth model where agents differ with respect to talent (or ability). When young, each agent is screened by an information system which provides him with imperfect information about his talent. The central issue of our study in this chapter is how more efficient screening in the education period affects the intragenerational income distribution.

Our intertemporal framework gives rise to various concepts of "income inequality" that differ by the timing of the appraisal. Recall that individual abilities are determined at birth even though abilities remain unknown until the agents enter their working periods. One may therefore be interested in how ex ante expected incomes (i.e., expected incomes *before* signals are observed) are distributed across agents with different abilities. Making this distribution more equal may be viewed as giving more "equal opportunities" to the younger generation (see Benabou and Ok, 2001). In Section 7.1, we will analyze how better screening information affects the distribution of income opportunities within a society.

An agent's conditional ex ante income expectation typically differs from his ex post income prospects. As a consequence, the distribution of income opportunities within a generation of agents differs from the distribution of actual income prospects. Section 7.2 elaborates on this difference by using an ex post concept of inequality: agents who have received the same signal, choose the same investment in education and, hence, have identical income prospects. That way, a distribution of income prospects across the signal groups is attained. In Section 7.2, we will explore the inequality of this ex post distribution of income prospects.

As a main result, we find that more efficient screening affects the inequality of income prospects and the inequality of income opportunities in different ways. Under plausible restrictions on the agents' attitudes toward risk, less inequality of income prospects involves more inequality of income opportunities.

7.1 INEQUALITY OF INCOME OPPORTUNITIES

We define the income opportunity of an agent with given ability as the agent's expected income before his signal is observed. The distribution of income opportunities then coincides with the intragenerational distribution of ex ante (i.e., before signals are observed) expected incomes, called income prospects, across groups of individuals with different abilities. Income opportunities are more unequal, if disparities in individual abilities are more consequential in determining the individuals' income prospects. In this section, we demonstrate that the inequality of income opportunities may either increase or decrease with better ability screening. More precisely, assuming constant relative risk aversion utility functions, we show that better screening increases (decreases) the inequality of income opportunities, if the relative measure of risk aversion is smaller (larger) than 1. Risk aversion plays such a crucial role, because it affects the behavior of the optimal effort level: the effort level increases (decreases) with the favorability of the information signal, if relative risk aversion is below 1 (above 1). Thus, better screening may either increase or decrease the dispersion of the distribution of investments in education—a fact which critically contributes to our result about the consequences of better screening for the inequality of income opportunities.

We also explore the role of risk sharing arrangements for the link between screening and the distribution of income opportunities. We find that risk sharing is of critical importance for the screening-inequality link. If the ability risks, on which the signals convey information, are insurable, then better screening always leads to more inequality of income opportunities.

7.1.1 Theoretical Framework

Building on the set up in Chapter 4, we consider an overlapping generations economy with a single commodity which is traded each period $t = 0, 1, \ldots$. The commodity can either be consumed or used as an input in a production process. The generations reproduce identically over time. Each generation consists of a continuum of individuals $i \in [0, 1]$ who live for three periods. In their first period ("youth") agents obtain education while they are still supported by their parents. In their second period ("middle-age") they work and spend part of the labor income for consumption; and in their third period ("retirement") they consume their savings. G_t is the generation of all agents born at date $t-1$.

Each agent earns labor income which depends on his human capital. Human capital, h, of an agent in G_t is determined by his innate ability, $A \in \mathbb{R}_+$, the effort $e \in \mathbb{R}_+$ invested in education by this individual, and the "environment" when education takes place represented by the average human capital of agents in the previous generation, H_{t-1}:

$$h = Ag(H_{t-1}, e). \tag{7.1}$$

$g : \mathbb{R}_+^2 \to \mathbb{R}_+$ is a twice differentiable function which is strictly increasing in both arguments.

Again, agents differ only with respect to the abilities assigned to them by nature. The distribution of abilities across agents is the same in each generation. $\nu(A)$ denotes the time-invariant (Lebesgue-) density of agents with ability A and, for convenience, the measure of agents in each generation is normalized to 1. The distribution ν is common knowledge. However, when young no agent knows the ability nature has assigned to him. Agents learn their abilities only at the beginning of their middle-age period.

Before an agent chooses optimal effort in the youth period nature assigns to him a deterministic signal $y \in Y \subset \mathbb{R}$ which contains information about his unknown ability. The signals assigned to agents are monotone in the sense of

Corollary 1.1 and are distributed according to the conditional density $f(\cdot|A)$. These conditional densities are known to all agents. Thus, by construction, the distributions of signals and of abilities across agents are correlated. Since an agent in his youth period is ignorant about what ability nature has assigned to him, he forms expectations on the basis of the signal. Therefore, an agent's decision about how much effort, e, to invest in education, will be based on the conditional distribution of A given his signal y. Hence, as agents in the same generation differ only with respect to (unknown) ability, any two individuals who receive the same signal choose the same effort level.

The agents are expected utility maximizers with von-Neumann Morgenstern lifetime utility function

$$U(e, c_1, c_2) = v(e) + u_1(c_1) + u_2(c_2). \tag{7.2}$$

Individuals derive negative utility from "effort" while they are young and positive utility from consumption in the working period, c_1, and from consumption in the retirement period, c_2.

We make the following assumption about the preferences:

Assumption 7.1. *The utility functions v and u_j, $j = 1, 2$, have the following properties:*

(i) $v : \mathbb{R}_+ \to \mathbb{R}_-$ *is decreasing and strictly concave,*
(ii) $u_j : \mathbb{R}_+ \to \mathbb{R}_+$ *is increasing and strictly concave,* $j = 1, 2$.

The structure of the production sector is the same as in Section 4.2 of Chapter 4: the aggregate production function $F(K, H)$ exhibits constant returns to scale, physical capital K is mobile between countries (the small country assumption), and the supply of labor is inelastic. $\bar{r}_t$ and w_t denote the exogenous interest rate and the wage rate.

Consider the optimization problem of an agent in G_t, given $\bar{r}_t, w_t$, and H_{t-1}. At date $t-1$, when "young," this individual chooses the optimal level of effort employed in obtaining education. This decision is made after the individual has observed his signal y and, hence, is based on the conditional distribution $\nu_y(\cdot)$ of ability. The decision about saving, s, to be used for consumption when "old" is taken in the second period, after the agent has learned his ability, A, and, hence, his human capital, h. Thus s will depend on h via the wage earnings, $w_t h$.

For given levels of h, w_t and $\bar{r}_t$, the optimal saving decision of the agent is determined by

$$\begin{aligned} &\max_s \; u_1(c_1) + u_2(c_2) \\ &\text{s.t. } c_1 = w_t h - s \\ &\qquad c_2 = (1 + \bar{r}_t)s \end{aligned} \tag{7.3}$$

and satisfies the necessary and sufficient first-order condition

$$-u_1'(w_t h - s) + (1 + \bar{r}_t)u_2'((1 + \bar{r}_t)s) = 0 \tag{7.4}$$

for all h. From Eq. 7.4 we find optimal saving as a function of each realized h, that is, $s = s_t(h)$. The optimal level of effort invested in education, e, is determined by

$$\max_{e} \; E[v(e) + u_1(c_1) + u_2(c_2)|y] \tag{7.5}$$
$$\text{s.t. } c_1 = w_t h - s$$
$$c_2 = (1 + \bar{r}_t)s,$$

where h is given by Eq. 7.1 and s satisfies Eq. 7.4. Note that from the perspective of the agent his (unknown) ability A is a random variable which is distributed according to $\nu_y(\cdot)$. Similarly, h is also perceived to be random as human capital depends on ability. Due to the Envelope theorem and the strict concavity of the utility functions, Problem 7.5 has a unique solution determined by the first-order condition

$$v'(e) + w_t g_2(H_{t-1}, e)E[Au_1'(w_t h - s)|y] = 0. \tag{7.6}$$

Since u_1' is a decreasing function we also conclude from Eq. 7.4 that $s_t(h)$ and $w_t h - s_t(h)$ are both increasing in h. This implies, in particular, that the LHS in Eq. 7.6 is strictly decreasing in e. Similarly, from Eq. 7.6 we obtain the optimal level of effort as a function of the conditional distribution ν_y, that is, $e = e_t(\nu_y)$. Note that any two agents in generation t who receive the same individual signal will choose the same effort level.

The aggregate stock of human capital at date t can be expressed as

$$H_t = E_y[\bar{h}_t(\nu_y)] = \int_Y \bar{h}_t(\nu_y)\mu(y)\,dy, \tag{7.7}$$

where

$$\bar{h}_t(\nu_y) := \bar{A}(\nu_y)g(H_{t-1}, e_t(\nu_y)) \tag{7.8}$$

is the average human capital of agents in G_t who have received the signal y.

Our analysis will be based on a screening reliability criterion that differs from Blackwell's concept of informativeness. Below we develop the reliability criterion and discuss how it is related to other information concepts. Given an information system f and an ability level A, define

$$L_f^A(z) := \int_{\frac{f_A}{f}(y|A)\le z} f(y|A)\,dy,$$

where f_A denotes the partial derivative. $L_f^A(z)$ is called the *likelihood ratio distribution* of an agent with ability A under information system f.

Lemma 7.1. $\frac{f_A}{f}(y|A)$ *is monotone increasing in y and, hence, the likelihood ratio distribution function can be written as*

$$L_f^A(z) = F\left(\left(\frac{f_A}{f}\right)^{-1}(z)\middle|A\right), \tag{7.9}$$

where $F(y|A)$ is the c.d.f. for the distribution of signals across agents with ability A.

Kim (1995) has shown that the likelihood ratio distribution under $\bar{f}$, $L^A_{\bar{f}}(z)$, is a mean preserving spread (MPS) of that under $\hat{f}$, $L^A_{\hat{f}}(z)$, if $\bar{f}$ is more informative (in the Blackwell sense) than $\hat{f}$:

Lemma 7.2. *Let $\bar{f}$ and $\hat{f}$ be two information systems such that $\bar{f} \succ_{\text{inf}} \hat{f}$. For any $A \in \mathbb{R}_+$, $L^A_{\bar{f}}(z)$ is an MPS of $L^A_{\hat{f}}(z)$. That is, both distribution functions have the same mean and*

$$\int^{z'} \bar{F}\left(\left(\frac{\bar{f}_A}{\bar{f}}\right)^{-1}(z)\middle| A\right) dz \geq \int^{z'} \hat{F}\left(\left(\frac{\hat{f}_A}{\hat{f}}\right)^{-1}(z)\middle| A\right) dz \quad \forall z' \in \mathbb{R} \quad (7.10)$$

with the strict inequality holding for some z'.

For a proof, see Kim (1995).

Equation 7.10 can be transformed into an integral condition that will turn out to be a useful tool for the analysis in this chapter.

Lemma 7.3. *Equation 7.10 is satisfied for all $z' \in \mathbb{R}$ if and only if the following integral condition holds for all $\vartheta \in [0, 1]$:*

$$S(\vartheta|A) := \int_0^{\vartheta} \left[\frac{\bar{f}_A}{\bar{f}}\left(\bar{F}^{-1}(s|A)\middle|A\right) - \frac{\hat{f}_A}{\hat{f}}\left(\hat{F}^{-1}(s|A)\middle|A\right)\right] ds \leq 0. \quad (7.11)$$

This lemma is a straightforward modification of Proposition 3 in Demougin and Fluet (2001). The proof is therefore omitted.

Being ignorant about what level of ability nature has assigned to him, a young agent perceives his ability as random. For clarity and in conformity with our notation in earlier chapters, we shall mark variables which are perceived to be random by a "˜." The subsequent analysis uses a special concept of informativeness for the screening process that is called "reliability":

Definition 7.1 (Reliability). *Let $\bar{f}$ and $\hat{f}$ be two information systems. $\bar{f}$ is more reliable than $\hat{f}$ (expressed by $\bar{f} \succ_{\text{rel}} \hat{f}$), if:*

(i) *[Adding Noise Reduces Reliability] For any $A \in \mathbb{R}_+$, the likelihood ratio distribution under $\bar{f}$, $L^A_{\bar{f}}(z)$, is an MPS of that under $\hat{f}$, $L^A_{\hat{f}}(z)$.*

(ii) *[Good News Become Better News Under More Reliability] For any $A \in \mathbb{R}_+$ and any increasing function $\pi : \mathbb{R}_+ \to \mathbb{R}_{++}$,*

$$\frac{E^{\bar{f}}[\pi(\tilde{A})|\bar{F}^{-1}(s''|A)]}{E^{\bar{f}}[\pi(\tilde{A})|\bar{F}^{-1}(s'|A)]} \geq \frac{E^{\hat{f}}[\pi(\tilde{A})|\hat{F}^{-1}(s''|A)]}{E^{\hat{f}}[\pi(\tilde{A})|\hat{F}^{-1}(s'|A)]} \quad (7.12)$$

holds for any two signals $s'' \geq s'$. If π is a decreasing function, then the inequality in Eq. 7.12 reverses.

According to Lemma 7.2, condition (i) is weaker than the Blackwell criterion, that is, condition (i) is implied by $\bar{f} \succ_{\text{inf}} \hat{f}$. Condition (ii) postulates that under a more reliable information system the conditional expectation of any increasing transformation of the state variable (ability) reacts more sensitively to changes in the (transformed) signal s. In this sense, an increase in the transformed signal s constitutes better news if the signal is more reliable. Note that

$$\frac{E^{\bar{f}}[\pi(\tilde{A})|\bar{F}^{-1}(s|A)]}{E^{\hat{f}}[\pi(\tilde{A})|\hat{F}^{-1}(s|A)]} \tag{7.13}$$

is monotone increasing in the signal s, if and only if condition (ii) holds.

Even though formally different, condition (ii) bears similarity with Lehmann's (1988) concept of *accuracy* (see also Persico, 2000). Intuitively speaking, a signal is more accurate, if it is more closely related (in a statistical sense) to the state variable. Our reliability concept admits a similar interpretation. The fact that the term in Eq. 7.13 is increasing in s means that a higher signal "improves" the posterior distribution of the state variable more if the system is more reliable. Therefore, a more reliable system can be interpreted as one where the signals are more closely related to the state variable.

Observe that any two information systems which can be ordered according to Blackwell's criterion, $\bar{f} \succ_{\text{inf}} \hat{f}$, satisfy the inequality in Eq. 7.12 for $s' = 0$ and $s'' = 1$. In particular, for increasing π, the term in Eq. 7.13 is less than 1 for $s = 0$ and larger than 1 for $s = 1$. This observation follows from the following assessment (for arbitrary $\hat{A} \in \mathbb{R}_+$):

$$\begin{aligned} E^{\bar{f}}[\pi(\tilde{A})|\bar{F}^{-1}(0|\hat{A})] &= E^{\bar{f}}[\pi(\tilde{A})|\underline{y}] = \int_{\mathcal{A}} \pi(A)\bar{\upsilon}_{\underline{y}}(A)\,\mathrm{d}A \\ &\leq \frac{1}{\hat{\mu}(\underline{y})}\int_Y \bar{\mu}(y')\lambda(\underline{y},y')\int_{\mathcal{A}} \pi(A)\bar{\upsilon}_{y'}(A)\,\mathrm{d}A\,\mathrm{d}y' \\ &= \int_{\mathcal{A}} \pi(A)\hat{\upsilon}_{\underline{y}}(A)\,\mathrm{d}A = E^{\hat{f}}[\pi(\tilde{A})|\hat{F}^{-1}(0|\hat{A})]. \end{aligned} \tag{7.14}$$

By a similar argument we get

$$E^{\bar{f}}[\pi(\tilde{A})|\bar{F}^{-1}(1|\hat{A})] \geq E^{\hat{f}}[\pi(\tilde{A})|\hat{F}^{-1}(1|\hat{A})], \quad \forall \hat{A} \in \mathcal{A}. \tag{7.15}$$

Equations 7.14 and 7.15 imply that the conditional expectations $E^{\bar{f}}[\pi(\tilde{A})|\bar{F}^{-1}(s|\hat{A})]$ and $E^{\hat{f}}[\pi(\tilde{A})|\hat{F}^{-1}(s|\hat{A})]$ cross at least once.

Thus the Blackwell criterion has important implications for the curvatures of conditional expectations under the information systems $\bar{f}$ and $\hat{f}$. These implications are strengthened by the condition in Eq. 7.12, which implies that the conditional expectations in Figure 7.1 have the single crossing property.

In many economic applications, signals are generated according to $\tilde{s} = A + \delta\tilde{\varepsilon}$. This specification implies that, as an approximation (which is exact if $\tilde{A}$ and $\tilde{s}$ are jointly normal or if the log of their densities is quadratic), conditional expectations can be represented as $E[\tilde{A}|s] = E\tilde{A} + \vartheta(s - E\tilde{s})$ with $\vartheta = \sigma_A^2/(\sigma_A^2 + \delta^2\sigma_\varepsilon^2)$. Typically, in these applications, ϑ is used as a measure of reliability. In such a framework, condition 7.12 is always satisfied: if $\bar{f}$ and $\hat{f}$

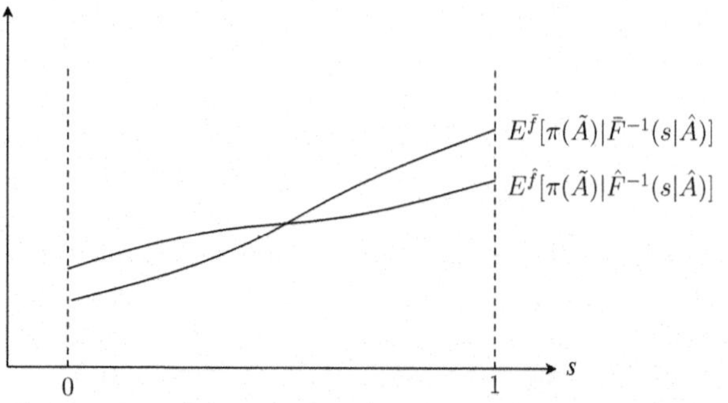

FIGURE 7.1 Conditional expectations under information systems $\bar{f}$ and $\hat{f}$.

are information systems corresponding to $\bar{\vartheta}$ and $\hat{\vartheta}$, $\bar{\vartheta} > \hat{\vartheta}$, then

$$\frac{E^{\bar{f}}[\pi(\tilde{A})|s]}{E^{\hat{f}}[\pi(\tilde{A})|s]} = \frac{E[\pi(\tilde{A})] + \bar{\vartheta}(s - E\tilde{s})}{E[\pi(\tilde{A})] + \hat{\vartheta}(s - E\tilde{s})},$$

which is increasing in s.

7.1.2 Screening and Inequality Without Risk Sharing

To facilitate the comparison of income distributions under different information systems we restrict the utility functions $u_1(\cdot)$, $u_2(\cdot)$, and $v(\cdot)$ to be in the family of CRRA:

$$u_1(c_1) = \frac{c_1^{1-\gamma_u}}{1-\gamma_u}; \quad u_2(c_2) = \beta\frac{c_2^{1-\gamma_u}}{1-\gamma_u}; \quad v(e) = -\frac{e^{\gamma_v+1}}{\gamma_v+1}. \tag{7.16}$$

γ_u and γ_v are strictly positive constants. γ_v parameterizes the curvature of the utility function in the youth period, v; and γ_u parameterizes the curvature of the utility functions in the middle-age period and retirement period, u_i, $i = 1, 2$.

We also assume that the function g in Eq. 7.1 has the form

$$g(H, e) = \hat{g}(H)e^{\alpha}, \tag{7.17}$$

where $\hat{g}$ is strictly increasing in H, and $\alpha \in (0, 1)$. Using the functional forms of $u_j, j = 1, 2$, in Eq. 7.16, it follows from Eq. 7.4 that, given $\bar{r}_t$ and w_t, the saving s is proportional to the human capital level h. In other words, for each t and for any agent in G_t we have:

$$s = m_t h, \quad 0 < m_t < w_t, \quad t = 1, 2, \ldots. \tag{7.18}$$

The specifications in Eqs. 7.16–7.18 allow us to solve Eq. 7.6 for the optimal effort level as a function of the conditional distribution ν_y:

$$e_t(\nu_y) = \delta_t\left(E\left[\tilde{A}^{1-\gamma_u}\middle|y\right]\right)^{\rho/\alpha} \tag{7.19}$$

where

$$\delta_t := \left[\frac{\alpha w_t(\hat{g}(H_{t-1}))^{1-\gamma_u}}{(w_t - m_t)^{\gamma_u}}\right]^{\rho/\alpha}; \quad \rho = \frac{\alpha}{\gamma_v + \alpha(\gamma_u - 1) + 1}.$$

We will discuss the role of screening information for the distribution of individual income opportunities. For that purpose we focus on the average income of all agents with given ability A. The distribution of these average incomes across different ability levels will serve as a measure of the inequality of income opportunities. In this sense, income opportunities are less equal, if expected incomes are more responsive to disparities in abilities.

Let

$$\begin{aligned} I_t^f(A) &:= \int_Y w_t h f(y|A)\,dy \\ &= w_t \hat{g}(H_{t-1})\delta_t^{\alpha} A \int_Y \left(E^f[\tilde{A}^{1-\gamma_u}|y]\right)^{\rho} f(y|A)\,dy \qquad (7.20) \end{aligned}$$

be the expected income, as of date $t-1$, of an agent in generation t with ability A. We measure the inequality of income opportunities by the elasticity of the expected income with respect to ability.

Definition 7.2 (Inequality of Income Opportunities). *Income opportunities under information system $\bar{f}$ are said to be more unequal than income opportunities under information system $\hat{f}$, if*

$$\varepsilon\left[I_t^{\bar{f}}, A\right] := \frac{\partial I_t^{\bar{f}}(A)}{\partial A}\frac{A}{I_t^{\bar{f}}(A)} \geq \frac{\partial I_t^{\hat{f}}(A)}{\partial A}\frac{A}{I_t^{\hat{f}}(A)} =: \varepsilon\left[I_t^{\hat{f}}, A\right] \qquad (7.21)$$

holds for all $t \geq 0$ and all A.

We will show below (cf. part (i) in Theorem 7.1) that for $\gamma_u \leq 1$ and given A the elasticity $\varepsilon[I_t^f, A]$ is bounded from below by $\varepsilon[I_t^{f^0}, A]$, where f^0 denotes the uninformative system. From Eq. 7.20 it is immediate that $\varepsilon[I_t^{f^0}, A] = 1$ for all A. Similarly, for $\gamma_u \geq 1$ the elasticity $\varepsilon[I_t^f, A]$ is bounded from below by $\varepsilon[I_t^{f^1}, A]$ where f^1 is the fully reliable system. Since under f^1 the signal reveals an agent's talent, Eq. 7.20 reduces to

$$[w_t \hat{g}(H_{t-1})\delta_t^{\alpha}]^{-1} I_t^{f^1}(A) = A^{1+(1-\gamma_u)\rho}$$

and, hence, $\varepsilon[I_t^{f^1}, A] = 1 + (1-\gamma_u)\rho = (1+\gamma_v)/[1+\gamma_v+\alpha(\gamma_u - 1)] > 0$. Thus the elasticities in Eq. 7.21 are strictly positive.

It should be pointed out here that the above definition of inequality of income opportunities implies the definition given by Atkinson (1970) in the sense that the normalized income under $\hat{f}$, $\|I_t^{\hat{f}}(A)\| := I_t^{\hat{f}}(A)/E[I_t^{\hat{f}}(A)]$, dominates in second degree stochastic dominance the normalized income under $\bar{f}$, $\|I_t^{\bar{f}}(A)\| := I_t^{\bar{f}}(A)/E[I_t^{\bar{f}}(A)]$. In other words, $\|I_t^{\bar{f}}(A)\|$ and $\|I_t^{\hat{f}}(A)\|$ differ by an MPS and, hence, the Lorenz curve for $\|I_t^{\hat{f}}(A)\|$ lies strictly above that for $\|I_t^{\bar{f}}(A)\|$.

It is useful to rewrite the criterion in Eq. 7.21 in a technically more convenient (albeit economically less intuitive) form. To this end, observe that

$$\operatorname{sign}\left(\varepsilon\left[I_t^{\bar{f}},A\right]-\varepsilon\left[I_t^{\hat{f}},A\right]\right)=\operatorname{sign}\left(\varepsilon\left[\bar{I}^{\bar{f}},A\right]-\varepsilon\left[\bar{I}^{\hat{f}},A\right]\right), \qquad (7.22)$$

where

$$\bar{I}^f(A) := I_t^f(A)/w_t\hat{g}(H_{t-1})\delta_t^{\alpha}A, \quad f=\bar{f},\hat{f}.$$

$\bar{I}^f(A)$ can be rewritten as

$$\bar{I}^f(A)=\int_0^1\left(E^f\left[\tilde{A}^{1-\gamma_u}|F^{-1}(s|A)\right]\right)^{\rho}f\left(F^{-1}(s|A)|A\right)\left(F^{-1}\right)'(s)\,\mathrm{d}s$$

$$=\int_0^1\left(E^f\left[\tilde{A}^{1-\gamma_u}|F^{-1}(s|A)\right]\right)^{\rho}\mathrm{d}s, \quad (f,F)=(\bar{f},\bar{F}),(\hat{f},\hat{F}). \qquad (7.23)$$

Differentiating Eq. 7.23, we obtain

$$\frac{\partial\bar{I}^f(A)}{\partial A}\frac{1}{\bar{I}^f(A)}=\frac{1}{\bar{I}^f(A)}\int_Y\left(E^f\left[\tilde{A}^{1-\gamma_u}\middle|y\right]\right)^{\rho}f_A(y|A)\,\mathrm{d}y$$

$$=\int_0^1\frac{\left(E^f\left[\tilde{A}^{1-\gamma_u}\middle|F^{-1}(s|A)\right]\right)^{\rho}}{\int_0^1\left(E^f\left[\tilde{A}^{1-\gamma_u}\middle|F^{-1}(\hat{s}|A)\right]\right)^{\rho}\mathrm{d}\hat{s}}\frac{f_A}{f}\left(F^{-1}(s|A)\middle|A\right)\mathrm{d}s. \qquad (7.24)$$

Now we are ready to state an alternative characterization of inequality of income opportunities. Even though less intuitive than condition 7.21, this characterization turns out to be a convenient tool for our analysis. Define

$$\Gamma^A(f|s):=\frac{\left(E^f\left[\tilde{A}^{1-\gamma_u}|F^{-1}(s|A)\right]\right)^{\rho}}{\int_0^1\left(E^f\left[\tilde{A}^{1-\gamma_u}|F^{-1}(\hat{s}|A)\right]\right)^{\rho}\mathrm{d}\hat{s}}; \quad (f,F)=(\bar{f},\bar{F}),(\hat{f},\hat{F}). \qquad (7.25)$$

Combining Eqs. 7.22 and 7.24 with Eq. 7.25 yields the following characterization.

Proposition 7.1. *Inequality of income opportunities in the sense of Definition 7.2 is higher under information system $\bar{f}$ than under information system $\hat{f}$, if and only if*

$$\int_0^1\left[\Gamma^A(\bar{f}|s)\frac{\bar{f}_A}{\bar{f}}\left(\bar{F}^{-1}(s|A)\middle|A\right)-\Gamma^A(\hat{f}|s)\frac{\hat{f}_A}{\hat{f}}\left(\hat{F}^{-1}(s|A)\middle|A\right)\right]\mathrm{d}s\geq 0, \qquad (7.26)$$

holds for all A.

If relative risk aversion, γ_u, is equal to 1, expected individual income is linear in ability due to constant effort and, as a direct consequence, inequality of income opportunities is not affected by more reliable information. To see this, observe that

$$\int_0^1 \frac{f_A}{f}\left(F^{-1}(s|A)\Big|A\right)\,\mathrm{d}s = \int_Y f_A(y|A)\,\mathrm{d}y = 0. \tag{7.27}$$

Equation 7.27 implies that Eq. 7.26 is satisfied with equality for all A provided that $\gamma_u = 1$. In that case, therefore, the inequality of income opportunities is the same for any two information systems $\bar{f}$ and $\hat{f}$.

Proposition 7.2. *If $\gamma_u = 1$, the inequality of income opportunities does not depend on the chosen information system.*

To understand the economic intuition behind this proposition, observe that for $\gamma_u = 1$ the individual effort level is not responsive to the information revealed by a signal (cf. Eq. 7.19). With fixed effort level, however, the sole channel is blocked through which the information system may affect the distribution of expected incomes across agents. Yet, when γ_u differs from 1, a more reliable information system may give rise to more or less inequality of income opportunities.

Theorem 7.1. *Let $\bar{f}$ and $\hat{f}$ be two information systems with $\bar{f} \succ_{\text{rel}} \hat{f}$.*

(i) *If $\gamma_u \leq 1$, the distribution of income opportunities is more unequal under $\bar{f}$ than under $\hat{f}$.*

(ii) *If $\gamma_u \geq 1$, the distribution of income opportunities is more unequal under $\hat{f}$ than under $\bar{f}$.*

Information affects the distribution of efforts at each date. From Eq. 7.19 we know that effort is increasing in the signal if $\gamma_u \leq 1$, and decreasing if $\gamma_u \geq 1$. To illustrate the consequences for inequality, consider the case $\gamma_u \leq 1$. Under a more reliable information system, signals more accurately reflect the agents' talents. As a consequence, due to more favorable signals, agents with high talents tend to choose higher effort levels; and agents with low talents tend to choose lower effort levels. This mechanism produces more inequality of income opportunities. Similarly, if $\gamma_u \geq 1$ the mechanism works in reverse and reduces the inequality of income opportunities.

On a more general note, better screening information leads to higher inequality of income opportunities whenever effort is increasing in the signal. If the utility functions u_1 and u_2 satisfy the restriction in Eq. 7.16, then assuming $\gamma_u \leq 1$ generates this monotonicity. Otherwise, additional assumptions are needed. If, for example, u_1 and u_2 are restricted to be in the family of CRRA, then effort is increasing in the signal if $\gamma_{u_2} \leq \gamma_{u_1} \leq 1$ holds; and effort is decreasing in the signal if $\gamma_{u_2} \geq \gamma_{u_1} \geq 1$ is satisfied. This claim can be verified through inspection of Eqs. 7.4 and 7.6.

7.1.3 Screening and Inequality with Risk Sharing

To make our model more realistic, we now allow that part of the perceived uncertainty of an agent's ability is insurable. Let $A = A_1 \cdot A_2$ with $(A_1, A_2) \in \mathcal{A} := \mathbb{R}^2_+$. We assume that the distributions of A_1 and of A_2 across agents in H_t are stochastically independent. Before agents make decisions about effort they can insure the perceived risk which is associated with the A_1-component of their (unknown) ability. Since there is no aggregate risk in the economy the insurance market for the A_1-component of ability will be unbiased, that is, the agents can share part of the perceived risk on fair terms. While in Section 7.1.2 the signals affected only uninsurable risks, in this section we assume that the signals contain only information about the insurable risk factor A_1.

In order to introduce the risk sharing market we need to assume that the A_1-component of individual ability is verifiable ex post by the insurers. The future income of each individual, perceived as random at young age, will then have an insurable component as well as an uninsurable component. Denote by $\bar{A}_1(\nu_y)$ the expected value of $\tilde{A}_1$ if the signal y has been observed,

$$\bar{A}_1(\nu_y) := \int_{\mathcal{A}} A_1 \nu_y(A)\,\mathrm{d}A. \tag{7.28}$$

Since the insurance market is unbiased, all agents find it optimal to completely eliminate the (perceived) A_1-risk from their incomes in the second period of life. Thus the optimal saving and effort decisions of an agent in G_t satisfy the following first-order conditions

$$(1+\bar{r}_t)u_2'\left((1+\bar{r}_t)s\right) - u_1'\left(w_t\bar{A}_1(\nu_y)A_2 g(H_{t-1},e) - s\right) = 0 \quad (A_2 \in \mathbb{R}_+) \tag{7.29}$$

$$v'(e) + w_t g_2(H_{t-1},e) E\left[\tilde{\bar{A}}(\nu_y) u_1'\left(w_t\tilde{\bar{A}}(\nu_y) g(H_{t-1},e) - s\right) \Big| y\right] = 0 \quad (y \in Y), \tag{7.30}$$

where

$$\tilde{\bar{A}}(\nu_y) := \bar{A}_1(\nu_y) \cdot \tilde{A}_2. \tag{7.31}$$

It is our aim to analyze the impact of more reliable screening information on the inequality of income opportunities, if agents are able to share part of the uncertainty about their random abilities. Using the functional specifications (Eqs. 7.16 and 7.19), the average income of an agent with ability $A = A_1 \cdot A_2$ is

$$\begin{aligned} I_t^f(A_1,A_2) &= w_t\delta_t^{\alpha}\hat{g}(H_{t-1})\left(E\left[\tilde{A}_2^{1-\gamma_u}\right]\right)^{\rho} A_2 \int_Y \left(E^f\left[\tilde{A}_1|y\right]\right)^{\tau} f(y|A_1)\,\mathrm{d}y \\ &= w_t\delta_t^{\alpha}\hat{g}(H_{t-1})\left(E\left[\tilde{A}_2^{1-\gamma_u}\right]\right)^{\rho} A_2 \int_0^1 \left(E^f\left[\tilde{A}_1|F^{-1}(s|A_1)\right]\right)^{\tau} \mathrm{d}s, \end{aligned} \tag{7.32}$$

where

$$\tau := 1 + \rho(1 - \gamma_u) = \frac{1 + \gamma_v}{\gamma_v + \alpha\gamma_u + (1 - \alpha)} > 0. \tag{7.33}$$

Since $I_t^f(\cdot)$ is linear in A_2 regardless of the information system, the elasticity of expected income with respect to A_1 is now the relevant measure of inequality: the distribution of income opportunities is more unequal under $\bar{f}$ than under $\hat{f}$ if $\varepsilon[I_t^{\bar{f}}, A_1] \geq \varepsilon[I_t^{\hat{f}}, A_1]$ holds for all $t \geq 0$ and $A_1 \in \mathbb{R}_+$.

Define

$$\Delta^{A_1}(f|s) := \frac{\left(E^f\left[\tilde{A}_1|F^{-1}(s|A_1)\right]\right)^\tau}{\int_0^1 \left(E^f\left[\tilde{A}_1|F^{-1}(\hat{s}|A_1)\right]\right)^\tau \, d\hat{s}}. \tag{7.34}$$

The same procedure as in Section 7.1.2 yields the following characterization.

Proposition 7.3. *Inequality of income opportunities is higher under information system $\bar{f}$ than under information system $\hat{f}$, if and only if*

$$\int_0^1 \left[\Delta^{A_1}(\bar{f}|s)\frac{\bar{f}_{A_1}}{\bar{f}}\left(\bar{F}^{-1}(s|A_1)\Big|A_1\right) - \Delta^{A_1}(\hat{f}|s)\frac{\hat{f}_{A_1}}{\hat{f}}\left(\hat{F}^{-1}(s|A_1)\Big|A_1\right)\right] ds \geq 0, \tag{7.35}$$

holds for all A_1.

In the absence of risk sharing opportunities, the impact of more reliable information on income inequality was shown to be critically dependent on the risk aversion parameter γ_u. By contrast, if the risks affected by the signals can be insured on fair terms, more reliable information will always increase the inequality of income opportunities.

Theorem 7.2. *Assume that an unbiased insurance market for the A_1-risk is available. Let $\bar{f}$ and $\hat{f}$ be two information systems with $\bar{f} \succ_{\text{rel}} \hat{f}$. The distribution of income opportunities is more unequal under $\bar{f}$ than under $\hat{f}$.*

If the signals convey information about *insurable* risks, more efficient screening (i.e., a more reliable information system) results in more inequality regardless of the measure of relative risk aversion. In Section 7.1.2, we found that the effect of screening information about *noninsurable* risks on the inequality of income opportunities depends on the agents' attitudes toward risk. Why is risk sharing so critical for the link between inequality of opportunities and the precision of screening information?

In the absence of risk sharing arrangements, agents use their effort decisions as a hedging instrument against talent risks: strongly risk-averse agents choose higher effort in response to a less favorable signal. This mechanism produces less inequality of income opportunities under a more reliable system. By contrast, moderately risk-averse agents choose higher effort when they receive a more favorable signal, which results in more inequality.

When an unbiased risk sharing market exists, screening information affects the distribution of income opportunities through a different channel. The availability of insurance against talent risks on fair terms obviously eliminates any incentives to use effort as a hedging device. Moreover, under unbiased risk sharing arrangements, agents with favorable signals (i.e., high expected ability) obtain insurance on better terms than agents with unfavorable signals (i.e., low expected ability). This mechanism produces more inequality of income opportunities under a more reliable information system, regardless of the agents' attitudes toward risk.

Along with the distribution of income opportunities, also economic growth is intricately related to screening information. Indeed, when risk sharing is possible, attitudes toward risk critically affect the link between growth and information. In Chapter 4, we found that more reliable information enhances growth when γ_u is less than 1; and more reliable information reduces growth when γ_u exceeds 1. Thus, in economies with low risk aversion ($\gamma_u < 1$) information induced growth comes at the cost of more unequal income opportunities. In strongly risk-averse economies ($\gamma_u > 1$), by contrast, growth and inequality of opportunities are inversely related.

7.2 INEQUALITY OF INCOME DISTRIBUTION

The distribution of ex ante income opportunities analyzed above constitutes a characteristic that can conveniently be used for normative welfare evaluations and policy recommendations. Despite this fact, ex post income inequality concepts are still popular in the theoretical literature, mainly because they are consistent with commonly used empirical inequality measures and with various remuneration schemes we find in the labor markets. In this section, we analyze whether and to what extent the choice of the inequality concept matters. That is, we compare the effects of screening information on ex post income inequality with the effects on inequality of ex ante income opportunities.

Our ex post inequality concept focuses on the distribution of expected incomes (called income prospects) after signals have been observed. Since all individuals in a given signal group choose the same investment in education, they all have identical income prospects. Income inequality is higher if the distribution of income prospects across signal groups is more unequal.

As a main result, we find that the implications of screening information for income inequality involve an inherent trade-off: under specifications which are consistent with empirical evidence for developed industrial countries, better screening can achieve less (ex post) income inequality only at the expense of more inequality in the distribution of (ex ante) income opportunities.

The reason why better screening affects the distributions of incomes and of income opportunities differently lies in the composition of the subgroups compared under each inequality concept. *Income opportunities* are the same for agents with identical abilities. By contrast, *income prospects* are the same for agents with identical signals. And while the members of a given signal group all react uniformly to better screening, the members of a given ability group react in a nonuniform manner according to their signals. The different patterns of investment behavior in the respective subgroups of agents may generate opposite effects of better screening on the inequality of incomes and the inequality of income opportunities.

7.2.1 The Framework and Assumptions

We slightly specialize the theoretical set-up of Section 7.1, assuming that human capital of individual $i \in G_t$ depends on random ability $\tilde{A}^i$ and on effort $e^i \in \mathbb{R}_+$ invested in education according to

$$\tilde{h}^i = B\tilde{A}^i e^i. \tag{7.36}$$

$B \in \mathbb{R}_{++}$ represents the impact of publicly provided schooling. Since the level and quality of public schooling is exogenous in our model, we set $B = 1$. We also assume that the signals assigned to agents conditional on their abilities have uniform marginal distribution on $[0, 1]$. This assumption does not imply any loss of generality (cf. Section 1.3.3).

Average ability of all agents who have received the signal y is

$$\bar{A}(y) := E[\tilde{A}|y] = \int_{\mathbb{R}_+} A\nu_y(A)\,\mathrm{d}A. \tag{7.37}$$

Recall from Section 4.1 that aggregate production $F(K, H)$ exhibits constant returns to scale and that agents are expected utility maximizers. Hence,

$$w_t = F_L\left(\frac{K_t}{H_t}, 1\right). \tag{7.38}$$

Moreover, the von-Neumann Morgenstern lifetime utility function

$$U(e, c_1, c_2) = v(e) + u_1(c_1) + u_2(c_2), \tag{7.39}$$

satisfies Assumption 7.1

Labor contracts are concluded *after* agents have learned their signals but *before* their abilities become known. Therefore, the wage income specified in a labor contract cannot be made contingent on individual human capital. As a consequence, agents are unable to appropriate the full marginal product of their human capital. Instead, individuals are grouped according to the signals they have received. And, in the absence of any further information, the market treats all agents in the same group identically. Under these circumstances each individual will receive a wage equal to the marginal product of the mean human capital of those with whom he is grouped. For all agents who have received the signal y, average ability is given by $\bar{A}(y)$ in Eq. 7.37. Therefore, the wage income of agent $i \in G_t$ with signal y is $w_t\bar{h}^i$, where

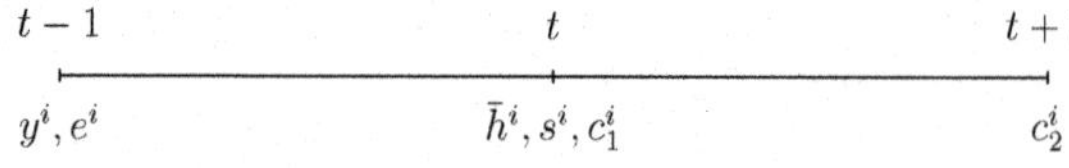

FIGURE 7.2 Timing of events.

$$\bar{h}^i = \bar{A}(y)e^i. \tag{7.40}$$

The timing of events and decisions is depicted in Figure 7.2.

For given levels of w_t and $\bar{r}_t$, the optimal saving and effort decisions of individual $i \in G_t$ are determined by

$$\max_{s^i, e^i} \; v(e^i) + u_1(c_1^i) + u_2(c_2^i) \tag{7.41}$$

$$\text{s.t. } c_1^i = w_t \bar{h}^i - s^i$$

$$c_2^i = (1 + \bar{r}_t)s^i.$$

Since income is determined by *average ability*, given the signal y^i and the effort level, saving s^i is based on average human capital $\bar{h}^i$ (and not on h^i); as a consequence, period 2 consumption c_2^i is nonrandom when e^i is chosen.

The necessary and sufficient first-order conditions are

$$-u_1'(w_t\bar{h}^i - s^i) + (1 + \bar{r}_t)u_2'((1 + \bar{r}_t)s^i) = 0 \tag{7.42}$$

$$v'(e^i) + w_t\bar{A}(y^i)u_1'(w_t\bar{h}^i - s^i) = 0, \tag{7.43}$$

where $\bar{h}^i$ is given by Eq. 7.40.

Observe that the signal y^i enters the first-order conditions only via the term $\bar{A}(y^i)$. Thus we may express the optimal decisions as functions of $\bar{A}(y^i)$ rather than as functions of the signal itself, that is, $s^i = s_t(\bar{A}(y^i))$, $e^i = e_t(\bar{A}(y^i))$. Similarly, in equilibrium we have $\bar{h}^i = \bar{h}_t(\bar{A}(y^i))$. This implies that all agents with signal y receive the same labor income $w_t\bar{h}_t(\bar{A}(y))$. Note, however, that individual incomes are affected by *both* the signals and the chosen effort levels. Therefore, agents do have incentives to choose positive effort levels. Notwithstanding this observation, *equilibrium labor incomes* depend only on the agents' signals because in this model any two agents with the same signal choose the same effort level.

The functions $s_t : \mathbb{R}_+ \to \mathbb{R}_+$, $e_t : \mathbb{R}_+ \to \mathbb{R}_+$, and $\bar{h}_t : \mathbb{R}_+ \to \mathbb{R}_+$, $\bar{h}_t(\bar{A}) := \bar{A}e_t(\bar{A})$ satisfy Eqs. 7.42 and 7.43, that is,

$$-u_1'\left(w_t\bar{h}_t(\bar{A}) - s_t(\bar{A})\right) + (1 + \bar{r}_t)u_2'\left((1 + \bar{r}_t)s_t(\bar{A})\right) = 0 \tag{7.44}$$

$$v'\left(e_t(\bar{A})\right) + w_t\bar{A}u_1'\left(w_t\bar{h}_t(\bar{A}) - s_t(\bar{A})\right) = 0, \tag{7.45}$$

for all $\bar{A} > 0$. In addition, $s_t(0) = e_t(0) = \bar{h}_t(0) = 0$.

Using Eq. 7.37, the aggregate stock of human capital at date t can be expressed as

$$H_t = E_y\left[\bar{h}_t\left(\bar{A}(y)\right)\right] = \int_0^1 \bar{h}_t\left(\bar{A}(y)\right)\,\mathrm{d}y, \tag{7.46}$$

where $\bar{h}_t(\bar{A}(y))$ is the average human capital of agents in G_t who have received the signal y.

Next we define a workable criterion of informativeness for this economy. Let $G(A|y)$ be the c.d.f. for the conditional density $\nu_y(A)$. Signal monotonicity implies that $G(A|y)$ is a decreasing function of y. To see why this property holds, choose $\hat{A} \in \mathbb{R}_+$ arbitrarily but fixed and define

$$U(A) = \begin{cases} 0; & A \leq \hat{A} \\ 1; & A > \hat{A} \end{cases}.$$

Since $EU(\tilde{A}|y) = 1 - G(\hat{A}|y)$ is increasing in y by signal monotonicity, $G(A|y)$ is decreasing in y for all $A \in \mathbb{R}_+$.

For later reference, we secure this monotonicity property in a Remark.

Remark 7.1. *By signal monotonicity, $G(A|y)$ is a decreasing function of y.*

Let us denote by $G_y(A|y)$ the partial derivative of the c.d.f. $G(A|y)$ with respect to y. An information system will be said to be strongly more informative, if the signal realizations have a uniformly stronger impact on the posterior distribution of states:

Definition 7.3 (Strong Informativeness). *Let $\bar{f}$ and $\hat{f}$ be two information systems with corresponding c.d.f's $\bar{G}(A|y)$, $\hat{G}(A|y)$ for the densities $\bar{\nu}(A|y)$, $\hat{\nu}(A|y)$. $\bar{f}$ is strongly more informative than $\hat{f}$ (expressed by $\bar{f} \succsim_{\text{s-inf}} \hat{f}$), if*

$$\bar{G}_y(A|y) \leq \hat{G}_y(A|y) \tag{7.47}$$

holds for all $A \in \mathbb{R}_+$ and $y \in (0, 1)$.

According to Remark 7.1, $G(A|y) = \text{prob}\ (\tilde{A} \leq A|y)$ is decreasing in the signal y. Equation 7.47 says that under a strongly more informative system the posterior distribution over states is more sensitive with respect to signal realizations. In recent papers, Ganuza and Penalva (2006) and Brandt et al. (2014) use information concepts which are also based on differences in posterior distributions. Some of these concepts can be shown to be equivalent to our notion of strong informativeness.

Note that our concept of strong informativeness does not involve any restrictions on the dispersion of abilities relative to the dispersion of test outcomes (signals). The distribution of abilities is exogenously given by $\nu(\cdot)$ and the test outcomes are uniformly distributed under any information system. Instead, condition 7.47 imposes a restriction on the correlation structure between these two distributions.

A few words relating our concept of strong informativeness to the literature are in order. In the economics literature, various concepts of informativeness have been used, dating back to the seminal work by Blackwell (1951, 1953) where the ordering of information has been linked to a statistical sufficiency criterion for signals. More recently, concepts have been developed which represent informativeness as a stochastic dominance order over conditional distributions of signal transformations (Kim, 1995; Athey and Levin, 2001; Demougin and Fluet, 2001). Some of these partial orderings contain the Blackwell ordering as a subset. For example, Kim's criterion can be shown to be strictly weaker than Blackwell's criterion.

Our concept of information in Eq. 7.47 imposes a restriction on the sensitivities of the posterior state distributions. This concept has an advantage in terms of tractability over the above mentioned criteria as it involves only signal derivatives of the posteriors rather than more complex measures of stochastic dominance. In dichotomies, that is, when the number of signals and the number of states are both equal to 2, the restriction in Eq. 7.47 is implied by the Blackwell criterion (Hermelingmeier, 2007). Yet, the Blackwell criterion is itself a restrictive concept that has been generalized in many directions. For a discussion of the relationships between the various extensions of the Blackwell information ordering see Jewitt (1997).

7.2.2 Formation of Human Capital and Income Inequality

In the sequel, we shall compare equilibria under different information systems with regard to the formation of human capital and the distribution of incomes. To avoid notational confusion, equilibrium values attained under information system f will be marked by an upper index f. We begin by analyzing the effects of better information on the formation of human capital. Aggregate human capital of generation t under information system f is

$$H_t^f = \int_0^1 \bar{h}_t(\bar{A}^f(y))\,\mathrm{d}y, \tag{7.48}$$

where

$$\bar{h}_t(x) := xe_t(x), \quad x := \bar{A}^f(y).$$

Since $\bar{h}_t \geq 0$ and $\bar{h}_t(0) = 0$, $e_t(x)$ is increasing (decreasing) in x if $\bar{h}_t(x)$ is a convex (concave) function of x. Depending on the well-known interaction between an income effect and a substitution effect, $\bar{h}_t(\cdot)$ may be convex or concave. The strengths of the income effect and the substitution effect depend on the elasticity of intertemporal substitution between the periods 2 and 3. In Section 7.2.3, we will consider the special case where preferences exhibit constant elasticity of intertemporal substitution. For such preferences, the income effect is dominant and hence $\bar{h}_t(\cdot)$ is concave, if the elasticity of intertemporal substitution is sufficiently small. As a consequence, a better signal results in lower effort. By contrast, the substitution effect is dominant, if the elasticity of intertemporal substitution is sufficiently high. In that case, $\bar{h}_t(\cdot)$ is convex which means that agents step up their efforts when they receive more favorable signals.

The expected marginal product of investment in education, $\bar{A}^f(y)$, is higher for agents with better signals. Thus, convexity of $\bar{h}_t(\cdot)$ (increasing effort function) would be more conducive to the formation of the human capital stock than concavity of $\bar{h}_t(\cdot)$ (which implies a decreasing effort function). We shall therefore call individual behavior *accumulation-inducing* if $\bar{h}_t(\cdot)$ is convex and, hence, good news (higher signal) induces higher investment in education. Similarly, individual investment behavior will be called *accumulation-impeding* if $\bar{h}_t(\cdot)$ is concave, a case where good news results in investing lower effort. This distinction leads to the following characterization.

Proposition 7.4. *Let $\bar{f}$ and $\hat{f}$ be two information systems such that $\bar{f} \succ_{\text{s-inf}} \hat{f}$. Consider the corresponding competitive equilibria under these two systems.*

- **(i)** *Under accumulation-inducing behavior better information (weakly) enhances human capital formation, that is, $H_t^{\bar{f}} \geq H_t^{\hat{f}}$ for all $t \geq 1$.*
- **(ii)** *Under accumulation-impeding behavior better information (weakly) reduces human capital formation, that is, $H_t^{\bar{f}} \leq H_t^{\hat{f}}$ for all $t \geq 1$.*

The characterization in Proposition 7.4 can be interpreted in terms of a simple economic mechanism. Consider part (i), that is, assume that investment behavior is accumulation-inducing. The implementation of a better information system enhances the reliability of the individual signals. As a consequence, high signals become even better news and induce higher investment in education. Similarly, under a better information system the bad news conveyed by a low signal becomes even worse (because now the news is more reliable). Hence, investment in education declines. Thus, under accumulation-inducing investment behavior, better information tends to increase the efforts of agents with high signals and decrease the efforts of agents with low signals. Since the expected marginal product of effort (in terms of human capital) is higher for agents with higher signals, aggregate human capital increases when the information system becomes more informative. If investment behavior is accumulation-impeding, the same mechanism results in lower aggregate human capital under a strongly more informative system.

Next we look into the effects of better information on income inequality. Our analysis of income inequality focuses on the distribution of labor incomes within a given generation G_t. Labor income depends both on the information system and on the signal received by an agent,

$$I_t^f(y) = w_t \bar{A}^f(y) e_t(\bar{A}^f(y)), \tag{7.49}$$

where

$$\bar{A}^f(y) := E^f[\tilde{A}|y]. \tag{7.50}$$

To study the impact of information on income inequality, we use an inequality concept which is based on the following comparison of distributions:

Definition 7.4. *Let Y and X be real-valued random variables with zero-mean normalizations $\check{Y} = Y - EY$ and $\check{X} = X - EX$. The distribution of Y is "more unequal" than the distribution of X, if $\check{Y}$ differs from $\check{X}$ by an MPS.*

This definition of inequality differs from the requirement that one Lorenz curve is strictly above the other one, which is equivalent to second degree stochastic dominance (see Atkinson, 1970). Instead, our definition (known as *absolute* Lorenz order) is based on a location-free concept of dispersion. The induced ordering is implied by the Bickel-Lehmann stochastic ordering (see Landsberger and Meilijson, 1994) which is a concept commonly used in statistics.

The following lemma facilitates the application of our inequality concept in Definition 7.4.

Lemma 7.4. *Let $\tilde{y}$ be a random variable that is distributed over the unit interval $[0, 1]$. Let $z : [0, 1] \to \mathbb{R}$, $x : [0, 1] \to \mathbb{R}$ be differentiable increasing functions such that*

(i) *$\tilde{z} := z \circ \tilde{y}$ differs from $\tilde{x} := x \circ \tilde{y}$ by an MPS,*
(ii) *$z(y) - x(y)$ is strictly monotone in y.*

Let $\vartheta : \mathbb{R} \to \mathbb{R}$ be a differentiable strictly increasing function. The distribution of $\vartheta \circ \tilde{z}$ is more unequal than the distribution of $\vartheta \circ \tilde{x}$, if ϑ is either convex or concave.

The claim in Lemma 7.4 remains valid, if z, x and ϑ are continuous (rather than differentiable) and if $z(y) - x(y)$ is monotone (rather than strictly monotone) in y. This can be shown by means of a straightforward extension of the proof of Lemma 7.4. We secure this observation for later reference in a Remark.

Remark 7.2. *Lemma 7.4 remains valid if z, x and ϑ are continuous and if $z(y) - x(y)$ is monotone in y.*

Our concept of income inequality is based on the dominance criterion for normalized distributions in Definition 7.4.

Definition 7.5. *Let $\bar{f}$ and $\hat{f}$ be two information systems. Income inequality under $\bar{f}$ is higher than under $\hat{f}$, if the distribution of $I_t^{\bar{f}}(y)$ is more unequal than the distribution of $I_t^{\hat{f}}(y)$ for all $t \geq 1$.*

Under a better information system individual ability can be assessed more accurately at the time when labor contracts are concluded. We may conjecture, therefore, first that the income distribution will be more discriminating with respect to differences in abilities, and second that it will be better in line with the distribution of human capital across agents. The following proposition confirms our first conjecture, that is, the informational mechanism results in higher income inequality.

Proposition 7.5. *Let $\bar{f}$ and $\hat{f}$ be two information systems such that $\bar{f} \succcurlyeq_{\text{s-inf}} \hat{f}$. Under both constellations, that is, accumulation-inducing behavior as well as accumulation-impeding behavior, the information system $\bar{f}$ results in more income inequality than $\hat{f}$.*

Even though the result in Proposition 7.5 confirms the above intuitive conjecture, it is not straightforward because the effort decision may be decreasing in the signal y if the elasticity of intertemporal substitution is small. In that case agents who are better talented (on average) invest less in education. This mechanism clearly involves a tendency toward less income inequality for any *given* information system. Yet, under a *better* information system, high signals become better news about abilities and income prospects, while low signals become worse news. This is why more reliable screening benefits high signal groups more than low signal groups in terms of human capital formation and incomes, thereby leading to more income inequality in favor of the more talented agents.

In Theorem 7.1 of Section 7.1.2, we found that more reliable screening reduces the inequality of income *opportunities* under the plausible assumption that the agents' preferences exhibit relative risk aversion larger than 1. This result is in striking contrast to Proposition 7.5 according to which better screening leads to more income inequality. To see where this asymmetry comes from, recall that income opportunities are the same for individuals with identical (albeit unknown) abilities. Since agents in a given ability group receive different signals, better screening implies "good news" for some of them and "bad news" for others. The effect of better screening on the distribution of income opportunities therefore depends on how agents adjust their investments in education in response to good news and bad news. Depending on relative risk aversion, these responses may go in either direction thus leading to more or less inequality of income opportunities. Income *prospects*, by contrast, are the same for individuals with identical signals. Better screening therefore implies "good news" for *all* agents in high signal groups and "bad news" for *all* agents in low signal groups, thus unambiguously increasing the inequality of income prospects.

The relationship between economic growth and income inequality has been widely debated in the literature in the last decade. Based on empirical evidence, Persson and Tabellini (1994) show that higher growth results in less income inequality—a finding that was challenged by other authors, for example, Forbes (2000) and Quah (2003). Our study contributes to this controversy with a narrow, information-based focus. By identifying the effects of information on indicators for human capital formation and income inequality we obtain the co-movements of both indicators due to changes in information.

From Propositions 7.4 and 7.5 we obtain, as a corollary, an information-induced link between human capital formation and income inequality:

Corollary 7.1. *As the result of an improvement of the economy's information system,*

(i) *under accumulation-inducing investment behavior, higher human capital formation is accompanied by more income inequality, and*
(ii) *under accumulation-impeding investment behavior, lower human capital formation is accompanied by more income inequality.*

Thus, human capital accumulation (i.e., growth in our framework) and income inequality are positively related if agents respond to better signals with higher investment in education. Yet, the model is also consistent with an inverse relationship between human capital formation and income inequality. Such a pattern arises when better signals induce agents to reduce investment in education.

In our model, an agent's noisy signal provides *imperfect* information about his ability, but *perfect* information about his income. Therefore, in a given signal group, agents differ in their abilities but they do not differ with regard to incomes. The diversity with respect to ability among agents in the same signal group declines as the signals become more reliable under a better information system. Under perfect information, that is, when the signal reveals the ability level, each signal group consists solely of agents with identical abilities. We have seen that less diversity within signal groups may increase or decrease human capital formation, depending on the shape of the accumulation function $\bar{h}_t(\cdot)$. On the other hand, the agents' incomes depend only on their signals, and the reliability of the signals determines how sensitively incomes vary across signal groups. For this reason, income inequality always increases under a better information system. In particular, under perfect information the economy exhibits a maximum degree of income inequality.

7.2.3 The Case of CEIS Preferences

To illustrate the critical role of the elasticity of intertemporal substitution for the information-induced link between income inequality and human capital formation we restrict the utility functions $u_1(\cdot)$, $u_2(\cdot)$, and $v(\cdot)$ to be in the family of Constant Elasticity of Intertemporal Substitution (CEIS).

$$u_1(c_1) = \frac{c_1^{1-\gamma_u}}{1-\gamma_u}; \quad u_2(c_2) = \beta\frac{c_2^{1-\gamma_u}}{1-\gamma_u}; \quad v(e) = -\frac{e^{\gamma_v+1}}{\gamma_v+1}. \tag{7.51}$$

γ_u and γ_v are strictly positive constants. $1/\gamma_u$ parameterizes the elasticity of intertemporal substitution in consumption.

Using the functional forms of $u_j, j = 1, 2$, in Eq. 7.51, it follows from Eq. 7.42 that, given $\bar{r}_t$ and w_t, the saving s^i is proportional to the human capital level h^i. In other words, for each t there is a constant m_t such that for all $i \in G_t$ we have:

$$s^i = m_t h^i, \quad 0 < m_t < w_t, \quad t = 1, 2, \ldots. \tag{7.52}$$

The specifications in Eqs. 7.51 and 7.52 allow us to solve Eq. 7.43 for the optimal effort level as a function of average ability $\bar{A}^f(y)$,

$$e_t\left(\bar{A}^f(y)\right) = \delta_t \left(\bar{A}^f(y)\right)^{\rho(1-\gamma_u)}, \tag{7.53}$$

where

$$\delta_t := \left[\frac{w_t}{(w_t - m_t)^{\gamma_u}}\right]^{\rho}; \quad \rho = \frac{1}{\gamma_v + \gamma_u}.$$

The income of an agent with signal y is

$$I_t^f(y) = w_t \delta_t \left(\bar{A}^f(y)\right)^{\tau}, \tag{7.54}$$

and aggregate human capital of generation t is

$$H_t^f = \delta_t \int_0^1 \left(E^f[\tilde{A}|y)]\right)^{\tau} \mathrm{d}y, \tag{7.55}$$

where

$$\tau := 1 + \rho(1 - \gamma_u) = \frac{1 + \gamma_v}{\gamma_v + \gamma_u} > 0. \tag{7.56}$$

Consider the expression in Eq. 7.53 for $x = \bar{A}^f(y)$. Clearly $\bar{h}_t(x)$ is convex if $1 + \rho(1 - \gamma_u) \geq 0$, namely if $\gamma_u \leq 1$. In that case, the effort function $e_t(x)$ is increasing. Similarly, $\bar{h}_t(x)$ is concave, that is, $e_t(x)$ is decreasing, if $\gamma_u \geq 1$. Proposition 7.4 therefore implies the following corollary.

Corollary 7.2. *Let $\bar{f}$ and $\hat{f}$ be two information systems such that $\bar{f} \succeq_{\text{s-inf}} \hat{f}$, and assume that the specifications in Eq. 7.51 are valid.*

(i) *High EIS: If $1/\gamma_u \geq 1$, then better information (weakly) enhances human capital formation, that is, $H_t^{\bar{f}} \geq H_t^{\hat{f}}$ for all $t \geq 1$.*
(ii) *Moderate EIS: If $1/\gamma_u \leq 1$, then better information (weakly) reduces human capital formation, that is, $H_t^{\bar{f}} \leq H_t^{\hat{f}}$ for all $t \geq 1$.*

By combining Proposition 7.5 and Corollary 7.2, we obtain a characterization of the information-induced link between human capital formation and income inequality.

Corollary 7.3. *Assume that the specifications in Eq. 7.51 are valid. As a result of an improvement of the economy's information system,*

(i) *higher human capital formation implies more income inequality, if the elasticity of intertemporal substitution in consumption is high, that is, $1/\gamma_u \geq 1$,*
(ii) *lower human capital formation implies more income inequality, if the elasticity of intertemporal substitution in consumption is small, that is, $1/\gamma_u \leq 1$.*

7.2.4 Discussion and Policy Implications

Due to the noise in the signals received by the agents, the screening process in the education sector involves a certain amount of misperception on the part of the individuals. By investing into activities that would improve the validity of the tests, the government can reduce the extent to which agents misperceive their abilities. Our analysis suggests that such policies may produce unwelcome effects with regard to human capital formation and the distribution of income. These effects critically depend on the elasticity of intertemporal substitution. More precisely, for small values of the elasticity of intertemporal substitution better information slows human capital formation and, at the same time, leads to more income inequality.

Empirical evidence suggests that in developed industrial countries the elasticity of intertemporal substitution is in fact small, and possibly close to zero (Hall, 1988). For developed countries our model therefore predicts that more efficient screening produces less human capital formation and more income inequality. At the same time, as we have seen in Section 7.1, the distribution of income opportunities becomes less unequal. Thus, abstracting from the impact on human capital formation, better screening in higher education involves an inherent trade-off: less inequality in the distribution of income opportunities can only be achieved at the expense of more inequality in the distribution of actual incomes.

Of course, ultimately it is a matter of value judgment whether the distribution of actual incomes or of income opportunities should be an issue of political concern. An important lesson to learn from our analysis is, therefore, to recognize the existence of a trade-off between these two goals: less inequality in the distribution of income opportunities comes at the expense of more inequality in the distribution of actual incomes.

APPENDIX TO CHAPTER 7

In this appendix, we prove Lemmas 7.1 and 7.4, Theorems 7.1 and 7.2, and Propositions 7.4 and 7.5.

Proof of Lemma 7.1. Define $h(y|A,\hat{A}) := f(y|A)/f(y|\hat{A})$. Obviously, $h_y(y|A,\hat{A}) = 0$, $\forall y$, if $A = \hat{A}$. Also, by signal monotonicity, $h_y(y|A,\hat{A}) > 0$, $\forall y$, if $A > \hat{A}$. From this observation we conclude

$$0 \leq \frac{\partial}{\partial A}\left(h_y(y|A,\hat{A})\right)\Big|_{A=\hat{A}} = \frac{\partial}{\partial y}\left(\frac{\partial h(y|A,\hat{A})}{\partial A}\Big|_{A=\hat{A}}\right) = \frac{\partial}{\partial y}\left(\frac{f_A(y|A)}{f(y|A)}\right),$$

which proves the claim. □

Below we establish some preliminary results before we proceed with the proofs of Theorems 7.1 and 7.2.

Lemma A.7.1. *Let $\theta : X := [\underline{x}, \bar{x}] \to \mathbb{R}$ be an integrable function satisfying*

$$\int_{\underline{x}}^{\hat{x}} \theta(x)\,\mathrm{d}x \le 0; \quad \int_X \theta(x)\,\mathrm{d}x = 0$$

for all $\hat{x} \in X$. Then

$$\int_X h(x)\theta(x)\,\mathrm{d}x \overset{(\le)}{\ge} 0$$

holds for any differentiable monotone increasing (decreasing) function $h : X \to \mathbb{R}$.

Proof. Integration by parts gives

$$\int_X h(x)\theta(x)\,\mathrm{d}x = h(x)\int_{\underline{x}}^{x} \theta(\hat{x})\,\mathrm{d}\hat{x}\Big|_{\underline{x}}^{\bar{x}} - \int_X h'(x)\int_{\underline{x}}^{x} \theta(\hat{x})\,\mathrm{d}\hat{x}\,\mathrm{d}x$$

$$= -\int_X h'(x)\int_{\underline{x}}^{x} \theta(\hat{x})\,\mathrm{d}\hat{x}\,\mathrm{d}x.$$

The last term is nonnegative if $h(x)$ is increasing; and it is nonpositive if $h(x)$ is decreasing. □

Lemma A.7.2. *Let $\bar{f}$ and $\hat{f}$ be two information systems with $\bar{f} \succ_{\text{rel}} \hat{f}$.*

(i)

$$\frac{\Gamma^A(\bar{f}|s'')}{\Gamma^A(\bar{f}|s')} \ge \frac{\Gamma^A(\hat{f}|s'')}{\Gamma^A(\hat{f}|s')}, \quad s'' \ge s',\ A \in \mathbb{R}_+ \tag{A.7.1}$$

holds for $\gamma_u \le 1$,

(ii)

$$\frac{\Gamma^A(\bar{f}|s'')}{\Gamma^A(\bar{f}|s')} \le \frac{\Gamma^A(\hat{f}|s'')}{\Gamma^A(\hat{f}|s')}, \quad s'' \ge s',\ A \in \mathbb{R}_+ \tag{A.7.2}$$

holds for $\gamma_u \ge 1$.

Proof. The claims in (i) and (ii) follow from part (ii) in Definition 7.1, if we set $\pi(\tilde{A}) = \tilde{A}^{1-\gamma_u}$. □

Corollary A.7.1. *Let $\bar{f}$ and $\hat{f}$ be two information systems with $\bar{f} \succ_{\text{rel}} \hat{f}$. Given any $A \in \mathbb{R}_+$ and any increasing function $V : [0, 1] \to \mathbb{R}$,*

$$\int_0^1 V(s)\Gamma^A(\bar{f}|s)\,\mathrm{d}s \overset{(\le)}{\ge} \int_0^1 V(s)\Gamma^A(\hat{f}|s)\,\mathrm{d}s$$

holds for $\gamma_u \overset{(\ge)}{\le} 1$.

Proof. By Lemma A.7.2, the densities $\Gamma^A(f,\cdot)$, $f = \bar{f}, \hat{f}$, satisfy a variant of the monotone likelihood ratio property (MLRP) in the sense of Eq. A.7.1 for

$\gamma_u \leq 1$ and Eq. A.7.2 for $\gamma_u \geq 1$. Therefore, the same reasoning as in the proof of Proposition 1 in Milgrom (1981) yields the result claimed in the corollary. □

Proof of Theorem 7.1. We apply the characterization in Proposition 7.1.

(i) According to Lemma 7.1, $\frac{f_A}{f}(F^{-1}(s|A)|A)$ is monotone increasing in s for $(f, F) = (\bar{f}, \bar{F}), (\hat{f}, \hat{F})$. The validity of the condition in Eq. 7.26 is then immediate from the following assessment:

$$\int_0^1 \frac{\bar{f}_A}{\bar{f}}\left(\bar{F}^{-1}(s|A)\Big|A\right)\Gamma^A(\bar{f}|s)\,ds \geq \int_0^1 \frac{\bar{f}_A}{\bar{f}}\left(\bar{F}^{-1}(s|A)\Big|A\right)\Gamma^A(\hat{f}|s)\,ds$$
$$\geq \int_0^1 \frac{\hat{f}_A}{\hat{f}}\left(\hat{F}^{-1}(s|A)\Big|A\right)\Gamma^A(\hat{f}|s)\,ds.$$

In the first of the above inequalities, we have used Corollary A.7.1. The second inequality makes use of Eq. 7.27, Lemma A.7.1, and the integral condition 7.11.

(ii) If $\gamma_u \geq 1$, the last two inequalities are reversed. Proposition 7.1 then implies the claim. □

Lemma A.7.3. *Let $\bar{f}$ and $\hat{f}$ be two information systems with $\bar{f} \succ_{\text{rel}} \hat{f}$.*

$$\frac{\Delta^{A_1}(\bar{f}|s'')}{\Delta^{A_1}(\bar{f}|s')} \geq \frac{\Delta^{A_1}(\hat{f}|s'')}{\Delta^{A_1}(\hat{f}|s')} \tag{A.7.3}$$

holds for all A_1, $s'' \geq s'$.

Proof. Since the information systems $\bar{f}$ and $\hat{f}$ satisfy signal monotonicity with respect to the state variable A_1, Inequality A.7.3 follows from part (ii) in Definition 7.1. □

Corollary A.7.2. *Let $\bar{f}$ and $\hat{f}$ be two information systems with $\bar{f} \succ_{\text{rel}} \hat{f}$. Given any increasing function $V : [0, 1] \to \mathbb{R}$,*

$$\int_0^1 V(s)\Delta^{A_1}(\bar{f}|s)\,ds \geq \int_0^1 V(s)\Delta^{A_1}(\hat{f}|s)\,ds$$

holds for all A_1.

Proof. By Lemma A.7.3, the densities $\Delta^{A_1}(f, \cdot), f = \bar{f}, \hat{f}$, satisfy a variant of the MLRP in the sense of Eq. A.7.3. The result follows by the same reasoning as in the proof of Proposition 1 in Milgrom (1981). □

Proof of Theorem 7.2. We apply the characterization in Proposition 7.3. Using Lemma A.7.3 and Corollary A.7.2, the proof proceeds as in part (i) of Theorem 7.1. □

Proof of Lemma 7.4. Assume that ϑ is convex, that is, ϑ' is increasing (we deal with the case where ϑ is concave in Step 5).

Step 1: Since $z(y) - x(y)$ is strictly monotone and $z \circ \tilde{y}$ is obtained from $x \circ \tilde{y}$ by an MPS, there exists y^* such that $z(y^*) = x(y^*)$ and

$$z(y) < x(y) \quad \text{for } y < y^*$$

$$z(y) > x(y) \quad \text{for } y > y^*.$$

Clearly the above inequalities are preserved under the strictly monotone increasing transformation ϑ, that is,

$$\vartheta \circ z(y) < \vartheta \circ x(y) \quad \text{for } y < y^*, \tag{A.7.4}$$

$$\vartheta \circ z(y) > \vartheta \circ x(y) \quad \text{for } y > y^*. \tag{A.7.5}$$

Step 2: We show that for $y \geqslant y^*$, $\vartheta \circ z(y) - \vartheta \circ x(y)$ is strictly monotone increasing.

$$\frac{\partial}{\partial y}\left[\vartheta \circ z(y) - \vartheta \circ x(y)\right] = \vartheta'(z(y))\, z'(y) - \vartheta'(x(y))\, x'(y) > 0. \tag{A.7.6}$$

The inequality is satisfied since $z'(y) > x'(y)$ holds by assumption; and since $\vartheta'(z(y)) \geqslant \vartheta'(x(y))$ holds due to the convexity of ϑ and due to the fact that $z(y) \geqslant x(y)$ for $y \geqslant y^*$.

Step 3: We show that the normalized random variables $\check{z}(y) := \vartheta \circ z(y) - E[\vartheta \circ z(\tilde{y})]$ and $\check{x}(y) := \vartheta \circ x(y) - E[\vartheta \circ x(\tilde{y})]$ satisfy

$$\check{z}(y) \neq \check{x}(y) \quad \text{for } y < y^*. \tag{A.7.7}$$

Since $z(y)$ is an MPS of $x(y)$ and ϑ is convex,

$$E\left[\vartheta \circ z(\tilde{y})\right] \geqslant E\left[\vartheta \circ x(\tilde{y})\right] \tag{A.7.8}$$

holds. Equations A.7.4 and A.7.8 then imply

$$\check{z}(y) < \check{x}(y) \quad \text{for } y < y^*.$$

Step 4: Since $\check{z}(\tilde{y})$ and $\check{x}(\tilde{y})$ have the same mean, there exists y^{**} such that $\check{z}(y^{**}) = \check{x}(y^{**})$. In view of Eq. A.7.7, $y^{**} \geqslant y^*$ holds. The intersection point y^{**} is unique since $\check{z}(y) - \check{x}(y)$ is strictly monotone increasing for $y \geqslant y^*$ according to Step 2. Thus we have shown that

$$\check{z}(y) \overset{(>)}{<} \check{x}(y) \quad \text{for } y \overset{(>)}{<} y^{**}. \tag{A.7.9}$$

These inequalities imply that $\check{z} = \vartheta \circ \tilde{z} - E[\vartheta(\tilde{z})]$ is obtained from $\check{x} = \vartheta \circ \tilde{x} - E[\vartheta(\tilde{x})]$ by an MPS and, hence, the distribution of $\vartheta \circ \tilde{z}$ is more unequal than the distribution of $\vartheta \circ \tilde{x}$.

Step 5: If ϑ is concave, then in Step 2 inequality (Eq. A.7.6) holds for $y \leq y^*$ and, consequently, in Step 3 we get $\check{z}(y) \neq \check{x}(y)$ for $y > y^*$. This implies $y^{**} < y^*$ in Step 4 from which, once again, the inequalities in Eq. A.7.9 follow. □

We prove two preliminary results before we proceed with the proofs of Propositions 7.4 and 7.5.

Lemma A.7.4 (MPS). *Let $\tilde{y}$ be a random variable which is distributed over $[0,1]$ according to the Lebesgue density ϕ. Let $z : [0,1] \to [\underline{t}, \bar{t}]$ and*

$x : [0,1] \to [\underline{t}, \bar{t}]$ be differentiable strictly increasing functions such that $E[z \circ \tilde{y}] = E[x \circ \tilde{y}]$, that is,

$$\int_0^1 z(y)\phi(y)\,\mathrm{d}y = \int_0^1 x(y)\phi(y)\,\mathrm{d}y. \tag{A.7.10}$$

Assume further that $z(y)$ and $x(y)$ have the single crossing property with $z(y^*) = x(y^*) =: t^*$ and $z(y) \overset{(\geq)}{\leq} x(y)$ for $y \overset{(\geq)}{\leq} y^*$. Then $Z := z \circ \tilde{y}$ differs from $X = x \circ \tilde{y}$ by an MPS.

Remark A.7.1. *If $z(y)$ and $x(y)$ are strictly decreasing and the other conditions in Lemma A.7.4 are satisfied, then $X = x \circ \tilde{y}$ differs from $Z = z \circ \tilde{y}$ by an MPS.*

Proof of Lemma A.7.4. Let G and F be the c.d.f.'s for Z and X. Denote by g and f the (Lebesgue) densities of G and F, and define $S := G - F$. From $z(y) \overset{(\geq)}{\leq} x(y)$ for $y \overset{(\geq)}{\leq} y^*$ we conclude $S(t) \overset{(\leq)}{\geq} 0$ for $t \overset{(\geq)}{\leq} t^*$ and, hence,[1]

$$\int_{\underline{t}}^{\bar{t}} S(t)\,\mathrm{d}t = \underbrace{tS(t)\Big|_{\underline{t}}^{\bar{t}}}_{=0} - \int_{\underline{t}}^{\bar{t}} t[g(t) - f(t)]\,\mathrm{d}t$$

$$= \int_0^1 [z(y) - x(y)]\phi(y)\,\mathrm{d}y = 0. \tag{A.7.11}$$

$$\int_{\underline{t}}^{\hat{t}} S(t)\,\mathrm{d}t = \int_{\underline{t}}^{t^*} S(t)\,\mathrm{d}t + \int_{t^*}^{\hat{t}} S(t)\,\mathrm{d}t \geq 0. \tag{A.7.12}$$

The inequality in Eq. A.7.12 follows from Eq. A.7.11 and the fact that $S(t) \overset{(\leq)}{\geq} 0$ for $t \overset{(\geq)}{\leq} t^*$. Equations A.7.11 and A.7.12 together imply that Z differs from X by an MPS. □

Lemma A.7.5. *Let $\bar{f}$ and $\hat{f}$ be two information systems with $\bar{f} \succcurlyeq_{\text{s-inf}} \hat{f}$. For any increasing differentiable function $\vartheta : \mathbb{R}_+ \to \mathbb{R}$ the random variable $\bar{\theta}(y) := E^{\bar{f}}[\vartheta(A)|y]$ differs from $\hat{\theta}(y) := E^{\hat{f}}[\vartheta(A)|y]$ by an MPS. Also, $\bar{\theta}(y) - \hat{\theta}(y)$ is monotone increasing in y.*

Remark A.7.2. *If ϑ is a decreasing function, $\hat{\theta}(y)$ differs from $\bar{\theta}(y)$ by an MPS.*

Proof of Lemma A.7.5. By the law of iterated expectations, $\int_0^1 \bar{\theta}(y)\,\mathrm{d}y = \int_0^1 \hat{\theta}(y)\,\mathrm{d}y$. Therefore, in view of Lemma A.7.4, it suffices to show that $\bar{\theta}(y) - \hat{\theta}(y)$ is increasing in y.

1. The first equality in the second line of Eq. A.7.11 follows from

$$\int_{\underline{t}}^{\bar{t}} tg(t)\,\mathrm{d}t = \int_{z^{-1}(\underline{t})}^{z^{-1}(\bar{t})} z(y)\underbrace{g(z(y))z'(y)}_{=\phi(y)}\,\mathrm{d}y = \int_0^1 z(y)\phi(y)\,\mathrm{d}y.$$

$$\bar{\theta}'(y) - \hat{\theta}'(y) = \int_{\mathbb{R}_+} \vartheta(A)\frac{\partial}{\partial y}\left[\bar{\nu}(A|y) - \hat{\nu}(A|y)\right] \mathrm{d}A$$
$$= -\int_{\mathbb{R}_+} \vartheta'(A)\frac{\partial}{\partial y}\left[\int_{\underline{A}}^{A} \left(\bar{\nu}(A'|y) - \hat{\nu}(A'|y)\right) \mathrm{d}A'\right] \mathrm{d}A$$
$$= -\int_{\mathbb{R}_+} \vartheta'(A)\left[\bar{G}_y(A|y) - \hat{G}_y(A|y)\right] \mathrm{d}A \geq 0.$$

The last inequality follows from Eq. 7.47, since $\vartheta' \geq 0$ has been assumed. □

Proof of Proposition 7.4. According to Lemma A.7.5, $\bar{A}^{\bar{f}}(y)$ differs from $\bar{A}^{\hat{f}}(y)$ by an MPS. In addition, if the investment behavior is accumulation-inducing (accumulation-impeding), $\bar{h}_t(\cdot)$ is a convex (concave) function. Therefore, see Rothschild and Stiglitz (1970),

$$\int_0^1 \bar{h}_t\left(\bar{A}^{\bar{f}}(y)\right) \mathrm{d}y \overset{(\leq)}{\geq} \int_0^1 \bar{h}_t\left(\bar{A}^{\hat{f}}(y)\right) \mathrm{d}y$$

holds and, hence, $H_t^{\bar{f}}$ in Eq. 7.48 is larger (smaller) than $H_t^{\hat{f}}$. □

Proof of Proposition 7.5. Incomes under the two information systems are given by

$$I_t^{\bar{f}}(y) = w_t\bar{A}^{\bar{f}}(y)e_t\left(\bar{A}^{\bar{f}}(y)\right), \quad I_t^{\hat{f}}(y) = w_t\bar{A}^{\hat{f}}(y)e_t\left(\bar{A}^{\hat{f}}(y)\right),$$

where

$$\bar{A}^{\bar{f}}(y) := E^{\bar{f}}[\tilde{A}|y], \quad \bar{A}^{\hat{f}}(y) := E^{\hat{f}}[\tilde{A}|y].$$

According to Lemma A.7.5, $\bar{A}^{\bar{f}}(y)$ and $\bar{A}^{\hat{f}}(y)$ differ by an MPS and $\bar{A}^{\bar{f}}(y) - \bar{A}^{\hat{f}}(y)$ is monotone in y. Below we show that $\bar{h}_t(\bar{A}) = \bar{A}e_t(\bar{A})$ is monotone increasing in $\bar{A}$. Lemma 7.4 (and Remark 7.2 following Lemma 7.4) then implies that the income distribution is more unequal under $\bar{f}$ than under $\hat{f}$.

First observe that $s_t(\bar{A}(y))$ and $w_t\bar{h}_t(\bar{A}(y)) - s_t(\bar{A}(y))$ are both co-monotone with $\bar{h}_t(\bar{A}(y))$. This observation is immediate from Eq. 7.42 since u_1' is a decreasing function. Now assume, by contradiction, that as $\bar{A}$ increases $\bar{h}_t(\cdot)$ declines. By co-monotonicity, $w_t\bar{h}_t(\cdot) - s_t(\cdot)$ declines as well. As a consequence, $\bar{A}u_1'(w_t\bar{h}_t(\cdot) - s_t(\cdot))$ increases and, according to Eq. 7.43, $e_t(\cdot)$ increases. However, in view of Eq. 7.40, an increase in $e_t(\cdot)$ contradicts our assumption that $\bar{h}_t(\cdot)$ declines as $\bar{A}$ increases. □

Bibliography

Aghion, P., 2002. Schumpeterian: growth theory and the dynamics of income inequality. Econometrica 70, 855-882.

Andolfatto, D., Gervais, M., 2006. Human capital investment and debt constraints. Rev. Econ. Dyn. 9 (1), 52-67.

Athey, S., Levin, J., 2001. The value of information in monotone decision problems. MIT, Department of Economics, Working Papers 98-24.

Atkinson, A.B., 1970. On the measurement of inequality. J. Econ. Theory 2, 244-263.

Azariadis, C., Drazen, A., 1990. Threshold externalities in economic development. Q. J. Econ. 105, 501-526.

Barr, N., Crawford, I., 1998. Funding higher education in an age of expansion. Educ. Econ. 6 (1), 45-70.

Barro, R., 1998. The Determinants of Economic Growth. MIT Press, Cambridge, MA.

Bassanini, A., Scarpetta, S., 2002. Does human capital matter for growth in OECD countries? A pooled mean-group approach. Econ. Lett. 74 (3), 399-405.

Becker, G., 1964. Human Capital: A Theoretical and Empirical Analysis, with Special Reference to Education. Columbia University Press, New York.

Benabou, R., 1996. Equity and efficiency in human capital investment: the local connection. Rev. Econ. Stud. 63, 237-264.

Benabou, R., Ok, E.A., 2001. Mobility as progressivity: ranking income processes according to equality of opportunity. NBER Working Paper 8431.

Berk, J.B., Uhlig, H., 1993. The timing of information in a general equilibrium framework. J. Econ. Theory 59, 275-287.

Bevia, C., Iturbe-Ormaetxe, I., 2002. Redistribution and subsidies for higher education. Scand. J. Econ. 104 (2), 321-340.

Blackwell, D., 1951. Comparison of experiments. In: Proceedings of the Second Berkeley Symposium on Mathematical Statistics, pp. 93-102.

Blackwell, D., 1953. Equivalent comparison of experiments. Ann. Math. Stat. 24, 265-272.

Blankenau, W., 2005. Public schooling, college subsidies and growth. J. Econ. Dyn. Control 29 (3), 487-507.

Brandt, N., Drees, B., Eckwert, B., Várdy, F., 2014. Information and the dispersion of posterior expectations. J. Econ. Theory 154, 604-611.

Cameron, S., Heckman, J., 1999. Can tuition policy combat rising wage inequality? In: Kosters, M. (Ed.), Financing College Tuition: Government Policies and Educational Priorities. American Enterprise Institute Press, Washington.

Canton, E., 2007. Social returns to education: macro-evidence. De Economist 155 (4), 449-468.

Carneiro, P., Heckman, J.J., 2002. The evidence on credit constraints in post-secondary schooling. Econ. J. 112, 989-1018.

Caselli, F., Esquivel, G., Fernando, L., 1996. Reopening the convergence debate: a new look at cross-country growth empirics. J. Econ. Growth 1 (3), 363-389.

Caucutt, E.M., Kumar, K.B., 2003. Higher education subsides and heterogeneity: a dynamic analysis. J. Econ. Dyn. Control. 27 (8), 1459-1502.

Chapman, B., 1997. Conceptual issues and the Australian experience with income contingent charges for higher education. Econ. J. 107, 738-751.

Chapman, B., 2006. Income contingent loans for higher education: international reforms. In: Hanushek, E., Welch, F. (Eds.), Handbook of the Economics of Education, vol. 2. North Holland, Amsterdam, pp. 1435-1500.

Checchi, D., 2006. The Economics of Education. Cambridge University Press, Cambridge.

Creedy, J., 1995. The Economics of Higher Education: An Analysis of Taxes Versus Fees. Edward Elgar Publishing Ltd., Hants.

Crémer, J., 1982. A simple proof of Blackwell's "Comparison of Experiments" theorem. J. Econ. Theory 27 (2), 439-443.

Cruces, G., García Domench, C., Gasparini, L., 2011. Inequality in education: evidence for Latin America. WIDER Working Paper, No. 2011/93, ISBN 978-929-230-460-7.

De Fraja, G., 2002. The design of optimal education policies. Rev. Econ. Stud. 69, 437-466.

Demougin, D., Fluet, C., 2001. Ranking of information systems in agency models: an integral condition. Econ. Theory 17, 489-496.

De Gregorio, J., Kim, S.J., 2000. Credit markets with differences in abilities: education, distribution and growth. Int. Econ. Rev. 41 (3), 579-607.

De La Croix, D., Michel, P., 2007. Education and growth with endogenous debt constraints. Econ. Theory 33, 509-530.

De Meulemeester, J.L., Rochat, D., 1995. A causality analysis of the link between higher education and economic development. Econ. Educ. Rev. 14 (4), 351-361.

Diamond, P., 1965. National debt in a neoclassical growth model. Am. Econ. Rev. 55, 1126-1150.

Dynarski, S., 2003. Does aid matter? Measuring the effect of student aid on college attendance and completion. Am. Econ. Rev. 93 (1), 279-288.

Epstein, L., Zin, S., 1989. Substitution, risk aversion, and the temporal behavior of asset returns: a theoretical framework. Econometrica 57, 937-969.

Eckstein, Z., Zilcha, I., 1994. The effects of compulsory schooling on growth, income distribution and welfare. J. Public Econ. 54, 339-359.

Eckwert, B., Zilcha, I., 1998. The value of information in some general equilibrium models. Foerder Institute for Economic Research, Working Paper No. 13-98, Tel Aviv University.

Eckwert, B., Zilcha, I., 2012. Private investment in higher education: comparing alternative funding schemes. Economica 79, 76-96.

Englebrecht, H.J., 2003. Human capital and economic growth: cross-section evidence for OECD countries. Econ. Rec. 79, 40-51.

Feldman, M., Gilles, C., 1985. An expository note on individual risk without aggregate uncertainty. J. Econ. Theory 35, 26-32.

Fender, I., Wang, P., 2003. Educational policy in a credit constrained economy with skill heterogeneity. Int. Econ. Rev. 44, 939-964.

Forbes, K.J., 2000. A reassessment of the relationship between inequality and growth. Am. Econ. Rev. 90 (4), 869-887.

Friedman, M., 1955. The role of government in education. In: Solow, R.A. (Ed.), Economics and the Public Interest. Rutgers University Press, Piscataway.

Friedman, M., 1962. Capitalism and Freedom. University of Chicago Press, Chicago.

Galor, O., Tsiddon, D., 1997. The distribution of human capital and economic growth. J. Econ. Growth 2, 93-124.

Galor, O., Zeira, J., 1993. Income distribution and macroeconomics. Rev. Econ. Stud. 60, 35-52.

Ganuza, J.J., Penalva, J.S., 2006. On information and competition in private value auctions. Working Paper, Department of Economics and Business, Universitat Pompeu Fabra.

Garcia-Penalosa, C., Wälde, K., 2000. Efficiency and equity effects of subsidies to higher education. Oxf. Econ. Pap. 52, 702-722.

Garrat, R., Marshall, J., 1994. Public finance of private goods: the case of college education. J. Polit. Econ. 102, 566-582.
Gary-Bobo, R.J., Trannoy, A., 2008. Efficient tuition fees and examinations. J. Eur. Econ. Assoc. 6, 1211-1243.
Glomm, G., Ravikumar, B., 1992. Private investment in human capital: endogenous growth and income inequality. J. Polit. Econ. 100, 818-834.
Gottardi, P., Rahi, R., 2014. Value of information in competitive economies with incomplete markets. Int. Econ. Rev. 55 (1), 57-81.
Green, J., 1981. The value of information with sequential futures markets. Econometrica 49, 335-358.
Greenaway, D., Haynes, M., 2003. Funding higher education in the UK: the role of fees and loans. Econ. J. 113 (February), F150-F166.
Hall, R.E., 1988. Intertemporal substitution in consumption. J. Polit. Econ. 96 (2), 339-357.
Hanushek, E., Kimko, D., 2000. Schooling labor force quality and the growth of nations. Am. Econ. Rev. 90, 1181-1206.
Hanushek, E., Leung, C.K.Y., Yilmaz, K., 2003. Redistribution through education and other transfer mechanisms. J. Monet. Econ. 50, 1719-1750.
Hare, P.G., Ulph, D.T., 1979. Education and income distribution. J. Polit. Econ. 87 (5, Part II), 193-212.
Hart, O.D., 1975. On the optimality of equilibrium when the market structure is incomplete. J. Econ. Theory 11, 418-443.
Hassler, J., Mora, V.R., 2000. Intelligence, social mobility, and growth. Am. Econ. Rev. 90 (4), 888-908.
Hermelingmeier, C., 2007. A note on comparing information structures using posterior state distributions. Working Paper, Department of Economics, Bielefeld University.
Hermelingmeier, C., 2010. Decisions Under Imperfect Information. Verlag Dr. Kovač, Hamburg.
Hirshleifer, J., 1971. The private and social value of information and the reward to incentive activity. Am. Econ. Rev. 61, 561-574.
Hirshleifer, J., 1975. Speculation and equilibrium: information, risk and markets. Q. J. Econ. 89, 519-542.
Huber, B., 1990. Staatsverschuldung und Allokationseffizienz: Eine Theoretische Analyse. Baden-Baden, Nomos.
Jacobs, B., 2007. Optimal tax and education policies and investments in human capital. In: Hartog, J., Maassen van den Brink, H. (Eds.), Human Capital. Cambridge University Press, Cambridge.
Jacobs, B., van der Ploeg, F., 2006. Guide to reform of higher education: a European perspective. Econ. Policy 21, 535-592.
Jewitt, I., 1997. Information and principal agent problems. Working Paper 97/414, University of Bristol.
Johnson, G.E., 1984. Subsidies for higher education. J. Labor Econ. 2, 303-318.
Jovanovic, B., Nyarko, Y., 1995. The transfer of human capital. J. Econ. Dyn. Control 19, 1033-1064.
Juhn, C., Murphy, K.M., Brooks, P., 1993. Wage inequality and the rise in return to skill. J. Polit. Econ. 101 (3), 410-442.
Kane, J.T., 1995. Rising public college tuition and college entry: how well do public subsidies promote access to college? NBER Working Paper 5164.
Kehoe, T., Levine, D., 1993. Debt-constrained asset markets. Rev. Econ. Stud. 60 (4), 865-888.
Kihlstrom, R.E., 1984. A "Bayesian" exposition of Blackwell's theorem on the comparison of experiments. In: Boyer, M., Kihlstrom, R.E. (Eds.), Bayesian Models of Economic Theory. Elsevier, Amsterdam, pp. 13-32.

Kihlstrom, R.E., Mirman, L.J., 1981. Constant, increasing and decreasing risk aversion with many commodities. Rev. Econ. Stud. 48, 271-280.

Kim, S.K., 1995. Efficiency of an information system in an agency model. Econometrica 63 (1), 89-102.

Kocherlakota, N.R., 1990. Disentangling the coefficient of relative risk aversion from the elasticity of intertemporal substitution: an irrelevance result. J. Finance 45 (1), 175-190.

Kuznets, S., 1955. Economic growth and income inequality. Am. Econ. Rev. 45 (1), 1-28.

Laitner, J., 1997. Intergenerational and interhousehold economic links. In: Rosenzweig, M.R., Stark, O. (Eds.), Handbook of Population and Family Economics. Elsevier, North Holland, Amsterdam.

Landsberger, M., Meilijson, I., 1994. Co-monotone allocations, Bickel-Lehmann dispersion and the Arrow-Pratt measure of risk aversion. Ann. Oper. Res. 52, 97-106.

Lehmann, E., 1988. Comparing location experiments. Ann. Stat. 16, 521-533.

Lemieux, T., 2006. Increasing residual wage inequality: composition effects, noisy data, or rising demand for skill? Am. Econ. Rev. 96 (3), 461-498.

Levhari, D., Weiss, Y., 1974. The effect of risk on investment in human capital. Am. Econ. Rev. 64 (6), 950-963.

Lewin, T., 2011. President to ease student loan burden for low-income graduates. Article, New York Times, October 25, 2011.

Lleras, M.P., 2004. Investing in Human Capital. Cambridge University Press, Cambridge.

Loury, G., 1981. Intergenerational transfers and the distribution of earnings. Econometrica 49 (4), 843-867.

Lucas, R., 1988. On the mechanics of economic development. J. Monet. Econ. 22, 3-42.

Milgrom, P.R., 1981. Good news and bad news: representation theorems and applications. Bell J. Econ. 12, 380-391.

Milne, F., Shefrin, H.M., 1987. Information and securities: a note on pareto dominance and the second best. J. Econ. Theory 43, 314-328.

Moretti, E., 2004. Human capital externalities in cities. In: Henderson, J.V., Thisse, J.F. (Eds.), Handbook of Urban and Regional Economics, vol. 1 (4). Elsevier, Amsterdam, pp. 2243-2291.

Newbery, D., Stiglitz, J., 1984. Pareto inferior trade. Rev. Econ. Stud. 51, 1-12.

Orazem, P., Tesfatsion, L., 1997. Macrodynamic implications of income-transfer policies for human capital investment and school effort. J. Econ. Growth 2, 305-329.

Peled, D., 1984. Stationary pareto optimality of stochastic asset equilibrium with overlapping generations. J. Econ. Theory 39, 396-403.

Perotti, R., 1996. Growth, income distribution, and democracy: what the data say. J. Econ. Growth 1 (2), 149-187.

Persico, N., 2000. Information acquisition in auctions. Econometrica 68, 135-148.

Persson, T., Tabellini, G., 1994. Is inequality harmful for growth? Am. Econ. Rev. 84 (3), 600-621.

Poutvaara, P., 2004. Educating Europe: should public education be financed with graduate taxes or income-contingent loans? CESifo Econ. Stud. 50, 663-684.

Quah, D., 2003. Some simple arithmetic on how income inequality and economic growth matter. In: Eicher, T., Turnovsky, S. (Eds.), Inequality and Growth: Theory and Policy Implications. MIT Press, Cambridge, MA.

Ramos, H.M., Ollero, J., Sordo, M.A., 2000. A sufficient condition for generalized Lorenz order. J. Econ. Theory 90, 286-292.

Restuccia, D., Urrutia, C., 2004. Intergenerational persistence of earnings: the role of early and college education. Am. Econ. Rev. 94, 1354-1378.

Rothschild, M., Stiglitz, J.E., 1970. Increasing risk: a definition. J. Econ. Theory 2, 225-243.

Rubinstein, Y., Tsiddon, D., 2004. Coping with technological change: the role of ability in making inequality so persistent. J. Econ. Growth 9, 305-346.

Sandmo, A., 1971. On the theory of the competitive firm under price uncertainty. Am. Econ. Rev. 61 (1), 65-73.

Schlee, E., 2001. The value of information in efficient risk sharing arrangements. Am. Econ. Rev. 91 (3), 509-524.

Shorrocks, A.F., 1983. Ranking income distributions. Economica 50, 3-17.

Sulganik, E., Zilcha, I., 1997. The value of information: the case of signal-dependent opportunity sets. J. Econ. Dyn. Control 21, 1615-1625.

Sylwester, K., 2002a. A model of public education and income inequality with a subsistence constraint. South. Econ. J. 69 (1), 144-158.

Sylwester, K., 2002b. Can education expenditures reduce income inequality? Econ. Educ. Rev. 21, 43-52.

Topel, R., 1999. Labor markets and economic growth. In: Ashenfelter, O., Card, D. (Eds.), Handbook of Labor Economics. North Holland, Amsterdam.

Viaene, J.M., Zilcha, I., 2002. Capital markets integration, growth and income distribution. Eur. Econ. Rev. 46, 301-327.

Woodhall, M., 1988. Designing a student loan programme for a developing country: the relevance of international experience. Econ. Educ. Rev. 7 (1), 153-161.

Index

Note: Page numbers followed by *f* indicate figures.

A

Aggregate income
  role of government, 134
  social optimum, welfare analysis, 89
Aggregate production function, 51, 72, 144

B

Bickel–Lehmann stochastic ordering concept, 160
Blackwell criterion, 4–9

C

Capital mobility, international, 106–107, 122
Complete risk sharing arrangements
  economic welfare, 21–22
  value of information, 23–26
Conditional Lebesgue density function, 4
Constant elasticity of intertemporal substitution (CEIS), 162–163
Credit constraints, 45–46
Credit funding equilibrium (CRE), 123–124
Credit markets
  competitive, welfare analysis, 83–84
  unrestricted access to, 72–74

D

Debt collection, 69
Direct welfare effect, 49
Diverse funding schemes
  credit funding equilibrium, 123–124
  equilibrium with funding diversity, 124–128
  financing costs, 120–121
  funding structure and individual behavior, 122–123
  government policy, 121
  income-contingent loans, 119, 120
  international capital mobility, 122
  policy implications, 132–133
  restricted participation FDE, 129–130
  social welfare and funding structure, 128–129

E

Economic development, 39–40
Economic growth
  absence of risk sharing, 53–56
  dynamic framework, 47–49
  indirect welfare effect, 60
  presence of risk sharing, 56–60
Economic welfare, 21–22, 29–30
Egalitarian income distribution, 71
Endogenous subsidization policies, 117
Equilibrium labor incomes, 156
Equilibrium with funding diversity (FDE), 124–128
Exchange economies
  ex ante expected utility, 14
  full information, 15
  Hirshleifer example, 15–18
  null information, 14–15
  Schlee's theorem, 13–14
Exogenous subsidization policies
  comparison, 116
  subsidizing student loans, 111–113
  subsidizing tuition fees, 114–115
Ex post inequality concept, 154

F

Financing. *See also* Higher education
  debt collection, 69
  human capital accumulation, 78–81
  income-contingent loans, 68
  individual income risk, 68
  investments, 67
  multiple funding schemes, 69–78
  private funding, 67
First-order stochastic dominance (FOSD), 3
Full information system, 15
Funding structure
  individual behavior, 122–123
  social welfare, 128–129

G

Γ-randomization, 4–5

H

Higher education
credit constraints, 45–46
economic development, 39–40
income inequality, 40–42, 43–45
High risk aversion, 55, 59
Hirshleifer effect, 15–18, 58–59
Human capital accumulation
aggregate investments, 80
financing schemes, 78
individual investments, 81
risk pooling, 79
Human capital formation, 48, 87–88, 158–162

I

ICLP. *See* Income-contingent loans program (ICLP)
Income-contingent loans, 68, 120
Income-contingent loans program (ICLP), 103
Income-contingent repayment scheme, 109
Income distribution
egalitarian, 71
income inequality, 42
interim, 112–113
role of government, 136
Income inequality
accuracy, 147
between-group variances, 40–41, 41*f*
CEIS preferences, 162–163
equal opportunities, 40, 142
income distributions, 42
likelihood ratio distribution, 145–146
normalized random variables, 167
overlapping generations economy, 143
policy implications, 164
reliability, 146
with risk sharing, 152–154
risk sharing arrangements, 42, 143
within-group variances, 41, 41*f*, 42*f*
without risk sharing, 148–151
Income opportunities
screening and inequality, without risk sharing, 148–151
screening and inequality, with risk sharing, 152–154
Incomplete risk sharing arrangements
aggregate capital stock, 28
information and economic welfare, 29–30
nontradable risk, 26, 30–31
tradable risk, 26, 31–34
Individual behavior and equilibrium, 108–110
Interim income distribution, 112–113

K

Kihlstrom theorem, 8
Kim criterion, 9–10

L

Labor supply, 51
Lifetime utility function, 50–51

M

Merit based screening, 108
MLRP. *See* Monotone likelihood ratio property (MLRP)
Moderate risk aversion, 55, 59
Monotone likelihood ratio property (MLRP), 3, 62
Multiple funding schemes
credit markets, 71
egalitarian income distribution, 71
government intervention, 71
implementation of regimes, 77–78
private investment, 69–70
public investment, 69–70
restricted insurance of loans, 76–77
unrestricted insurance of loans, 74–75

N

Nontradable risk, 30–31
Null information system, 14–15

O

Overlapping generations (OLG), 48–49

P

Private education institutions, 48
Production economies
complete risk sharing arrangements, 19–26
incomplete risk sharing arrangements, 26–34
resource allocation, 18
Production function, aggregate, 51, 72, 122, 144
Public schooling system, 48

R

Real state and signal spaces, 4
Repayment scheme
income-contingent, 93, 109
welfare analysis, 84
Restricted insurance of loans, 76–77
Restricted participation FDE (RP/FDE), 129–130
Risk aversion, 17
Risk-neutral pricing, 16
Risk sharing, 56–60
Role of government
diverse funding schemes, 119–133
endogenous liquidity constraints, 102
exogenous borrowing constraints, 102
government budget constraint, 135
income distribution, 136
subsidizing tuition *vs.* subsidizing student loans, 102–119

S

Schlee's theorem, 13–14, 18
Screening. *See also* Income inequality
aggregate investment, 87
direct welfare effect, 60
education loans, 85–86
human capital formation, 87–88
indirect welfare effect, 60
restricted insurance of loans, 84–85
value function, 61
welfare, 88–93
Social investment optimum, 107–108
Social welfare, 130–131
Students Loans Institution (SLI), 84–85
Subsidization policies
endogenous, 117
exogenous. *See* (Exogenous subsidization policies)

T

Tax-deductible investment, 117–118
Tax-financed subsidization regime, 104
Tradable risk, 31–34

U

Uncertainty and screening
Bayes' formula, 10
Blackwell criterion, 4–9
information system, 2–3
Kim criterion, 9–10
uniform signal distribution, 10
Unrestricted access to credit markets, 72–74
Unrestricted insurance of loans, 74–75

V

Value of information
exchange economies, 13–18
production economies, 18–34
von-Neumann Morgenstern (vNM)-utility function, 6, 13–14, 106

W

Welfare analysis
aggregate human capital, 82
capital formation function, 83
competitive credit markets, 83–84
economic efficiency, 82
education and human capital stocks, 84
equilibrium risk allocation, 83
ex ante expected utility level, 89
income-contingent loan-repayment scheme, 93
repayment schemes, 84
risk aversion, 88–89, 90
screening-induced efficiency gains, 92
screening-induced welfare gains, 91
social optimum aggregate income, 89
value function, 81–82, 83
Welfare effect, direct/indirect, 49, 60

Printed in the United States
By Bookmasters